Unleashing the Power of eBay®

Other books by Dennis L. Prince

How to Sell Anything on eBay® . . . and Make a Fortune!

How to Sell Antiques and Collectibles on eBay® . . . and Make a Fortune! coauthored by Lynn Dralle

How to Sell Music, Collectibles, and Instruments on eBay® . . . and Make a Fortune! coauthored by William M. Meyer

Unleashing the Power of eBay®

Dennis L. Prince

McGraw-Hill
New York Chicago San Francisco
Lisbon London Madrid Mexico City Milan
New Delhi San Juan Seoul Singapore
Sydney Toronto

The McGraw-Hill Companies

1 2 3 4 5 6 7 8 9 0 DOC/DOC 0 9 8 7 6 5 4

ISBN 0-07-144518-8

Unleashing the Power of eBay® is in no way authorized by, endorsed, or affiliated with eBay or its subsidiaries. All references to eBay and other trademarked properties are used in accordance with the Fair Use Doctrine and are not meant to imply that this book is an eBay product for advertising or other commercial purposes.

Readers should know that online auctioning has risks. Readers who participate in online auctions do so at their own risk. The author and publisher of this book cannot guarantee financial success and therefore disclaim any liability, loss, or risk sustained, either
directly or indirectly, as a result of using the information given in this book.

McGraw-Hill books are available at special quantity discounts to use as premiums and sales promotions, or for use in corporate training programs. For more information, please write to the Director of Special Sales, Professional Publishing, McGraw-Hill, Two Penn Plaza, New York, NY 10121-2298. Or contact your local bookstore.

Library of Congress Cataloging-in-Publication Data

Prince, Dennis L.
Unleashing the power of eBay / Dennis L. Prince.
p. cm.
ISBN 0-07-144518-8 (alk. paper)
1. eBay (Firm) 2. Internet auctions. I. Title.
HF5478.P756 2004
381'.177—dc22 2004019847

This book is printed on recycled, acid-free paper containing a minimum of 50% recycled, de-inked fiber.

For my loving wife, Diane, in constant thanks
for her support and belief in my entrepreneurial capabilities.

Contents

Acknowledgments

Though only my name is credited on the cover of this book, the truth is that any good book one person writes is made better by the team with which he works. Certainly, my case is no exception, and it's my duty, no, my pleasure to extend my deepest thanks to those with whom I've worked to bring this book to completion.

At McGraw-Hill, I must first recognize my project editor, Donya Dickerson, whom I've had the continuing pleasure to work with in developing this exciting new book. Your never-ending enthusiasm and positive attitude have made writing this book another excellent experience for me. I sincerely hope we can work together on many more projects. Also, my deep thanks to the rest of the incredible McGraw-Hill team with whom I've had the pleasure to partner on this project: Mary Glen, Anthony Sarchiapone, Brian Boucher, and all the fine folks on the McGraw-Hill sales and marketing teams, who have shown an exceptional proficiency in preparing, presenting, and promoting this book. Thanks to each of you.

Next, my thanks to Deborah Masi at Westchester Book Group for the excellent production editing. Thanks for your sharp eye and energetic input that resulted in such a fine interior layout.

And last but certainly not least, thanks to all the hardworking and industrious eBay sellers and business owners who graciously shared their stories and successes, many of which are included in this book, which have helped to illustrate the best ways to unleash the power of eBay. You've all been sources of inspiration not only to me but to the millions of others around the world who look to you as the shining examples of how successful an eBay business can be. Thanks for keeping the online auction business revving at top speed and for working with me as, together, we develop new ways to expand our online ventures and show others how exciting and rewarding this endeavor is.

Introduction

It was September 5, 1995, when entrepreneur Pierre Omidyar unveiled his unassuming auction Web site, one that would go on to define the online experience, ultimately account for billions of dollars in annual online sales, and become the primary motivation for millions of individuals to venture into cyberspace (many of whom confess they would never have attempted the journey otherwise). Originally known as AuctionWeb, Omidyar's brainchild, eBay, needs little introduction today.

Much has changed on eBay since that Labor Day weekend launch, most notably the opportunity for would-be and established businesspeople to open a virtual storefront and reap the benefits of a worldwide marketplace. Many experienced sellers (who often are equally astute buyers) have found success on eBay, have matured in their familiarity with online buying and selling, and are ready to explore and apply new methods to further tap this growing marketplace. For you, this book is your step up, your primer to reach the next level of conducting business on eBay. Of course, if you're already in business but haven't fully employed the potential eBay offers to increase your overall sales and profits, this book is your guide in harnessing all that the online market has to offer, no matter how large or how small your existing enterprise. If you're interested in unleashing the power of eBay and the online marketplace to further your business goals, this book will show you how to make major strides with your business with just a few keystrokes and mouse-clicks.

WHAT'S DIFFERENT ABOUT THIS BOOK?

Although so much has already been written about eBay and online bidding and selling, there is so much that people who want to tap its full potential need to know about. And, because eBay is an ever-growing, ever-changing entity, new opportunities spring up every month (it's true) to better serve and satisfy the growing base of consumers—soon to top the 100 million mark—who turn to eBay every day to find the items they want and the goods they need. I've made it my goal to keep up with these changes and to continually

let readers know about the "latest and greatest" tools in the world of eBay, and I'm presenting this information to ensure that *you* are likewise prepared to grow your business and effectively respond to the sea of eager buyers out there. I will show how you can take command of the incredible income potential every step of the way.

Unlike some books that discuss eBay with all the charm of a straight-faced exposition on quantum physics—or worse, those that speak to you as though you're a "dummy" or an "idiot," which you're not—this book delivers clear instruction and is written in an everyday manner that will give you the confidence and competence to succeed in your personal endeavors without feeling left behind, laughed at, or lost somewhere in the translation. Yes, much of what you'll read is technical in nature, much more so, in fact, than an introductory eBay text, but that's no reason to fear the finer points of online merchandising and computer-based commerce. This book is written with *your* success in mind and, to achieve this goal, you'll find that this book speaks *to* you, not at you; it *shows* you how to succeed, not just tells you; it *encourages* you to try new tools and techniques, so you can see that you possess the same aptitude as the thousands of current eBay PowerSellers who have realized terrific results. If you're seeking the details for improved success on eBay, this book has the information you need. You bring only the desire to succeed and the determination to apply what you'll learn. This book will provide the rest.

WHY YOU? WHY ME?

The fact that you're reading this book says that you're likely ready to move your eBay experience—and your online or brick-and-mortar business—forward. This book assumes that you're familiar with computers and their related tools, you're equipped to access the Internet, and you know the basics of and have experience in buying and selling on eBay (so if you need introductory information on how to get started on eBay or would like the opportunity to brush up on the basics, please see my previous book, *How to Sell Anything on eBay . . . and Make a Fortune!*). With that experience under your belt, you're ready to distance yourself from the casual users and take the next big step to sharply increase your bottom-line results.

So why am I the one to lead you on this advanced journey? I've been using eBay on a consistent basis since December 1995, just three months after the site went live and it was still the no-frills AuctionWeb site. I was fortunate to see eBay right at the beginning and have been lucky enough to see the site evolve every step of the way. Not only have I seen eBay grow and change, I've also seen the entire online industry evolve, from the introduction of complementary sites and services such as PayPal (formerly X.com) that make using eBay even easier and the numerous third-party auction management tools to the various would-be contenders who gave their best efforts to compete with

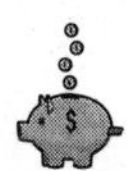

eBay, the veritable 800-pound gorilla. Through it all, I've written numerous texts and provided regular analysis and offered insights for several industry-centric auction service sites, including Vendio (formerly AuctionWatch), Auctiva, and CNET. Through the incredible dot-com boom, the difficult dot-com bust, and the stabilization of the online economy, I've ridden along the sometimes bumpy but always exciting road of online auctions and e-commerce. As the industry has reshaped and often reinvented itself, I've kept pace so folks like you can make the most of what eBay has to offer without having to focus your valuable time and energy to learn the monthly—even weekly—changes. In short, I've done the hard digging for you.

WHAT'S WAITING FOR YOU INSIDE

In my years of writing about and instructing others in the mastery of eBay and online merchandising, I've seen that folks are looking for easy-to-use resources that clearly outline tools and techniques in a logical and step-by-step manner. I've seen that presenting information in a way that is easy to recall and review and that providing quick answers when and where they're needed is critical to an eBay user's ongoing success. In order to make this book as useful a resource as possible, I've broken down the information into the following easy-to-access sections:

Part 1: eBay: It's Not Just for Cleaning Out the Attic Anymore

To take the next step in your eBay adventure, begin by learning to think "outside the box." Sure, you've come to know eBay as that funky Web site where you can buy collectibles and curiosities, but that's merely the tip of the iceberg. In this part of the book, you'll learn how eBay has evolved and how its base of sellers has likewise evolved and even driven change in the auction realm. You'll learn about the innovative new ways eBay is being utilized, about the best new tools you should be using to propel your online profits, how traditional brick-and-mortar companies are including eBay into their business model, and how to keep on top of what's selling, what's not, and where you should be positioned to make the most of what eBay can deliver.

Part 2: Build a Better Business, eBay Style

Since stepping up your efforts to use eBay entails sales increases and business growth, this part of the book guides you through taking your business to the next level. From establishing a solid business plan to controlling your eBay fees, from protecting and boosting your online reputation to staying ahead of the latest online frauds and scams, this section will serve you well as you strive to build your online empire and position yourself for the even greater profits and opportunities that await you.

Part 3: eBay Innovators: Build Your Profits Using the Newest Tools and Strategies Available

Here is where I'll unleash the hidden (or, at least, less obvious) powers of eBay and online merchandising. If you seek to excel in your online business and sharpen your auction acuity, this section of the book will hone your skill set and boost your bottom line. You'll learn how to utilize third-party (non-eBay) tools to maximum benefit, uncover new inventory sources to ensure you'll always have compelling goods to sell, and even how to master the art of selling goods *you don't even have* (it's legal and it's how many PowerSellers consistently earn thousands of dollars every month!).

I'M ON YOUR SIDE

Like all my other works, this book is an advocate for you, the seller or buyer, not necessarily for eBay, the venue. With *your* best interests always as its focus, this book continually reveals what will best serve advanced users on eBay, and what doesn't. It leads you to the best features the site has to offer, identifying and steering you away from less effective functions and gimmicks. It identifies the services that are worth paying for and exposes others that would needlessly eat away at your profits. As you advance through the levels of online merchandising, your time and your profits need to be maximized every step of the way. That thought is at the forefront of this book's delivery and message at all times.

REMEMBER, CHANGE IS GOOD

Longtime eBayers know that eBay, like the Internet itself and modern technology in general, is constantly changing. Early on, many of eBay's faithful decried the "tinkerings and tamperings" that altered the buying and selling experience, sometimes slightly, sometimes significantly. But eBay will continue to change and, by doing so, it offers astute businesspeople like yourself the opportunity to change and grow, too. With that in mind, recognize that, on occasion, some of what you read here or some images you'll find within this book may be slightly different from what you're seeing on the eBay site. Fear not, though: the changes you'll encounter will likely be minor, and the instruction provided in this book will help you spot and navigate effectively regardless of any future changes.

As always, and as your personal advocate for success, I welcome and encourage your thoughts, questions, and feedback regarding this book and your online experiences. Feel free, then, to drop me a line at *dlprince@bigfoot.com* to share an anecdote, sound off on an important matter, or just to say hi. I've

always enjoyed interacting with the eBay community and, regardless of its exponential growth since its halcyon days, I'm still eager to meet and greet my online peers and friends.

So let's get started. If you're ready to unleash the power of advanced eBay auctioning, I'm ready to show you how.

PART 1

eBAY: IT'S NOT JUST FOR CLEANING OUT THE ATTIC ANYMORE

1

A Fresh Look at an Old Mainstay: A Decade of eBay

Before leaping forward into any new endeavor, I like to take a quick moment to look back, so I can understand where I am now and how I managed to get here. If you've been active on eBay for around a year or more (or maybe for as little as six successful months) and you're ready to march forward to the next level of this online opportunity, take a moment to understand, *How* did I get here? *Why* am I here? and *What* got me here in the first place?

The answer to that last question has a simple answer: eBay. The site has become the now-solid foundation upon which millions of people have started or enhanced their own businesses—no matter how large or how small—thanks to the progressive vision of those in the eBay boardroom. And, as you look to grow your business to greater heights, consider how eBay itself—the once-quirky virtual flea market—has significantly evolved, serving as an example to follow (hey, Pierre never dreamed this could happen, right?). The history of eBay offers many lessons for emerging businesses and the entrepreneurial stalwarts behind them (that's you). This chapter provides that quick look back, providing you with a moment to brush up on eBay's history and the key developments that have made the site the untouchable pinnacle of dot-com success whose triumphs and travails offer valuable insights you might want to inject into your own path to fortune.

FROM EXPERIMENT TO ECONOMIC REVOLUTION

Be an enzyme—a catalyst for change. . . .

Pierre Omidyar, May 19, 2002,
Commencement address, Tufts University

Though not the sort of pronouncement that may someday be emblazoned at the foot of a bronze statue, and actually in reference to Pierre Omidyar's wife Pam's biology-based postulations of enzymes existing as "nature's activists," it's clear by his statement that eBay's legendary founder is driven at his core by Utopian principles, those that promote ideas of positive world change, excellence in individuals, and the potential for community-based achievement. Indeed, young Pierre was hardly able to prevent these deeply held beliefs of his from infiltrating his grand economic experiment, AuctionWeb at eBay, when he launched the site from the back bedroom of his apartment on Labor Day 1995. Word of his unique little site for bidding and selling computer parts, collectibles, and other items spread quickly among the Internet's earliest merchants, many having previously done business exclusively within the Usenet's staggering population of newsgroups. Omidyar soon determined that he needed to ensure his creation could be somewhat self-sufficient if he was going to remain successful at his day job.

During his commencement speech to the 2002 graduating class of Tufts University, Pierre and Pam's alma mater, Omidyar spoke of new ways to develop tools and services that would serve people and, by design, could grow and change as people's needs also changed (see Figure 1-1). He believed that

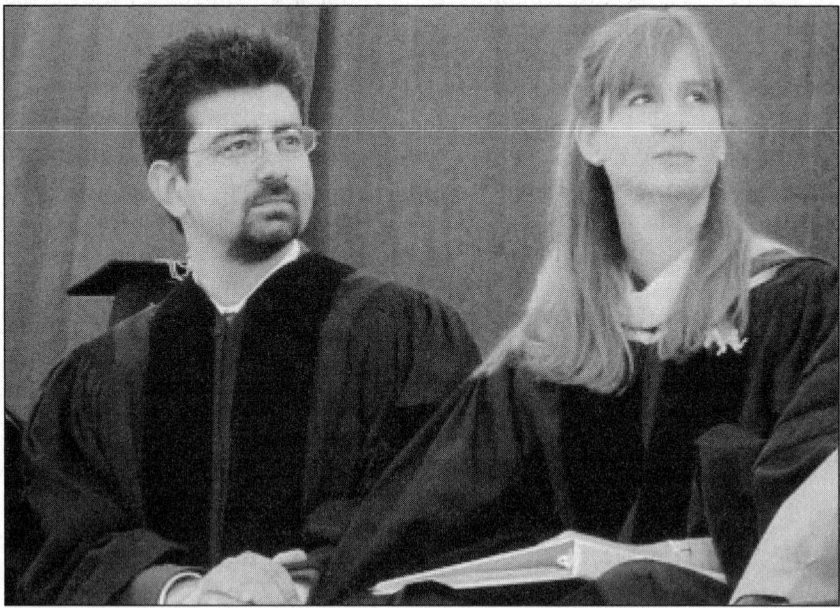

Figure 1-1 Pierre and Pam Omidyar in preparation for their individual commencement speeches at the 2002 Tufts University commencement ceremony.

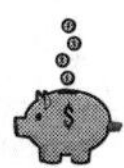

for his Web site to be successful it should be a prime mover for positive change and developed by utilizing a practical and theoretical platform that, like that idealistic Utopian society, could deftly adapt to change and would retain constant awareness of community values that would dutifully uphold "an organic, evolving, self-organizing web of individual relationships, formed around shared interests."

That's pretty lofty, but I just came here to auction some stuff.

Some have snickered a bit at Omidyar's grand vision, yet there's no denying the success the site enjoyed when all those years ago, the participants embraced this notion of community value and good, honest trade. Though his ideals may sail over the heads of many of us, somehow they have all come to serve the growth and resilience of his otherwise modest experiment.

The original AuctionWeb (see Figure 1-2) community grew and the site eventually became known as eBay, a multibillion-dollar-a-year business. It's clear that Omidyar was on to something when his site auctioned its first item, Pierre's own broken laser pointer, which sold for $14.

Today, you and I routinely think "eBay" whenever we're seeking some oddball artifact or hard-to-find item or we need a platform to quickly and inexpensively reach a potential buying market nearly 100 million strong (and growing), offer our goods, test the waters of commerce, and devise new and better merchandising methods.

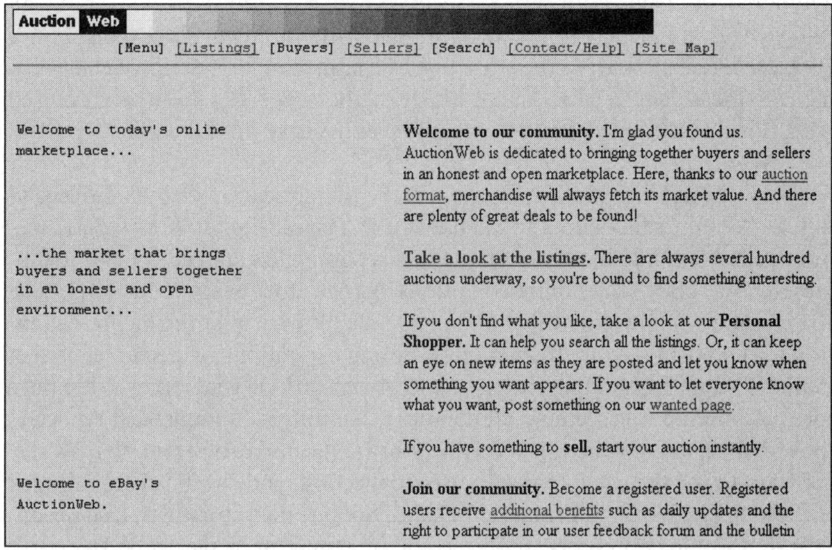

Figure 1-2 The humble beginnings of eBay, shown in the rather bland layout of the original AuctionWeb home page. Hardly Utopia, at the time, anyway.

What Pierre's example demonstrates, and what this means to you, is that there's definite value in carefully considering the reason for your business, the goals you hope to realize, and the approach you'll use to reach success. No, you don't have to have goals as lofty as Pierre's, admirable though they are, but clearly he had a vision and used it to drive his decisions in developing his business.

While our main goals in using eBay are to sell stuff and make money, dig a bit deeper to see if you're doing so in order to improve your quality of life, provide more stability for your family or other loved ones, or even improve the lives of those to whom you'll offer your products and services. No, it's not dopey to ponder your deepest motivations because, once you've clearly defined them, you'll likely find it easier to take the necessary steps to achieve your goals.

Yoga postures and deep breathing exercises are optional at this stage.

THE PEZ LEGEND—DEBUNKED!

If you've studied eBay lore for long, you've likely heard the story of how eBay got started. Omidyar created the revolutionary site so that his then-fiancée, Pam Wesley, could trade PEZ characters (you know, those hydrocephalic toy dispensers that produce tiny sugar candies when their noggins are forced back to neck-breaking extremes). Wesley had recently relocated from Boston to Silicon Valley and was disheartened at the difficulty she encountered in striking up new connections to buy, sell, and talk about all things PEZ in her new home. Over dinner with Omidyar, she expressed her PEZ predicament and, as the story goes, he launched his AuctionWeb experiment to please her. It's become the story of the new economy, a tale suffused with chivalry, romance, adoration, and inventiveness—and it's a lie.

What?!

Yes, even I was a sucker for the plucky prefabrication of the PEZ legend but, as Adam Cohen noted in his book, *The Perfect Store—Inside eBay* (recommended reading, by the way), the tale is completely untrue, a myth manufactured by eBay's first public-relations perpetrator, Mary Lou Song. The Korean-born pitchwoman was finding it difficult to attract the media's attention for Omidyar's groundbreaking yet boring aspirations to create the perfect market within the budding Internet, and Song's task of generating a true buzz for AuctionWeb was seeming all the more daunting as uninterested reporters looked elsewhere for their next feature stories. It's no lie, however, that Wesley *did* want to use the site to build her PEZ collection, and she did share this idea with Song. With that information in hand, Song spun a story with true sex appeal that would capture the attention and imagination of the press. The result was a kind of love story of what a man will do for his betrothed, generating a collective sigh of, "Ahhhh, that's so sweet." And it worked, didn't it?

It's still a nice story and one made potentially more interesting due to the fact that longtime eBayers fell for it, hook, line, and sinker. The take-away here, though, is not a feeling of betrayal or that your heart-strings have been played like a harp all these years. Instead, consider the effectiveness of the little white lie—nobody was truly harmed by the fortuitous fib—and how it helped buoy AuctionWeb's personality, a community where nice people come together to buy and sell nice things in a nice way. As you look at *your* business, consider the effectiveness of marketing angles you can use. (Although I don't encourage anyone to lie, a little bit of well-placed pitch can go a long way). It's a marketing mentality that helps lift businesses to the next level of success, and throughout this book I'll revisit this very important ingredient to your business's success.

PIERRE AND HIS MERRY MEN

As AuctionWeb/eBay rode the crest of the dot-com wave in the mid-1990s, Pierre quickly enlisted the help of a longtime associate and shrewd businessman, Jeff Skoll, to take the site to new heights. Once a free service, AuctionWeb had to begin charging its users small commissions on sales to support the hardware costs of this burgeoning Web destination. Skoll convinced Omidyar to drop three other home pages hosted on the eBay server—a biotech startup, a page for the San Francisco Tufts Alliance, and an odd tribute page to the Ebola virus—and rename AuctionWeb eBay.

eBay TIP: The name eBay is not derived from *Bay Area* but is actually an abbreviated version of EchoBay, the site name Pierre originally wanted but that had already been claimed.

Despite his philanthropic desires to keep eBay free and his worries that users might flee upon being asked to pay for usage, the site continued to flourish and eBay was soon generating thousands upon thousands of dollars each month. Pierre's invention had tapped an underserved need in the marketplace, and the growing stable of users gladly paid the reasonable fees to maintain access to this incredible opportunity. In fact, it was his philanthropic drive, I contend, that helped him identify and step forward to serve this market. Pierre had locked in on a breakthrough method of enabling (in a positive sense!) eager businesspeople, including many people who had never dared dream of starting their own business. Soon, the site was big and the profits impressive, but hard-driving Jeff Skoll, a self-avowed workaholic, wasn't satisfied: eBay needed to play among the "big boys."

MEG AGAINST THE MACHINE

By 1998, the Internet was in full commercial bloom. While venture capitalists were becoming the supermen and superwomen of the day, the growing executive staff at eBay saw an opportunity to significantly expand the site. All that was required was money, and lots of it.

At the time, IPOs (initial public offerings) were the rage of the exploding stock market, and eBay's chiefs decided it was time to go public. In order to gain the trust of potential shareholders and of Wall Street itself, eBay needed a new CEO, one readily recognizable and with a proven track record in the tough world of business.

Meg Whitman, fresh off a stint with Hasbro, Inc., was named the new CEO in March 1998. For better or worse, she brought corporate structure and stability to eBay. Able to thwart bids by both Amazon.com and Yahoo! to acquire eBay, Whitman and Omidyar marched ahead to lay the groundwork for the company's IPO.

eBay TIP: Did you know there was a proposal for online giant Yahoo! to acquire eBay? Negotiations ultimately reached an impasse, and eBay strode ahead on its own merits. In a potentially retaliatory move, Yahoo! Auctions was unveiled just days before eBay's IPO, hoping to steal some of the thunder and dilute the IPO price. The ploy failed.

On September 23, 1998, eBay began trading on Wall Street under the symbol *EBAY*. As the dot-com boom continued, eBay's stock price soared. Despite some controversial moves on eBay's part, such as permanently banning all forms of firearms from the site, the venue continued to prosper, attracting thousands of new users every month.

POP! GOES THE CULTURE

Today, eBay has become as commonplace in peoples' lives as television, CD players, and perhaps even the toaster. While it's probably not about to replace the dog as man's best friend, it has become a staple ingredient in the day-to-day activities of millions upon millions of everyday consumers, shrewd bargain hunters, established business owners, and the growing population of entrepreneurial businesspeople. The site has gone far beyond gaining the coveted brand recognition and mind share in the consumer consciousness; it has become a trusted and reliable resource for goods and services, as routine as the corner grocery store.

Beyond the business potential and serving as a clearinghouse for nearly everything and anything under the sun, eBay has also emerged as something

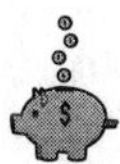

of a cultural barometer. Think about the rage several years back when adults clamored and clawed to acquire the elusive Tickle-Me Elmo or the flurry of activity over those hard-to-find Pokemon cards. Fact is, if it's hard to find, a have-to-have, or a stunning new product in the mind of the consumer, eBay has become a valued resource and reliable indicator of what is hot and what is not, used daily by private sellers, small businesses, and even giant corporations to quickly respond to and even anticipate shifts in consumer demands.

eBay TIP: In Chapter 4, you'll learn how valuable eBay has become in tracking and even steering economic trends and attitudes.

WHY DOES ALL THIS MATTER TO YOUR BUSINESS?

So, as I put forth at the beginning of this brief history lesson, the evolution of eBay and the emergence of the e-commerce revolution is rich with case studies that you and I can easily apply to our own endeavors, whether they are already in progress or are exciting new prospects yet to be launched. The key to keeping the pulse on eBay's history and upcoming developments is to constantly look, listen, learn, and—most important—leverage what you encounter into your own business goals. Pay close attention to how eBay's new functions or policy changes reflect the needs and wants of its marketplace (see Figure 1-3). Do your direct customers and business associates want or need something similar, such as easier ways to buy products, faster methods of delivery, or greater assurance of a safe and secure transaction? Keep an ear to the ground regarding which programs or promotions on eBay *don't* succeed as well as others. Is there something you should alter in the way you do business, based on what is not working? Maintain open communication with the buyers and sellers with whom you interact. Do they share any past successes or former failures that you can learn from? The point here is that there is so much *real-time* information and research that you can use for your business and, if you keep your eyes and mind open to what the market is telling you, you'll be off to a great start in advancing your eBay endeavors and unleashing the potential eBay has to offer.

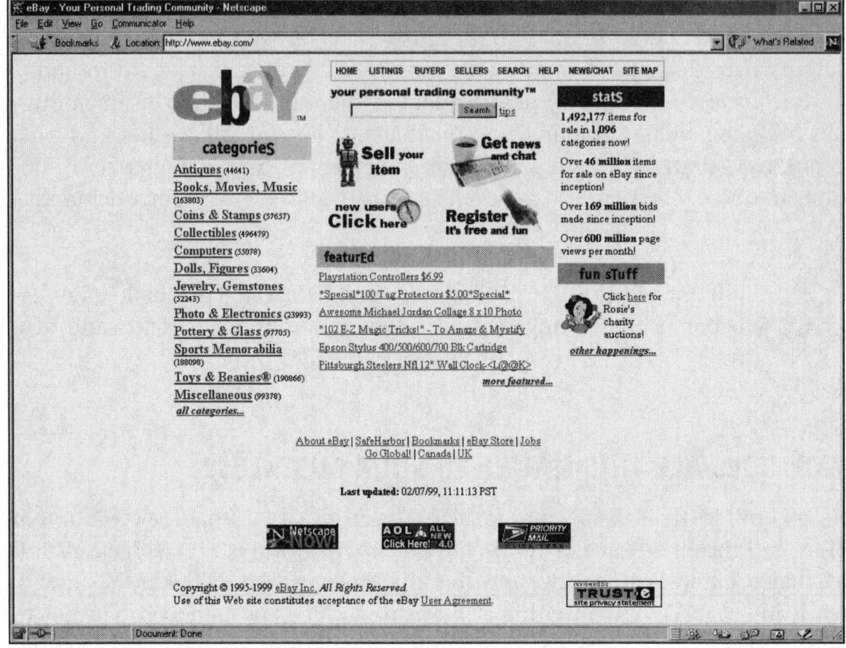

Figure 1-3 The vastly improved eBay user interface design, unveiled in June 1999, responded to users' need for ease of use and created more visual interest to encourage activity.

In the next chapter, I'll show you many of the innovative new ways folks are using eBay, including improvements in conducting day-to-day auction activities and much, much more.

2

New Ways to Use eBay, Day by Day

Yes, eBay has come a long way from being just a Web site to sell broken laser pointers, buy Beanie Babies, or stem boredom by providing hours of entertaining Net surfing. As Pierre had originally hoped (or mystically envisioned?), eBay actually grew and adapted in pace with the wants and needs of its growing base of users. The users were quite vocal in expressing how eBay was serving them well and how it was coming up short, and Pierre and company responded by making changes to the site as needed and often as requested. And even though the arrival of Meg Whitman challenged the homey community feel the once-grassroots site embodied, her vision for eBay has served millions of people worldwide and established eBay as a key ingredient in the way people and businesses buy, sell, and interact online.

And while it's clear that eBay has become a hub where you can buy or sell just about anything, is there anything so innovative about the mere growth in the number of items being offered at the site? Actually, there is, because eBay no longer offers just items for bid or sale, it offers solutions to the day-to-day needs of folks all around the globe. Look closely and you'll discover the interesting new ways that people are using eBay, then see if the examples presented in this chapter can help you adapt, adjust, and advance your own merchandising approach.

NECESSITY IS STILL THE MOTHER

During the dot-com bust of 2000 and further into what has been described as the jobless economic recovery of 2004, big businesses, small businesses, and private individuals were sometimes becoming hard-pressed to keep their income flowing, their businesses edging upward, and their overall expenses in

check. Following the lead of eBay, the most visible survivor of the dot-com shakeout, many folks looked to retool their business approach, expand their product offerings, secure new supply sources, and ultimately reach the millions of buyers who flocked to eBay in search of a way to buy the items they needed without having to visit a store in person. Savvy and attentive merchandisers, small and large, quickly discovered the need to become visible within eBay as more and more buyers turned to the site as another, and sometimes better, way to find the goods they sought. The sellers who recognized this fact of the new economy saw that eBay wasn't just an online curio shop anymore; it had become an important new marketplace to penetrate, vital in its potential to uphold and enhance a business's earnings.

Most significant to this point is that, in the years since Internet commerce began to surface, consumers have increasingly embraced the online market as a new and more convenient way to buy goods. When the world economy began to sputter with the arrival of the new millennium, businesses and individuals began working more and more hours just to maintain their level of income and profit. More hours working meant fewer hours to do much of anything else, including shop at traditional brick-and-mortar stores. However, e-commerce made it easy for these consumers not only to buy goods quickly and have them delivered to their doorsteps, it also made comparison shopping a breeze because of the simplicity of hopping from Web site to Web site to see where the best values could be found (see Figure 2-1). It became a buyer's market practically overnight and, for those astute innovators, it also became a service-provider's market as well, benefiting those people who developed and delivered online tools that made Internet shopping and bargain hunting easier. Here, again, the astute businessperson, especially the brick-and-mortar shop owner, recognized the potential to improve sales by venturing into online merchandising rather than relying on time-constrained buyers to push away from their computers and travel to shops. Maybe they would but perhaps they wouldn't; better to meet consumers on their own turf.

The example of DVD Price Search illustrates how an innovator recognized a trend in consumerism (an inclination to buy DVDs online), identified an efficiency need (a way to easily compare online prices), and then set about to develop and deliver the solution. Think about it: up to this point, consumers would need to study sales advertisements, call stores about products and prices, or spend hours visiting different stores to determine who had the best price and the stock on hand. Many consumers opted to settle on any store, a favorite store, or the first store that had the goods on the shelf, price comparison being traded off for the quickest availability. Hardly a well-researched purchase, right?

Now, to put this in the context of eBay, consider the site's introduction of the Item Watching feature, which can be used to identify items of interest and to monitor the bidding easily from the *My eBay* console. This

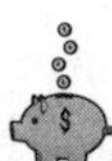

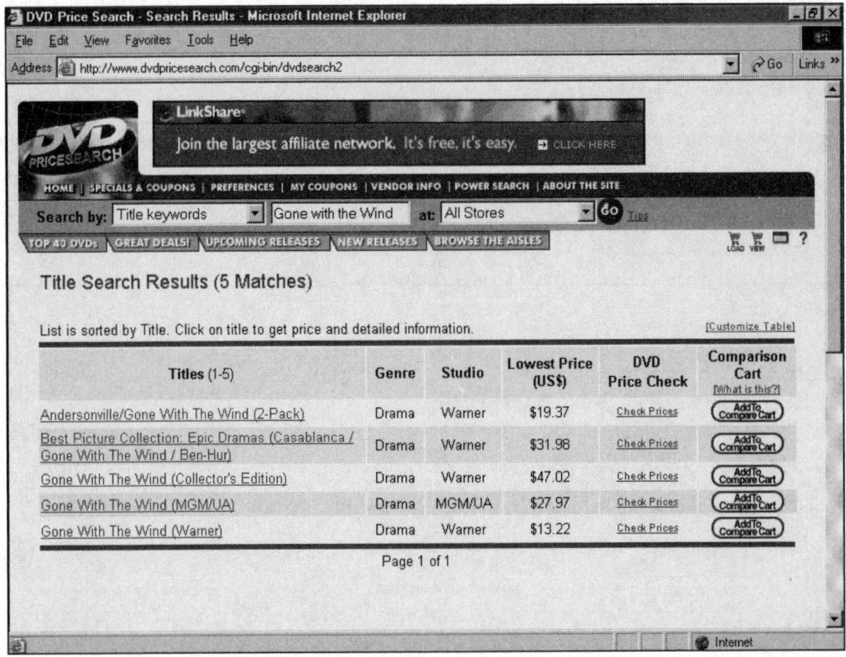

Figure 2-1 The introduction of the DVD was bolstered significantly by online shopping. DVD Price Search (*dvdpricesearch.com*) helps buyers quickly find the site offering best prices for favorite films.

effectively frees shoppers from having to continually look up a specific item and also allows them the ease of tracking it without even having to bid on it. Going a step further, the Favorites feature, also found within the *My eBay* console, relieves frequent shoppers from entering search terms time and time again. It allows favorite searches to be specified once and offers automatic e-mail notification when new items that match the search terms appear (see Figure 2-2).

As you look at your own activity as a seller on eBay and perhaps elsewhere on the Internet, look for ways to innovate and simplify the shopping and buying experience for your customers and maximize their shopping results with a minimal of shopping effort. Employ ways to make buying easier, perhaps through the use of online payment systems such as PayPal; provide price, quality, and service comparisons between your offerings and maybe those of a major retailer; offer links that lead shoppers to information sites where they can learn more about the goods they're interested in buying, encouraging them to return to your site for the final purchase or to ask more questions before they buy. Do all of this and you will have implemented a

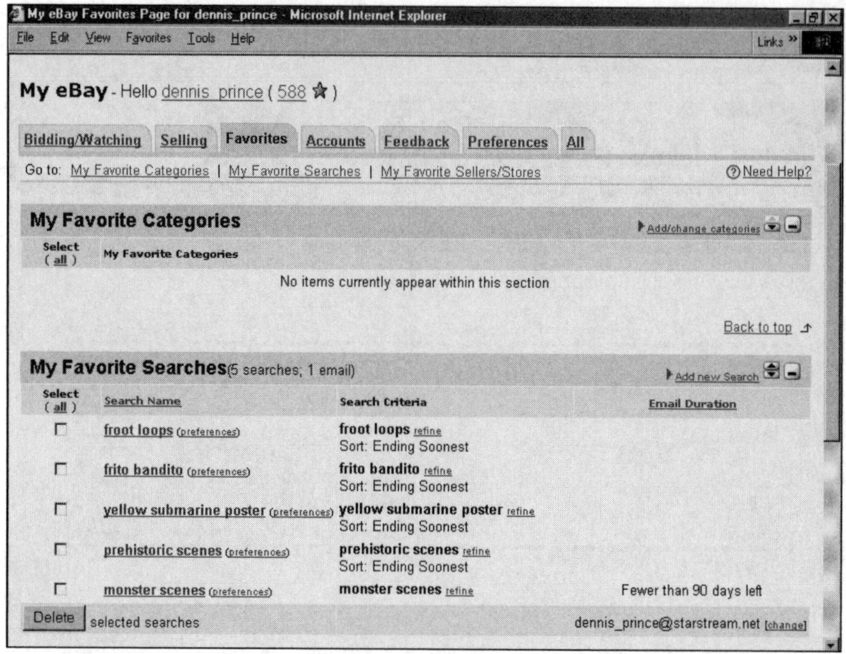

Figure 2-2 Visit the *My eBay* console to specify favorite search terms, then let eBay do the searching for you.

customer-centric shopping experience that will not only help you make a sale but also earn you a good reputation and encourage repeat customer visits.

eBay TIP: The easiest way to identify how to improve the shopping experience for your customers is to ask yourself what *you* would prefer to see in an auction listing, an eBay store, or any commercial Web site. Sellers are usually the toughest critics of all and, if you honestly apply that criticism to your own selling portals, you'll be certain to develop an experience that will be both pleasing and productive for your online patrons.

IT'S NOT THE SAME OLD eBAY ANYMORE

Since eBay's introduction back in 1995, it seems that a generation of pre-Internet users and consumers has passed through its virtual doors, while the new generation of Internet-ready users is venturing in with gusto. Given the

speed at which the Internet has grown and become a staple of our lives, this might not be too much of an exaggeration of time elapsed. What's different about eBay today is the interesting new ways in which buyers and sellers use the site. No longer a flea market setting where folks simply pass the time and trade unique wares, eBay has been molded into something of a problem solver, a site where folks can quickly and easily tend to their material needs. Consider these examples of how folks are using eBay for day-to-day purchases.

The Butcher, the Baker, the Beer-Commercial Maker

As consumers have come to embrace the ease and convenience of shopping online and bidding for just about anything in an effort to save money, they're turning away from the local butcher's block and, instead, visiting the auction block to purchase beef, poultry, and fish. Omaha Steaks has offered its 100 percent guaranteed meats on eBay and even participated in eBay's 2001 "The Ultimate Dining Experience" promotion. Superior Meats, likewise, has positioned its Ring Bell for Service sign on eBay, offering what it deems the "best steaks on eBay" by hosting regular auctions of USDA Choice Black Angus meats and also including a highly visible eBay link at its own online store, *www.steaks4less.com.*

After a nice meal, how about dessert? The Schwan Food Company, famous for its steady service of bringing all manner of goods directly to consumers' doorsteps since the 1950s, broadened its offerings of postentrée treats when it acquired Mrs. Smith's in 2003. Though other 1990s versions of home-delivered groceries, such as those of Webvan and supermarket chains, failed to flourish, Schwan's is growing faster than ever and is eagerly pursuing new and more effective ways to deliver tasty goods through what it refers to as alternate distribution channels, including eBay auctions and mail delivery.

Finally, after you've pushed away from the table, how about a cold beer to relax with? Well, alcohol sales are prohibited on eBay, but beer makers have still turned to the site for help in promoting their product. Production designer Michael Borthwick turned to eBay when filming a commercial for a well-known Canadian lager. "Believe it or not, we needed some stuffed chipmunks and squirrels for a beer commercial up here [in Canada]. It's illegal to stuff a chipmunk up here. . . . Apparently too many taxidermists were creating little baseball scenes and bowling teams out of the little fellas so I had to go on eBay and find a guy in Minnesota who could deliver. Trouble for production is we need everything yesterday, and usually waiting for an eBay auction to end wasn't an option. We found what we were looking for, contacted the guy, and he agreed to end the auction early. Thanks to him, we kept our shoot on schedule." Borthwick went on to share how other production designers like himself are turning to eBay more and more to acquire unique and essential props and set pieces. "Another designer I know was

shooting a bank commercial set circa Christmas 1962. She went to eBay and found a mint Easy-Bake Oven that ultimately featured prominently in the commercial."

It seems there's no end to the emerging usefulness of eBay.

Something Old, Something New, Something Found on eBay, Too!

Whenever two people are struck by Cupid's arrow and decide that a storybook wedding is the only cure for their blissfully lovesick pangs, their cloud of love dissipates quickly once they discover the often exorbitant costs imposed by the "wedding industry." That was yesterday, though, because today eBay serves love-struck couples who are finding creative new ways to tie the knot in grand fashion. Bride-to-be Sarah Manongdo of Chicago, Illinois, has taken a more direct approach in preparing for her May 2005 wedding, shunning the usual wedding spending holes and shopping on eBay instead.

"I started shopping on eBay to purchase some of my wedding items a few months ago (my wedding is a year and a half away). Just for fun, I made an Excel worksheet on how much I spent per item (including shipping) and compared it to how much I *would* have spent if I hadn't used eBay and had gone to the mall/bridal shops instead. Currently I've spent $300 in items and $100 in shipping yet, compared to the retail price total of $3,000, I've trimmed 90% off my costs already. And I'm just getting started." Clearly, Sarah's husband-to-be, Dan Joya, is a lucky guy to have such a cost-conscious, Net-savvy new bride.

Now consider the phenomenal results Liz Hoffswell of Holland, Michigan, has achieved since she decided to cater to the growing online matrimony market and began selling wedding dresses on eBay. Starting with just ten new dresses at an investment cost of $500, she's since established a lucrative business on eBay that earns her $1 million a year. Liz shared some of the details of her unexpected success: She began buying wedding dresses from closeout merchants and reselling them on eBay. "Before I knew it, I was buying 20, 50 and 500 wedding dresses at a time and reselling them on eBay. I was in the wedding dress business, and I didn't even have a store." Hoffman will garner nearly $1 million dollars in sales this year by offering eager new brides beautiful wedding dresses at roughly 25 percent of retail cost. Plus, she gains the added benefit of helping a new bride walk proudly down the aisle.

eBay as the New Virtual Catwalk for Fashion Designers

Having premiered in February 2001, eBay's Apparel Division quickly soared to become yet another of the site's $1 billion-a-year commodity segments. Thanks to its success in other noncollectible categories, eBay has also become a de facto stopping point for shoppers on the hunt for all manner of designer handbags, shoes, pants, and other clothing items and accessories. And

Figure 2-3 A search for hot fashionables from Prada revealed over 2000 chic items ready for bid.

while buyers eagerly scoop up the usual clothing goods available at the nearby department stores and clothing outlets, many more have turned to eBay to score great deals on more select items like Balenciaga cargo pants, Birkin bags, Marc Jacobs military jackets, and Yves Saint Laurent Mombasa bags, whether new or gently used (see Figure 2-3). Consumers have made eBay a regular venue to visit when seeking affordable apparel.

Don't think this billion-dollar bidding frenzy has gone unnoticed by some of the world's most prominent fashion designers, either. On the contrary, due to its growing popularity with dyed-in-the-wool fashionistas—those who identify themselves with only the finer fashions in life—top designers are now diverting their offerings from the crowded New York runways to the bustling eBay stage. In a promotional procession during February 2004, the sizzling new design team Proenza Schouler paraded their fashionable fleece on eBay *six months before their designs hit the stores*. How's that for recognition of eBay's credentials? In response, motivated high-end fashion buyers clamored at the chance to attend an online trunk show, scoring hot new designs ahead of the public at large (and paying top prices to do so). Sure, eBay is well known as a discount site of sorts, but it has also successfully showcased its finer side as fashion items from Prada, Kate Spade, and

Louis Vuitton can now regularly be found up for bid. It's practically becoming a black-tie and silver-sequin affair.

Home Sweet Home

When you're not dressing up yourself, how about turning to eBay to dress up your home? Like practically every other major category on the site, eBay's Home category has also boomed, hosting all manner of house and garden goods. From items as mundane as vacuum cleaner bags and bathroom fixtures to high-end rugs and chandeliers, eBay has moved into the market for domestic items. The wide range of availability is the reason for this growth: on eBay, you could conceivably furnish an entire house, from paint to flooring and everything in between. And it's not just serving up garage sale castoffs: major retailers like Sears and Sharper Image have employed the site to move goods quickly, whether they're new in the box and fully warranteed or factory refurbished and ready for a second go-around. These big-time businesses have seen the merits (and profits) of adding specialized staff personnel to list and manage online auctions (check the offerings from Seller ID "sears" and see how this retailer once regarded as stodgy is developing a significant presence in the auction marketplace).

Recently, a Los Angeles–based home contractor turned to eBay when he decided to renovate and resell a small Palm Springs home. Reportedly inclined to give the domicile a 1950s retro appeal, he sharpened up the home and turned a clear profit for his effort. Sellers of home goods are jumping into this growing category with both feet, offering direct-from-manufacture goods such as Pottery Barn and House and Garden offerings and reselling with success where the new breed of home shopper is actively buying (see Part 3 for more information on sourcing goods to resell on eBay).

eBay for Everything

The list is virtually endless in cataloging the inventive and insightful new ways that eBay is being used: banks selling certificates of deposit, museum curators uncovering strange new finds (without a pickax or shovel), and news services gleaning information on any and every new trend in our culture. It offers unending potential for sellers, buyers, economists, educators, designers, writers, and, yes, even the mildly curious onlooker. Fast becoming the standard destination for folks seeking just about anything, from goods to services to information, and with a population of nearly 100 million, eBay is practically a world unto itself.

YOU, THE NEXT INNOVATOR

So while learning of the impressive successes of others is quite interesting, the obvious next question is, What does it all mean to *me*? Glad you asked.

The point of all this is to help you broaden your view and open your mind to new and different ways to use eBay beyond its previous online-bazaar mentality. The examples you've read about here just skim the surface of eBay's potential in our new world economy. Now it's time to look at your business, whether it's new on the block or existing and ready to expand, and identify new ways to reach customers, service their wants and needs, and grow your profit potential. Therefore, understand that the key to utilizing eBay is to go into it completely unafraid; that is, to dare to do something different and explore the previously unexplored. Because the costs and risks are incredibly low as compared with attempting a brave new venture in the brick-and-mortar world, the only thing holding you back at this point is your own imagination.

eBay TIP: Here's a truly unusual account, but it makes a strong point nonetheless. Reportedly, Jennifer Glass stumbled across, of all things, two discarded prosthetic limbs beside a trash bin. Unfazed at the oddness of her find, she offered them up for bid on eBay.

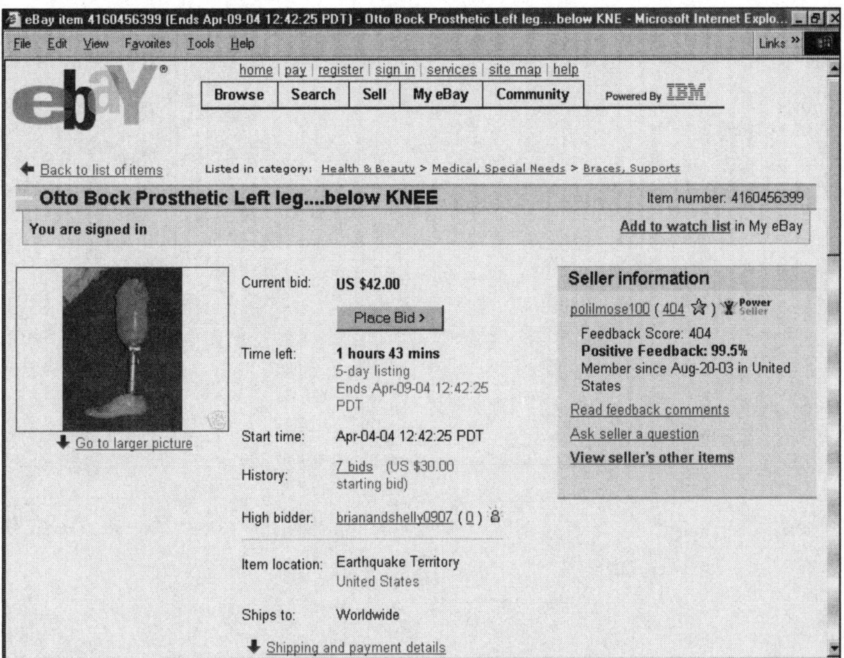

Figure 2-4 If you want to get a "leg up" on the competition, open your mind to selling or specializing in just about anything on eBay.

Strange but true, she earned $76 for one of the artificial legs, $29 for the other. On the surface, this may seem just another of those sick eBay stories, but a closer examination reveals that *anything* can draw a market at the world's largest online marketplace. And for Jennifer, it *didn't* cost her an arm and a leg to make a couple of quick sales (see Figure 2-4).

3

Cool New eBay Tools

Following the discussion of innovation in Chapter 2, it's easy to want to be innovative, to strive toward identifying and developing new marketing approaches and compelling product offerings, and to blaze the newest trails in online merchandising. But it takes time to innovate, and as I've always maintained, time *is* money. Your time required to break into new online auctioning and selling opportunities is extremely valuable, more so when you find yourself already very busy managing your current eBay and other online selling efforts and unable to allot the time to tap into new and potentially lucrative markets. When you find yourself in this potential business quagmire, you're subject to taking losses in areas where additional monies can be made but that lie just out of reach. This is the concept of opportunity cost, that is, the actual cost you bear when you're *not* able to investigate and implement new selling strategies or product offerings because of the precious time your current activities consume; and that cost could be significant.

Your challenge is to find ways to streamline your existing selling activities (you don't want to cut off the flow of income you've already established) to free up more time to further develop your business and take advantage of those profit-bearing opportunities that are ripe for the harvesting, while simultaneously enhancing the appeal of your offerings through improved style and design. Sure, it's a lot to juggle, keeping the current business running at full tilt while blazing new paths to profits, but it's being done every day by sellers just like you. The secret is no secret at all: look to improve the tools and methods you use to run your online business and you'll be better positioned to expand your business without missing a beat.

Every month, on eBay and many other non-eBay sites, better tools that significantly improve your market potential are being introduced. This chapter will explore some of the newer eBay tools that will help you advance your

online efforts, the ones that can save you time in your current business, improve the style and appeal of your business's products, and ultimately make it easier to lift your business to the next level of success.

THE BASIC ITEM-LISTING PAGE, UPDATED

Why not start with the eBay basics: your item-listing pages. Assuming you're fully at ease with listing items for auction or for direct sell (using the increasingly popular Buy It Now feature), take another look at how eBay has made it easier to add a bit of polish and organization during the item-listing process.

Though you're probably quite familiar with it, take a look at eBay's item-listing page (the Describe Your Item step of the listing process), as shown in Figure 3-1.

The first thing to notice is that the item title has now been expanded to 55 characters; that's 10 additional characters now available for key words that can increase the number of hits or views your items receive in buyer searches. Then, notice the new Subtitle option that allows you the flexibility to enter additional text that will appear in a search list just below your item's main title.

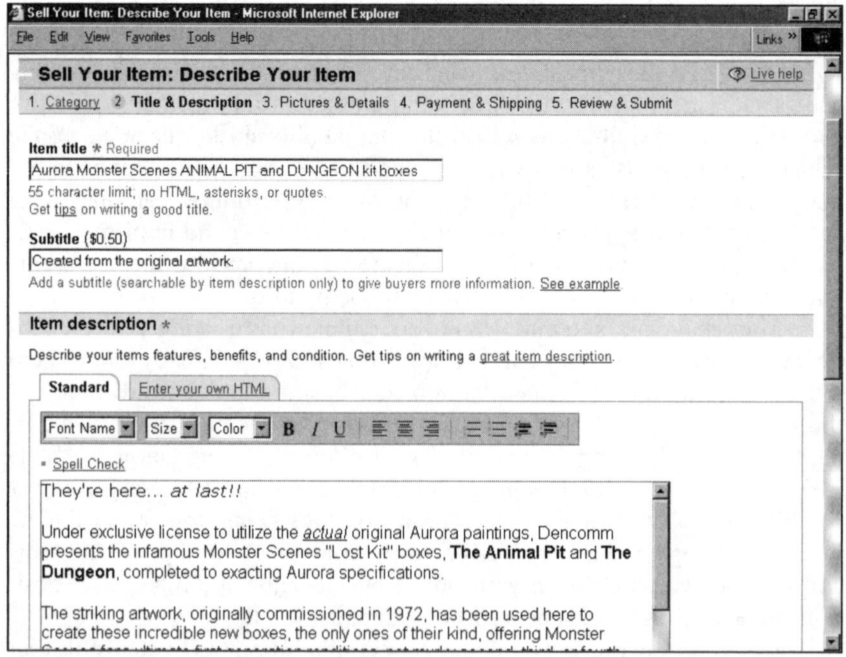

Figure 3-1 Some little changes can make a big difference. The Describe Your Item page now includes a longer title, a Subtitle option, and an easy text editor for your item description.

The keywords you include in the subtitle can only be searched if the buyer elects to include the Search Item Description option in the query for keywords. And, looking a bit further down, notice that the description section of the Describe Your Item page now includes a simple text-formatting bar that lets you select font style, size, color, and justification, and even create bulleted or numbered lists, all without resorting to HTML. There's even a spell-checker included! Look again at my sample text in Figure 3-1 and you'll see I altered text size and added a few simple effects to draw more attention to key details.

eBay TIP: Whether using eBay's easy description-formatting tools or stepping up to HTML design, use text fonts that are common to most computers. Of course, you can never know if your customers will have the same text-font library that you have, so try to utilize the most common fonts, such as Arial, Courier New, Verdana, or the old standard, Times New Roman. Though you may not get as dazzling a listing by using such plain, "vanilla" fonts, you'll be better off knowing that what you see is most likely what your customers, worldwide, will see. And, to keep up on what fonts are used most, make it a point to visit *www.codestyle.org/css/font-family/sampler-WindowsResults.shtml*; it's a terrific font-usage survey results page presented by Philip Shaw.

Of course, if you're interested in using HTML (hypertext markup language, the techno-dialect that makes up the World Wide Web), simply click on the HTML tab in the Describe Your Item page and begin entering your own custom code. Notice that if you've already entered text and added some enhancements using the text formatting bar, switching to the "Enter Your Own HTML" tab will display that same text with all the HTML tags that created those text effects. If you're looking for an easy head start on your HTML listings, this is a perfect opportunity (see Figure 3-2). Try it!

You've likely found that while HTML-created item descriptions appear a bit odd at first, HTML coding is quite straightforward for creating relatively simple yet effective listings. The key to effective HTML is style, not programming prowess. That is, while you can create some pretty stunning effects with HTML, you can also create a real visual mess of multicolored text, blinking images, and all manner of color mismatches that will leave a listing that looks like something from a gaudy Yuletide display, usually to the detriment of your ultimate sales success. While I can't effectively delve deeply into the best practices to use in creating your HTML listings, I can offer this: visit other listings and study other Web sites (those that you're likely to shop on) and notice which effects are most pleasing to you and which make the details of whatever it is you might be inclined to bid on or buy easiest to discern. Try to take note of colors, effects, or overall layouts that seem cumbersome, diffi-

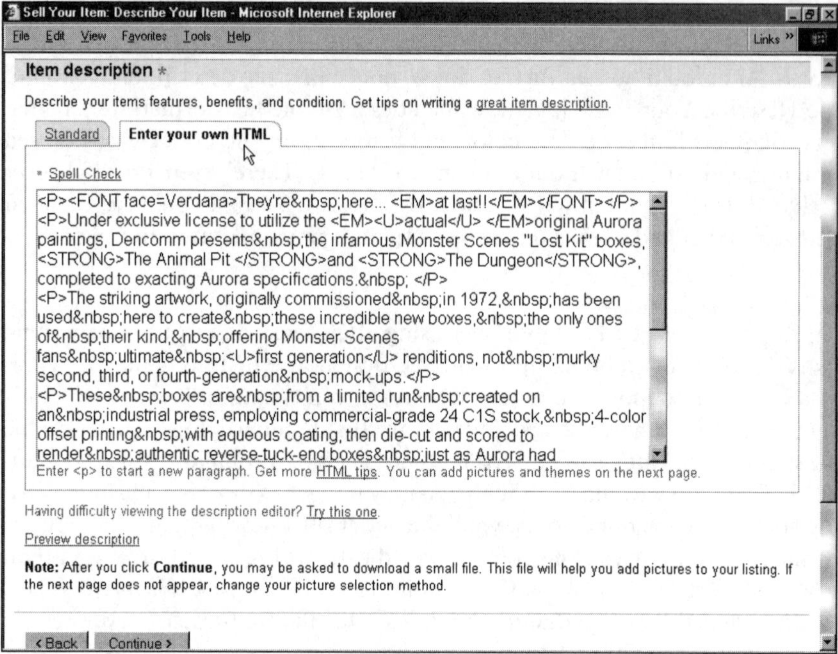

Figure 3-2 The text you see here was created using the text formatting bar, but now, with the HTML tab switched on, the screen displays the HTML equivalent for an easy head start to description customizing.

cult to read, or generally distracting, then avoid those methods. Even though HTML can produce some sterling results, try to keep things simple for your shoppers.

NEW ONE-DAY LISTINGS FOR FAST SALES

Another new feature available on eBay is the ability to host 1-day auctions. Previously, you selected from 3-, 5-, 7-, and 10-day auction durations, but now you can list an item and complete the auction in a mere 24 hours. In the past, I've always maintained (and still do) that auctions need to run at least 5 to 7 days in order to gain the greatest visibility to the potential market of bidders and buyers; however, 1-day auctions can be very effective, and I highly recommend them in the following situations:

- You are selling time-sensitive items such as event tickets, airline tickets, or other such dated goods that may suffer from an extended auction duration.

- You have a seasonal offering that buyers will want to be able to win quickly, such as that hot and have-to-have toy that needs to get under the Christmas tree in time for December 25.
- You have an inventory of identical items that you want to list simultaneously and allow buyers to buy quickly. eBay restricts all buyers from listing more than 10 identical items at any given time. In the case of 3-day auctions, you could only offer 30 identical items each week. Now, with auctions closing within 24 hours, you can host up to 70 identical items each week with 10 listings starting every day.

PREFILLED FORMS FOR FAST LISTINGS

Leveraging from the features of eBay-owned Half.com, the site where sellers can offer books, movies, music CDs, video games, and so much more in an easy-to-manage fixed-price setting, eBay has implemented *pre-filled* information for similar types of goods to be offered for auction. If you're selling books, compact discs, movies, or other items that bear a UPC (Universal Product Code) or ISBN (International Standard Book Number), all you need

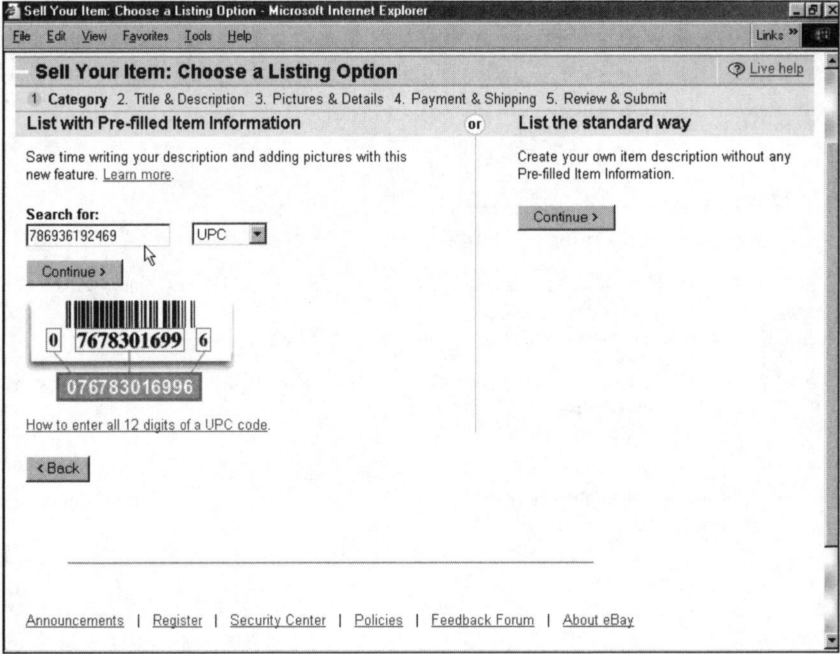

Figure 3-3 When listing a DVD for auction, enter the UPC number and let eBay provide the bulk of the description for you.

to do is enter that code, and eBay will load the majority of information for you (see Figure 3-3).

After I selected the "Continue" button, shown in Figure 3-3, eBay located the item, suggested an item title, provided a stock image of the DVD cover, and added production information for the film (see Figure 3-4); all I typed was the UPC number.

eBay TIP: If you don't wish to use eBay's pre-filled information for this sort of item, simply select the alternate "Continue" button you see in Figure 3-3 so you can "List the standard way." Take special care when using pre-filled information, especially stock pictures that eBay might provide, if that information misrepresents your item in any way. If your item features different packaging or contents, or is in a lesser condition, the pre-filled information promises something different than what your buyer will receive, so it's best in those cases to make all those specifications yourself, including providing a picture of the actual item you're listing.

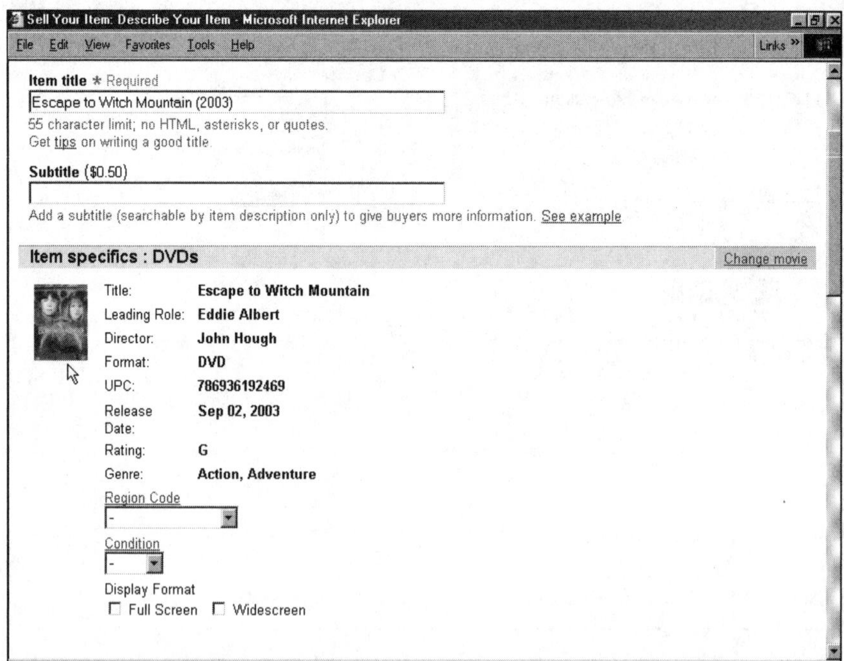

Figure 3-4 All I provide is a UPC number, and eBay provides the detailed information you see in this example.

BULKING UP YOUR BULK LISTINGS

If you're looking to grow your eBay business, you'll surely be needing to list 100 or more items each week. Using the single-item listing form is simply too time consuming for that level of activity, and so you've likely switched to bulk listing using eBay's Turbo Lister utility, the tool that allows you to define large collections of goods outside of eBay's item-listing pages and then easily upload large batches of items whenever you're ready. If you're using Turbo Lister today, terrific, but are you sure you're getting the most from the tool? As you advance your sales, make sure you advance your use of Turbo Lister. Here are a few considerations you should confirm in your use of the tool.

Have You Upgraded Lately?

As noted earlier in this chapter, eBay has made some enhancements to the listing form and, as a result, you may need to upgrade your version of Turbo Lister to ensure that your bulk listings are up-to-date with the site features. Just visit eBay's *Site Map* link (a text link located at the top of every eBay page), locate the Turbo Lister link on the Site Map page (or go directly to *pages.ebay.com/turbo_lister/*). From there, click the *Download Now* link and select *Turbo Lister Web Setup*. If you already have Turbo Lister installed on your computer, this setup wizard will upgrade your installed components and bring you up-to-speed with the latest listing features.

Duplicate Your Efforts

Although this sounds like the antithesis if good time management, it makes excellent business sense to duplicate your efforts with Turbo Lister. Notice the toolbar at the top of the Turbo Lister screen (see Figure 3-5) and you'll see the "Duplicate" and "Duplicate As" buttons. If you've never used these, start now. These button will save you time by doing the following:

- *Duplicate.* When an item in your current Turbo Lister inventory is selected, this button will create additional inventory entries automatically, allowing you to decide *how many* additional inventory entries you want. If you're selling identical items on eBay, let this function create the multiple listing items for you; all you need to decide is when you want to launch the new batch of the same goods.
- *Duplicate As.* This copying function performs just as "Duplicate," except it allows you to create another listing for a same item but in a different format. You'll be able to indicate quickly and easily if you want the duplicated entry to be created as an auction listing rather than a fixed-price offering. This is an easy way to convert auction items to eBay Stores inventory, or vice versa, with just a couple of clicks of the mouse.

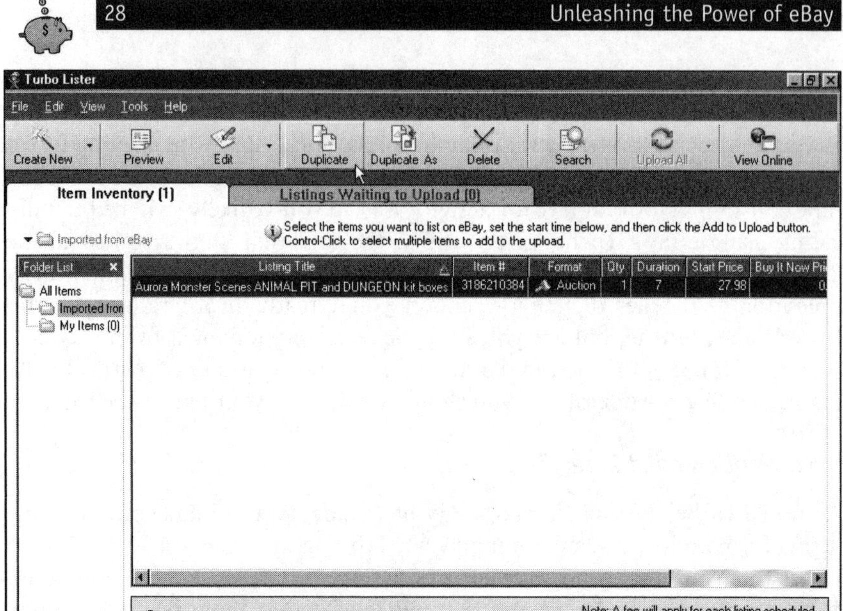

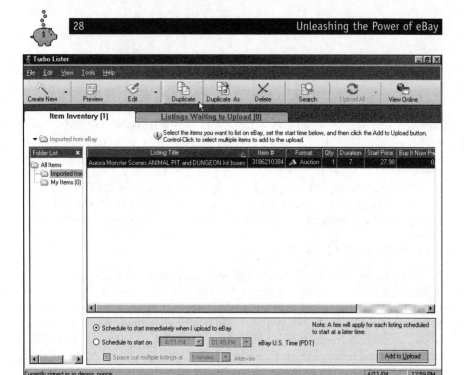

Figure 3-5 Use Turbo Lister's "Duplicate" and "Duplicate As" buttons to quickly add identical items to your inventory.

Folder Fodder

Depending on the sorts of items you'll be selling, you'll see that using the Turbo Lister folders is an easy way to group similar or complementary items in your inventory pages. As you acquire new items to offer, you can easily create a Turbo Lister inventory entry for each item and file it in an appropriate folder consisting of like items. This way, you can launch your folders of items in a single action, strategically listing your goods to coincide with seasonal appeal, the eBay Merchandising Calendar (see Chapter 5), or any other such designation you choose so that your goods will be in highest potential demand. I like to launch movie memorabilia items in a group batch, Christmas-related items during the holiday in one fell swoop, and auction-related tools and supplies year-round. Using the Turbo Lister inventory folders, this is easy and time efficient.

Pre-filled for Fast Listing

Great news! Turbo Lister has also been upgraded to allow you to benefit from pre-filled information for books, compact discs, DVDs, and other such items bearing UPC or ISBN codes. Just as you learned in the discussion earlier in

this chapter, pre-filled information can save you tremendous amounts of time whether you list individually or in bulk. All you have to do is type in the UPC or ISBN, and all the key information is automatically filled in for you.

Import Your Current eBay Listings

If you're already hosting a block of items on eBay but haven't begun to use Turbo Lister just yet, the good news here is that you can easily import the details of your current auctions directly from eBay and into a Turbo Lister item inventory. It's as simple as this: after you've started up Turbo Lister, simply click on the menu choice "File," select "Import items" from the drop-down menu, then select "From eBay listings" on the final menu. Turbo Lister will access eBay, locate your active auctions, and pull the data into your item inventory. This is excellent news for sellers who have been using eBay for some time and already have a host of auction or fixed-price items active on the site. With this import feature, there's no need to waste time rekeying the items into Turbo Lister. That equals more time saved for you.

Time Is on Your Side

Remember that, just as with listing items one-by-one on eBay, Turbo Lister allows you to specify a start date and time for your collections of offerings. If you'll be out of town or even away from the computer just temporarily, you can specify precisely when you want your bulk uploaded listings to commence on eBay, allowing you to begin your auctions at optimal times, even if it's not exactly optimal for you to be in attendance.

eBAY'S SHIPPING CALCULATOR

Ever since the advent of online buying, customers have been faced with paying additional fees to cover shipping costs. For many eBay buyers, this has been a source of confusion and sometimes frustration in cases where they were unclear about how much they'd be expected to add to their winning bid amount to ensure the delivery of their prize. Sellers, as a result, have also been faced with the challenge of calculating those fees quickly and accurately, sometimes erring on the side of excess and conceivably angering their customers or underestimating the costs and unwittingly siphoning off their profits in the process. That's all changed now that eBay's Shipping Calculator is available. It allows buyers to determine for themselves the costs of shipping, giving sellers the confidence that there will be no surprises in collecting these fees.

Including the Shipping Calculator in your auctions and fixed-price listings is easy: while listing a single item or creating an inventory entry in Turbo Lister, simply check on the "Calculated shipping rates" tab in the Payment and Shipping screen (see Figure 3-6).

When enabling the Shipping Calculator, you specify package size and

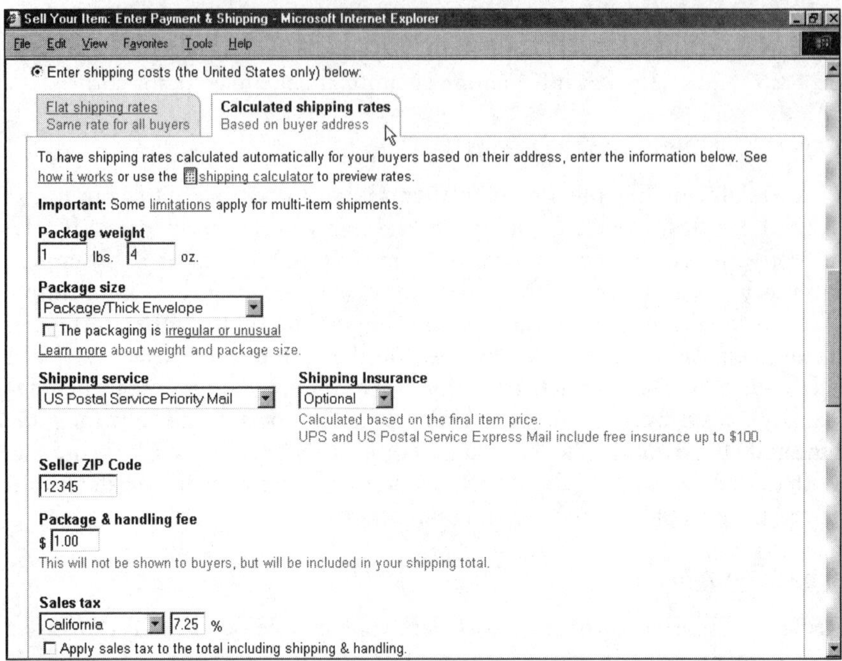

Figure 3-6 Using the eBay Shipping Calculator, you'll let your bidders and buyers calculate shipping for themselves.

weight characteristics, the carrier service you'll use, plus insurance, your charge for packaging and handling, and sales tax. In your auction listing, bidders will be able to enter *their* ZIP codes and, based on the information you've specified about the item, its packaging, and any additional fees you've included, they will be provided with the shipping fee that will be added to the final selling price. What's most useful about this tool is it allows your buyers to make a more informed decision about their potential final cost *before* they bid or buy. To this end, you've given them more information up front and have eliminated the need to respond to e-mail messages from buyers about these fees. Again, you've saved time and effort that you can instead apply elsewhere in your business.

eBay TIP: There are a few sensitive areas about the Shipping Calculator. First, you make the call in regard to the carrier service you'll be using; buyers may ask, on occasion, if you'll ship via a different method. But the decision is still up to you. Second, try to be very honest and accurate when specifying package characteristics; no one likes the butcher who slyly puts his thumb on the scale. Next, the package and han-

dling fee is an optional one you'll specify if you plan to charge for your packing supplies and/or shipping preparation time; that's a decision you'll need to make for yourself, but understand that if it's too high your potential bidders and buyers may balk at the shipping costs. Finally, collecting sales tax is only allowed if you are a bona-fide business and possess a valid Seller's Permit. Collecting taxes falsely is a federal offense. Oh, and typical protocol is to apply sales tax only to the item price, not the combination of item plus shipping costs. That is up to your discretion.

On a final note, when using the Shipping Calculator, your bidders and buyers will not be able to see the specifications you entered regarding your shipping ZIP code nor any package specifications or additional fee designations. This is good thinking on eBay's part, allowing sellers to maintain control and discretion over the way they specify and collect shipping costs.

POSTAGE FROM YOUR PRINTER

Just as you can easily view and print restaurant menus from your computer or buy and print movie tickets before you even step up to the theater box office, you can also easily buy and print postage and shipping labels directly from your home office. This is perhaps one of the best new features eBay has implemented, providing even more seamless functionality for sellers. It's simple to use, and you can pay through your PayPal account for the postage you buy. Here's how: When your auction or fixed-price listing sells, simply go to My eBay and find the Items I've Sold area (see Figure 3-7).

As you see in Figure 3-7, the "Shipment Status" column contains a button allowing you to "Print Shipping Label." Upon clicking the button, you'll be redirected to PayPal to select the carrier you wish to use (I'm using the U.S. Postal Service, as shown in Figure 3-8).

eBay TIP: To save time, you can establish a default carrier selection in the PayPal "Shipping Preferences" section.

From the screen shown in Figure 3-8, click the "Continue" button and proceed to specifying the details of the package to be shipped (see Figure 3-9).

If the buyer paid you using PayPal, his or her confirmed shipping address (the one they specified when they registered with PayPal) will automatically be populated in the shipping label screen for use on the label. If your buyer did not pay using PayPal or isn't a registered PayPal user, you'll merely need to fill in his or her address information yourself. Confirm the address information and click the "Continue" button; you'll see a confirmation screen, as shown in Figure 3-10.

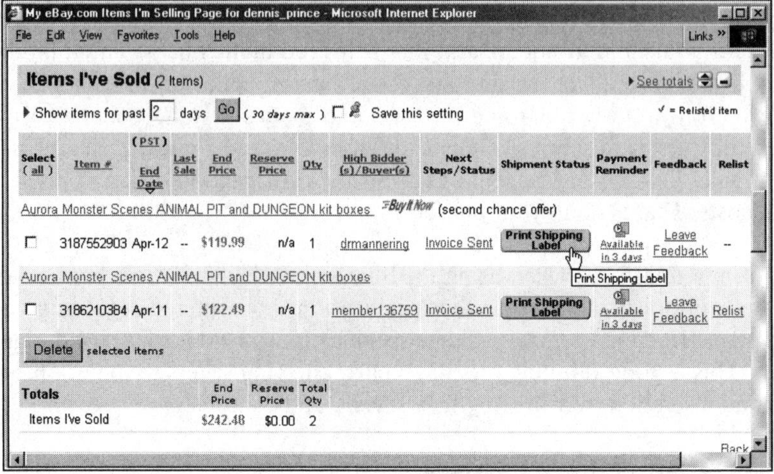

Figure 3-7 To create a shipping label from your computer, locate the appropriate pushbutton in the My eBay screen.

Figure 3-8 The next step is to select the carrier method you wish to use for shipping.

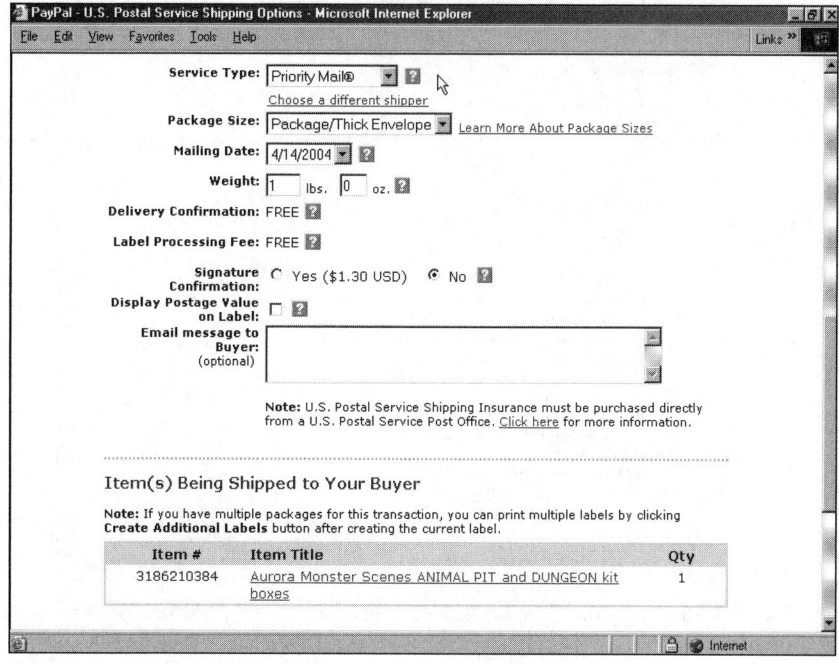

Figure 3-9 Enter the package specifications on this screen.

Figure 3-10 shows the details of the label you'll purchase and print for use in shipping the package. Review it carefully, then click the "Pay and Continue" button. After a short moment, you'll see a new pop-up window display a sample of the label you just created and for which the postage amount has been calculated and deducted from your PayPal account. All you need to do now is click on the "Print Label" button as shown in Figure 3-11, attach the label to your package, and send it on its way. No waiting in lines to buy postage, no licking numerous stamps, no overpaying for postage because you miscalculated; it's this easy. Just drop off your package in a nearby drop-box, take it to the post office or authorized postal collection station (found in many supermarkets) or just hand it to your postal carrier; it's paid for and ready to ship.

With this new feature, I've already shaved considerable time from my online-selling exploits. By and large, other sellers I speak with share the same sentiment: the packing and shipping process takes way too much time. Half of that problem—the postage and shipping process—is now under my control, no longer requiring the hit-or-miss uncertainty of visiting my post office or local shipping station and standing far too long at the back of a long line (at the supermarket, it seems everyone brings in their lottery tickets on

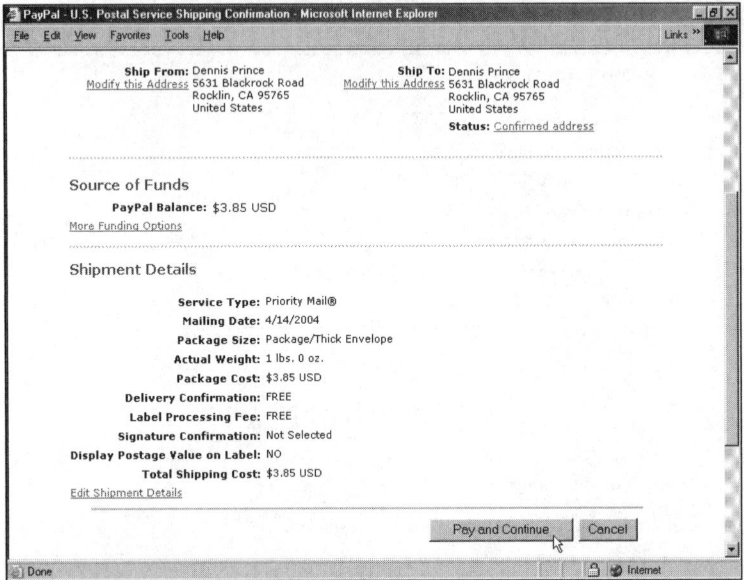

Figure 3-10 Verify the "Ship To" address of your buyer, verify the package specifications and the postage cost, and then proceed to create the label by clicking on the "Pay and Continue" button.

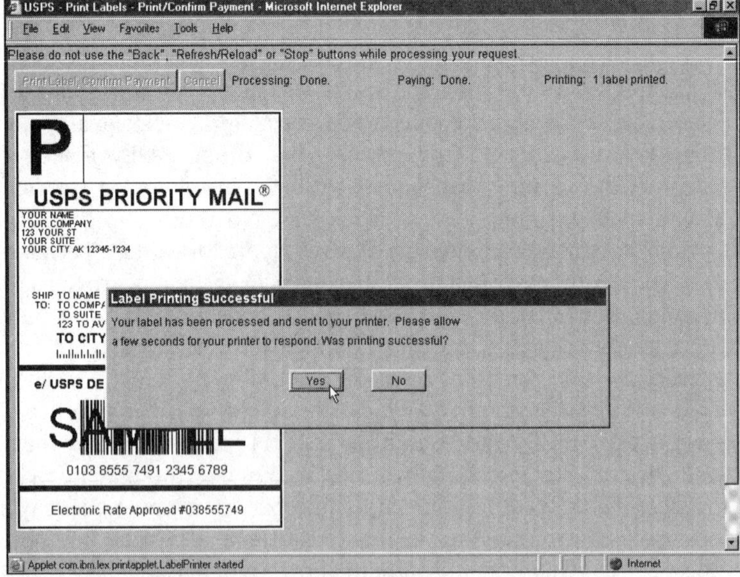

Figure 3-11 The shipping process just got easier thanks to online postage purchase and label printing.

the day I want to ship). In Chapter 12, I'll explain some ways to streamline packing.

Now, the eBay/PayPal online postage solution isn't the only show in town. If you've been in the online auction fray for long, you're likely aware of other services like Stamps.com, but that one incurs a monthly fee for continued service (although you will receive a free digital scale). The eBay/PayPal solution is a better choice since there is no usage fee and, as you saw previously, it brings your buyer's address information from eBay to auto-populate the form and save you more time. All other features, including 24/7 access to buy and create labels, free delivery confirmation, ability to suppress postage value from printing on the label, and online package tracking are part of both solutions.

OTHER COOL TOOLS OFF eBAY

Just so you know that all of what I'm stating here isn't some sort of commercial for the eBay site, here are some excellent non-eBay tools that you may also find of particular benefit. Remember, I'm here to advocate your success first and foremost, not necessarily eBay's. To that end, here are some handy tools that will help maximize your selling efforts.

Fee Calculators

If you're not using Turbo Lister or aren't interested in starting it up to take a look at the potential fees for a single auction, there are many free calculators available on the Web to help you determine how much of a cut eBay will be taking from your bottom line. Of the many calculators out there, here are the best I've seen so far:

- *HammerTap's Fee Finder.* Perhaps the most comprehensive fee calculator, this one calculates regular and Dutch auction fees, PayPal fees, and even shipping costs. *www.hammertap.com/FeeFinder.html*
- *The Bid Floor eBay Auction Fee Calculator.* A basic eBay auction fee calculator. *www.thebidfloor.com/ebay_calculator/ebay_auction_fee_calculator.php*
- *The Net Outpost Auction Fee Calculator.* Servicing the UK in British Pounds. *www.netoutpost.f2s.com/auction/*
- *The eTopps Clubhouse.* Designed for trading-card sellers; a tool that calculates the combined cost of eBay and PayPal fees. *www.etoppsclubhouse.com/expenses.htm*

These are some of the better fee calculators I've seen. Search the Web for "eBay Fee Calculator" and take your pick from the numerous choices. And, as you continue through this book, I'll point out other non-eBay tools that will help you in your business's growth.

A Little Java Goes a Long Way

Java is one of the more advanced HTML languages and is responsible for some of the nifty things you see when you visit well-designed Web pages. Although I won't attempt to turn you into a deep-coder at this point, there is one Java script (a piece of Java code that performs a self-contained function) that I think you'll appreciate. If ever you've been irked when you see an auction listing that unashamedly features one of *your* images, either from an eBay listing or from a Web site of your own, you'll want to find a way to fight back and keep those picture pilferers from swiping your images. The following short Java script can help you do just this: it prevents the image from being saved when a right-mouse-click is used (that's how you usually view the properties and ultimately save an *unprotected* image). Here's the simple code:

```
<head>

<script language="JavaScript"> <!—
// Script Description:
// Prevent right-click image copy script
// End of description

var message="Copyright (c)2004 DENCOMM"; // Message for the alert box

// Script function below

function click(e) {
if (document.all) {
if (event.button = 2) {
alert(message);
return false;
}
}
if (document.layers) {
if (e.which = 3) {
alert(message);
return false;
}
}
}
if (document.layers) {
document.captureEvents(Event.MOUSEDOWN);
}
```

```
document.onmousedown=click;
//—> </script>

</head>
```

Read this script carefully and you'll see that it prevents right-click mouse functions, delivering a pop-up copyright message instead of image details, as shown in an example from a Web site of my own (see Figure 3-12). Just add this code into your Web-page HTML or item-listing HTML just after the Header <head> tags and before the core of your design code.

Of course, this Java script isn't fail-safe, and those hardcore coders and hackers can likely find a way around it. However, for your uses in online selling and in order to prevent the majority of picture grabbers from using your images, this little script is a handy deterrent.

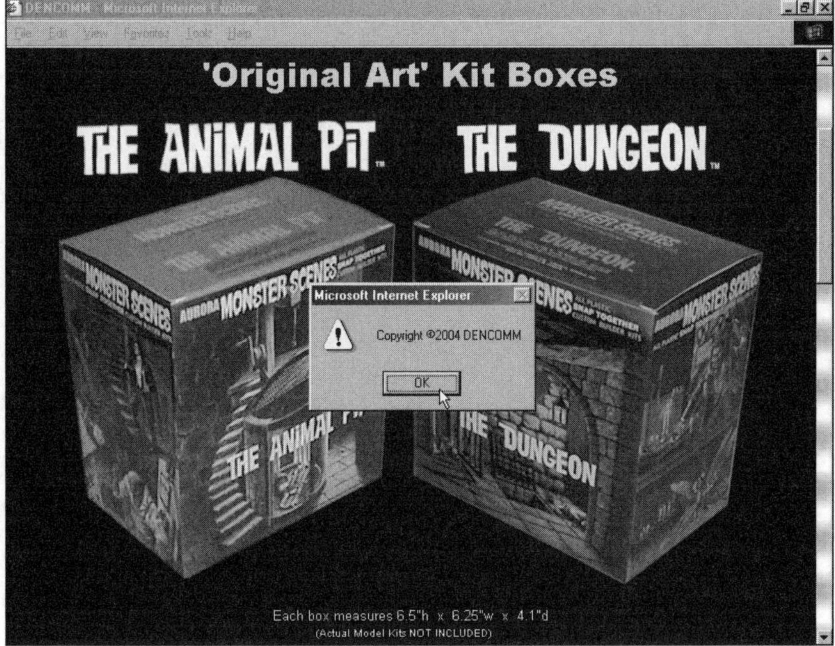

Figure 3-12 A simple Java script effectively displays my copyright ownership over the images I include on my business Web site as well as within my eBay listings.

NEW TOOLS AROUND EVERY TURN

There are plenty more services and tools, including auction management suites (I'll cover those in Chapter 15), both within and outside of eBay. For the purposes of this chapter, the goal was to ensure you were aware of the tools that I've found easiest to use (you can learn and apply them in a single sitting) and that will have the most immediate benefit to your business, either in saving you time, saving you money, or both. Next up, I'll show you the economic impact eBay has had the world over and why it makes good sense to build a new business or boost an existing enterprise in this bustling online market. That discussion and more is coming up in the next chapter.

4

Understanding the eBay Economy

You know, as a kid, I always hated math—until I learned it would help me count money. I'd venture there was a time for all of us when a topic like applied economics held absolutely no immediate appeal, and the only reason we might gravitate toward it at all was because is was part of our collegiate requirements. Well, assuming you've been busy on eBay for six months or longer (either actively selling or just actively browsing), you've likely become quite a fan of economic principles whether you realize it or not. The interesting thing about eBay and other outlets for online merchandising is that, now that we have the power to go into business for ourselves in a way that's infinitely easier than similar prospects of 10 or 20 years ago, economics is suddenly quite enjoyable because now it's *our* economics, the study of *our* business activity, successes, and statistical potential. Don't be surprised if you feel suddenly compelled to bid on economics textbooks on eBay.

While eBay has long been used by mom-and-pop outfits eager to eke out a few dollars in the large yet still presumably hobby economy, it's interesting to note that the site has now come onto the radar of professional economists, business analysts, and investment counselors. By remaining resilient through economic instabilities, eBay has remained as stable as ever and has proven its worth as a foundation for business and its ability to withstand the ebb and flow of the sometimes frenzied, often fickle, consumer marketplace. This chapter will reveal some of the buzz that eBay has created in the economic think tanks and why that spells even greater success for you, who has already discovered this as the perfect footing upon which to build your business.

eBAY: THE HUB OF A SELF-CONTAINED ECONOMY

Since its start in September 1995, the site has grown not just in number of items up for bid or swelling numbers of registered users: it has become an

economic entity in and of itself. Defining eBay as its own "self-regulating economy" (as stated by CEO Meg Whitman) goes well beyond the income the site generates for itself; it has actually become the catalyst for other businesses that have also become established and grown impressively *because of* eBay's existence. That's impressive and it's reassuring to you, the budding businessperson who's looking for firm ground upon which to launch your enterprise.

Doing Business at the Speed of eBay

If you look at the numbers, eBay appears to be unstoppable, thumbing its nose to every dot-com refugee and economic naysayer. Its results are the envy of its peers and would-be imitators. These are statistics from its 2003 consolidated financial report:

- Consolidated net revenues totaled a record $2.17 billion, an increase of 78 percent over 2002's $1.21 billion.
- Item listings totaled 971 million, 52 percent higher than the 638 million reported from 2002.
- Gross merchandising sales (the value of all goods sold on the site) totaled a record $24 billion, a 60 percent increase from the $15 billion reported from 2002.
- U.S. net transaction revenues totaled $291.6 million, a 38 percent year-over-year growth, while international net transaction revenues totaled $210.5 million, a 96 percent year-over-year growth.
- Confirmed registered users at the end of 2003 totaled 94.9 million, a 54 percent increase over the previous year.

Any questions? Any doubts? eBay *is* the platform of choice for easy entry into the small-business world and for low-cost expansion into multiregion, multinational markets. No wonder business analysts and economists the world over have started to take a serious look at this undeniable eBay economy.

HERE COME THE NIELSENS

Here's some tantalizing data to chew on: when ACNielsen conducted a 2004 survey among small businesses, it asked about planned growth to businesses that use eBay to sell their products and to those that do not. Of the respondents, 70 percent of small businesses that use eBay firmly indicated their plans to grow, while only 58 percent of businesses that don't use eBay to sell their goods were aspiring to expand in their land-based efforts. More compelling, additional survey data revealed that as many as 7 percent of the non-

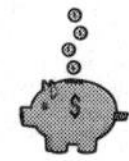

eBay businesses were concerned that the overall economy would determine actual growth success while a mere 2 percent of the eBay businesspeople gave any thought about the latest job data or global monetary rates as having any impact on their business's expansion.

Are these eBayers crazy? Don't they know economic times have been frightening, or at best uncertain, since the dot-com meltdown of 2000? Surely they're just a bunch of Inter-nuts who have their head in the digital sand, too foolish to know the ripple effect of a sluggish economy. Well, how about a few more facts about the rate of business that takes place on eBay, day in and day out:

- As eBay reports it, roughly 250,000 individuals are full-time eBay sellers, drawing their entire income from their eBay-based enterprises.
- At the end of 2003, eBay served as host to approximately 154,000 fixed-price eBay Stores worldwide, contributing around $2 billion to the site's gross merchandising sales.
- An estimated $729 worth of goods is sold on eBay every second.
- An estimated 10,000 people visit eBay Motors every month.
- An estimated 19 million items are available at any given time, more than 300 times the number of stockkeeping units in a typical Wal-Mart store.
- The $20 billion of goods sold on eBay in 2003 is $6.5 billion more than the annual revenue of Gap clothing stores.

If those are the statistics of the crazy businessperson, lock me up with the rest of them. Despite economic downturns or Wall Street skittishness, the eBay economy is somehow shielding itself from the typical pressures of the open-market system and has enabled millions of individuals and businesses combined to withstand the inclement economic weather outside eBay's doors.

A MICROECONOMY

So how has the once-amateurish AuctionWeb evolved into the microcosm known as eBay? The answer is that it *is* a microcosm, an economic and cultural world all to itself in some way, self-contained and impressively large, yet still nimble enough to alter direction at almost a nanosecond's notice. Briefly, here are the ingredients that have allowed eBay to evolve at its own blistering rate, benefits that you may or may not have fully stopped to appreciate:

- *eBay Established a New Free Market.* In his original concept, Pierre Omidyar determined that he would establish a marketplace where sellers would decide for themselves what they would sell and buyers

would decide what they would pay. This is the core ingredient that has enabled eBay to grow organically.

- *eBay Established a "Light Legislation."* Another of Pierre's original concepts was that of self-governance, the seed that germinated and produced eBay's Feedback Forum, which allows users to rate one another and clearly instills a reliance on maintaining a positive reputation to support business growth. A few of eBay's own governing tools and methods to thwart fraud and other illicit actions have been added, but with relative discretion to avoid upsetting the ongoing trading and transacting.
- *eBay Yielded to the Voice of the Community.* Certainly, the site hasn't been without fault in some of its developments, enhancements, and evolutionary steps, yet by and large it has demonstrated an awareness of the need to solicit user feedback, host in-person meetings with groups of sellers (Whitman entertains them personally by e-mail invitation on a monthly basis), and closely monitor questions, complaints, and ideas from the various site forums.

    Though the site has grown far beyond those days of small-town trading, it still embodies that "come on in, help yourself, and do things your way" way of thinking.
- *eBay Established Its Own Banking System.* When eBay acquired PayPal in 2002, it created a seamless transition from bidding and buying to payment and collection. By doing so, the site solidly addressed one of its inherent failings: while auctions could be conducted at the speed of the Internet, payment was still dragging at a snail-mail's pace. And now that online postage is in effect, the site has also created something akin to a virtual post office, again adding speed and elegance to that otherwise sluggish step in transacting (recall the discussion of online postage from Chapter 3).
- *eBay Established an Education System.* Since many people are still new to eBay and are searching for ways to quickly come up to speed with the other 100 million users, eBay created its traveling training camp, eBay University. Hosted over a weekend and appearing throughout the year in numerous major cities, eBay helps new users get started and current users get growing. Although the instruction doesn't get into the advanced information that you'll find in these pages, it nonetheless smooths some of the rough spots for new and experienced eBay business people.
- *eBay Promotes Global Trade.* With acquisition of new sites in countries such as Germany, China, Britain, and others, eBay has broadened its reach and thereby has broadened the reach of every buyer or seller within its community, enabling global trading in a way never before imagined.

All of this has led to an explosion in the new wave of microbusinesses, small businesses that can be initiated by a single individual and can operate at the same or similar level of a conventional small business. The most exciting element of starting, operating, and growing a microbusiness is that it can typically be done with little, if any, formal business experience. Operating overhead has all but been eliminated by eBay's ready-to-use business model and captive audience of consumers. New businesses can get started on minimal inventory investment (I started my ventures with the accumulated goods stowed away in my own closets, garage, and attic) and can often support lower sales prices while providing reasonable profits, because office space, storage facilities, and other such income siphons can be avoided. Most encouraging about all of this is that you and I can effectively spread the word of our up-and-coming business ventures for practically pennies by floating our marketing balloon in front of the eyes of 100 million registered eBay users. *That's* good business, *that's* a strong economic situation, and *that's* the reason the eBay economy is alive and well and ready to help you advance your business goals.

5

What's Selling on eBay and Who's Selling It?

The perennial question of practically all eBay sellers still seems to be, What should I sell on eBay? Though it's the most obvious question to ask, especially to those who are new at venturing into online auctioning, it's sometimes the most difficult to answer. While I contend that you can sell practically *anything* on eBay (and make a fortune), sellers looking to advance their businesses, whether they are strictly online or existing brick-and-mortar establishments, will want to carefully study the online market and just as carefully consider what they'll attempt to market. This chapter will introduce you to the newest tools that can help to acquire and analyze eBay data and, in the end, put you in a more confident position to decide what's selling and whether you'll sell it too.

RESEARCH THE MARKET, CONSTANTLY

You can never research consumer trends enough. Fickle as we buyers are, our attitudes can change overnight due to the never-ending influence of world events, the entertainment industry, the technology sector, and myriad other reasons that would have us buy Brand B tomorrow when yesterday we'd never settle for anything other than Brand A. To keep up with the changing wants and needs of buyers, especially within the realm of eBay, you'll need to constantly monitor the market, the offerings, and the prices being paid for the sorts of goods you'll expect to sell.

Browsing the Category Offerings

Simply enough, start by looking over the details of offerings within the eBay categories and sub-categories. The easiest way to do this is to click the *Browse* button located on the eBay main toolbar that you see at the top of the eBay home page as well as at the top of most other eBay pages (see Figure 5-1).

When you search all categories in this fashion, you'll see a listing of category headers and sub-category headers, each of which includes parenthetical numbers that indicate how many different listings are currently available (see Figure 5-2).

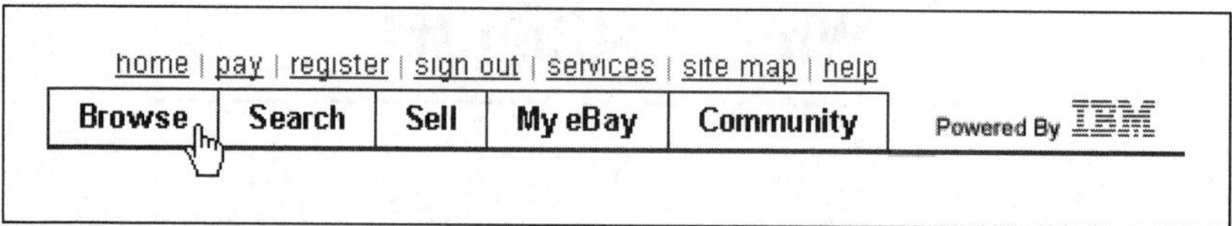

Figure 5-1 Click the *Browse* button on the eBay main toolbar to begin researching the number of items currently available in each of the eBay item categories and sub-categories.

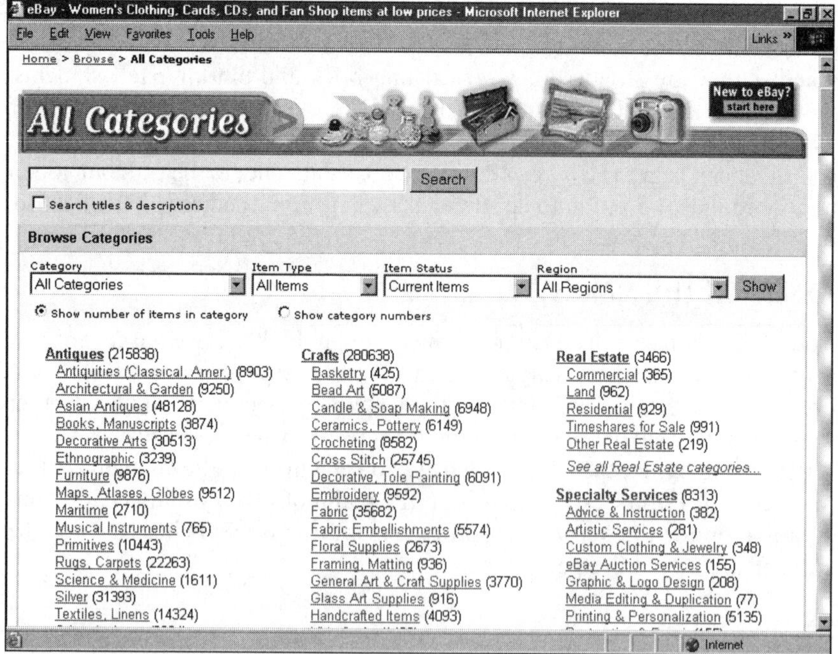

Figure 5-2 Search all categories to see how many active listings are currently underway.

As you browse the different categories, take note of which seem to contain the highest number of listed items (the *Collectibles* category has traditionally been tops in this regard, but other categories are nearly ready to take the lead), then drill into the subcategories and explore the types of items being offered. This is a useful exercise because it gives you a view into where sellers are concentrating their efforts, working on the assumption that they wouldn't be offering it if it wasn't selling. Even though the number of listings doesn't directly equate to the actual number of items sold, you can gain an immediate pulse on where the action is, what categories seem to be up-and-coming, by monitoring the change in their numbers of active listings, and which areas are either less active or (pay attention here) prime for development.

Investigating Completed Items

Having investigated what's currently available by searching the category listings, refine that search by looking at what transactions have recently been *completed* on eBay. For this analysis, you'll need to narrow your search using key words, terms, and phrases that will deliver results lists for items you're interested in marketing yourself. If you're curious about how popular outdoor tiki torches, perhaps, are on eBay, search for those in the current listings then, on the results page, select the *Completed listings* checkbox you'll see in the left-hand column in the Search Options area (see Figure 5-3).

In reviewing the completed listings for tiki torches, I found that 141 auctions have recently closed, and I have the details at my fingertips regarding number of bids, bid amounts, and sellers who are peddling such wares. Completed listings are hugely useful in your research of what's hot and what's not on eBay in that they allow you to determine how well particular items are selling, what prices buyers are earning for these items, how many bidders seem to be bidding on these goods, and how much room there is for another player to offer similar goods (that would be you). Unfortunately, due to the millions upon millions of listings available on eBay at any given time, you can only drill the site for completed items dating back two weeks; any more and the site would probably choke if it tried to maintain information on such a huge amount of closed listings.

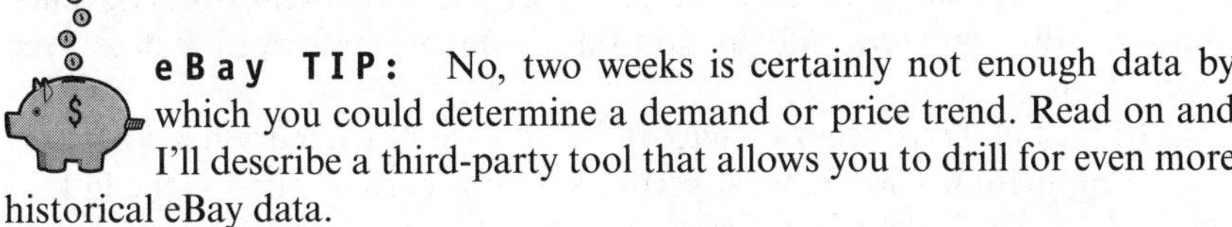

eBay TIP: No, two weeks is certainly not enough data by which you could determine a demand or price trend. Read on and I'll describe a third-party tool that allows you to drill for even more historical eBay data.

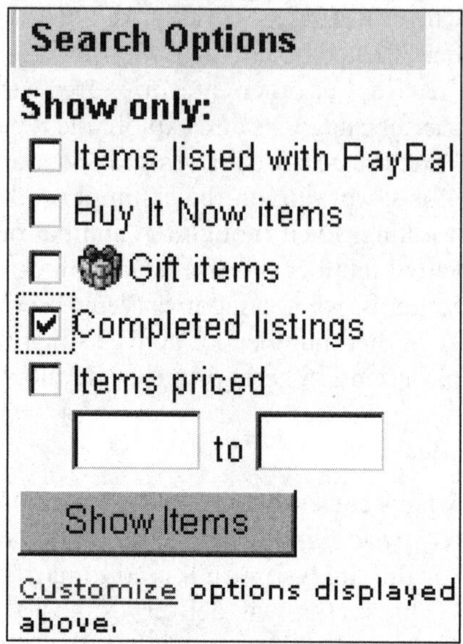

Figure 5-3 On a current-listings search result, select the *Completed listings* checkbox to check results of recently completed auctions.

Learning about Popular Searches

Sometimes the difficulty about determining what sells and what, ultimately, you'll sell lies in our limitations of knowing what buyers are searching and shopping for. You and I can use our own indications about what we like, what interests us, and what *we* believe will be popular among buyers, but *only the buyers themselves can reveal what's hot and what's not*. To crack this particular nut, you need to understand what search terms and keywords are used most on eBay. Thankfully, eBay provides a snapshot of this critical data.

It's difficult to find, this treasured information, so begin by visiting eBay's Site Map, then click on the *Seller Central* link you'll find on the Site Map page. From there, click on the *Sell by Category* link and you'll advance to a page that provides information on a category-by-category basis (see Figure 5-4).

In the Sell by Category page, you'll see various category headings and links to more information. Most pertinent to our current quest is the link *In Demand*, on which the pointer is positioned in Figure 5-4. For this example, I'll follow the link under *Antiques*. Clicking the *In Demand* link advances you to a page such as the one in Figure 5-5 where, upon scrolling down just a bit, you'll see that eBay has compiled a collection of buyers' top search terms.

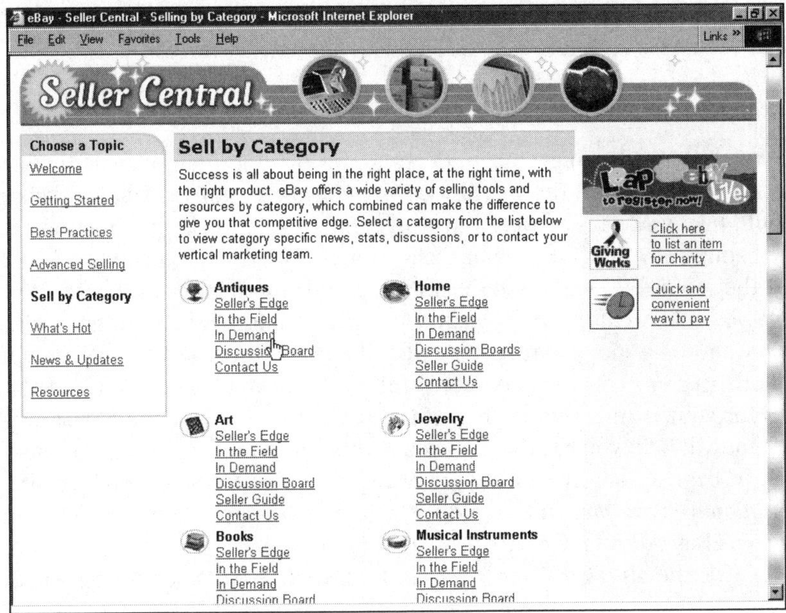

Figure 5-4 The Sell by Category page leads you to learn the most popular search terms for particular types of goods.

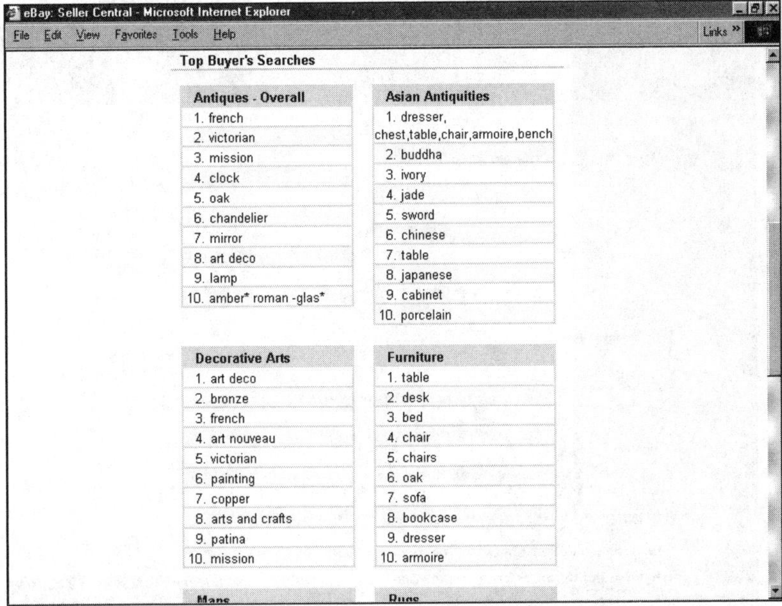

Figure 5-5 On the In Demand page, scroll down to find a collection of buyers' top search terms.

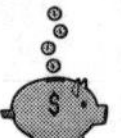

Bingo! Now you can refine your marketing approach by further exploring the results of such search terms to see if this is the market for you.

Tracking the Sell-Through Statistics

The next step in honing your understanding of eBay market demands and trends is to wrestle out the actual *sell-through statistics* of recent eBay listings. It could take you days or weeks to painstakingly cull through numerous category listings, trying to determine sell-through, or which items actually sold, what they sold for, and which sellers seem to be more successful than others. (Note: *key* information can by gleaned by understanding the successful sellers; you'll want to be sure you recognize what it is about those sellers' offerings and methods that makes them so successful, and you may want to adopt those traits for your own listings.) Fear not, because there are a couple tools available that will help you sift through what could become a mountain of data.

To begin, start by visiting the Medved Quote Tracker Web web site at *www.quotetracker.com*. In the middle of its home page, Medved offers a link to a free eBay Auction Counts Site (see Figure 5-6).

Click the *Auction Counts Site* link and you'll advance to the Auction

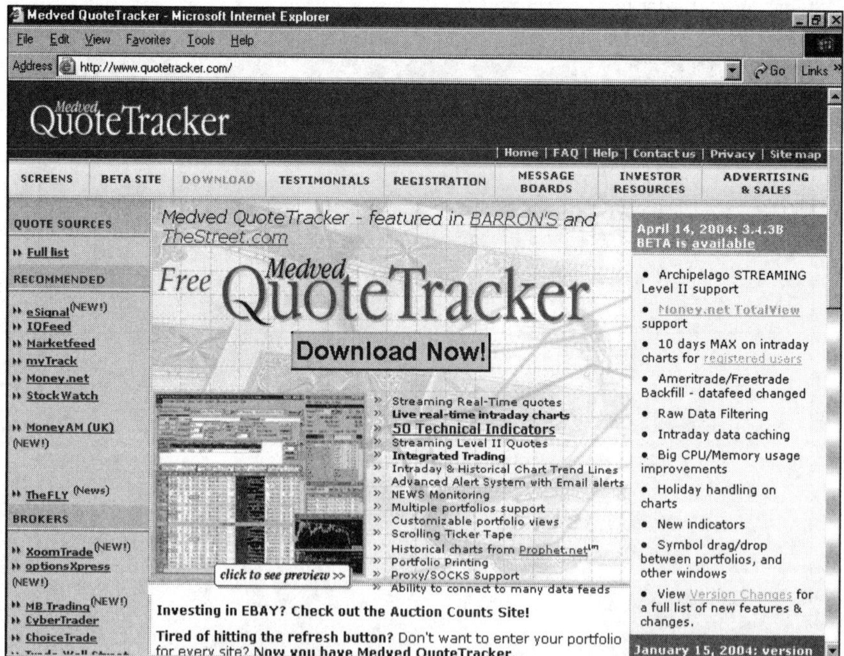

Figure 5-6 Medved's Quote Tracker site is your portal to the useful Auction Counts Site.

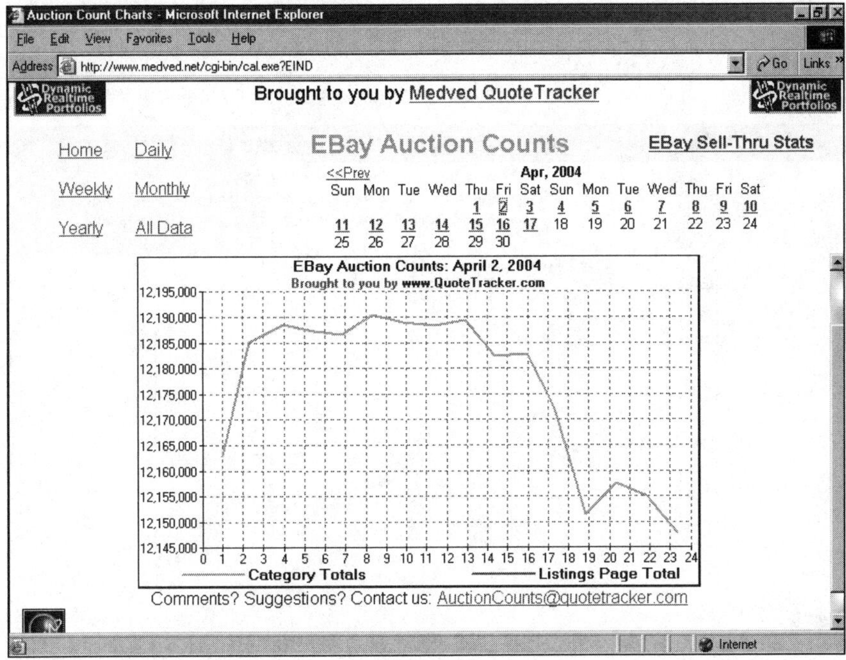

Figure 5-7 The Auction Counts chart details the number of listings and when they were launched on eBay for a given month and day.

Counts chart (see Figure 5-7) where you can, by month and day, review the statistics for the number of total listings and the time when the listings were launched on eBay, which is good sideline data to interpret as you're considering the best times to launch your listings.

To return to the topic of sell-through statistics, though, click on the text link, *EBay Sell-Thru Stats* as you see it at the top right corner of the screen in Figure 5-7. This will take you to a new screen where you can specify month, year, and specific category to see a graphical representation of listings and their rate of bids or buy-it-now purchases on eBay (see Figure 5-8).

What's most useful about the data you can cull from Medved's Auction Count charts and Sell-Thru Stats pages is that it's captured and updated every 1.5 hours and has been collated since 1999. Although eBay isn't keeping such statistics available for public use on their site, Medved has the data ready for access.

You want more granular data, though, don't you? That's fine because there's still more data ready for you to review. This time, we'll use a tool called HammerTap's Deep Analysis. This tool was developed to sift through data from eBay auctions—active or completed—and extract and report details

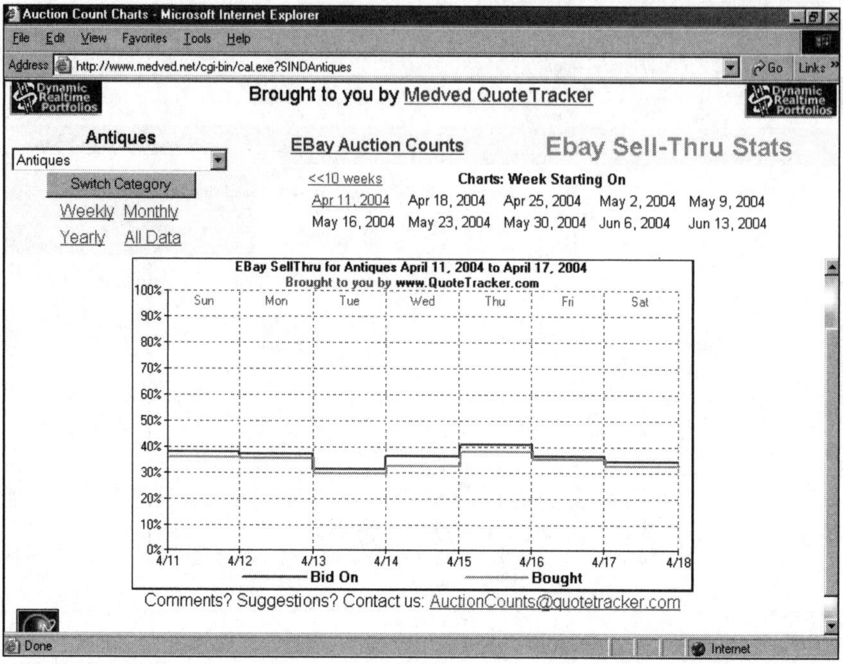

Figure 5-8 The Sell-Thru Stats page depicts items, by category, and the rate at which they were bid on or purchased outright. In this case, I searched for *Antiques*.

about items sold: the selling price, the number of bids, and sellers who offered them. Here's your tool to determine exactly how popular and profitable items are on eBay and which sellers seem to have found the key recipes for success, based on the reported sales statistics that Deep Analysis provides. This is a tool that you can really sink your teeth into because it provides the final level of detail for your market research, the key data that lets you easily and effectively analyze the activities and successes (or misses) of other sellers within the marketplace (see Figure 5-9).

eBay TIP: Be forewarned, the HammerTap Deep Analysis tool will chug along for quite some time as it gathers and collates its valuable data. Try using smaller query sizes (you can specify the number of auctions you'll analyze) and running the extraction at a time when you can step away from the computer for a little while.

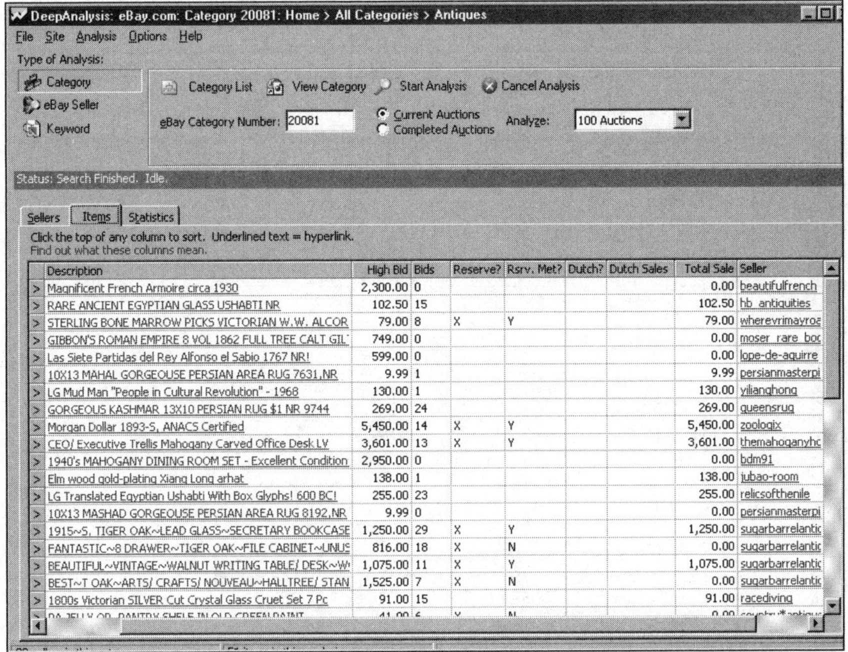

Figure 5-9 HammerTap's Deep Analysis tool provided this in-depth level of detail on eBay sales data for antiques.

MAKING USE OF THE eBAY "HOT ITEMS" LIST

Let's go back to eBay now to see what other sales data is readily available for your market research and merchandise planning. eBay has recognized the need to provide more in-house sales details to its vast user base, in order to make the selling experience more seamless within the eBay environment and not force users to venture outside the site to get the sort of useful data every expanding business needs (though always be on the lookout for a good third-party tools you can use). Knowing that sellers want to know "what's hot" on eBay, the site provided the aptly named *Hot Items by Category* report that distills sales activity for the past three months. To find it, visit Seller Central again (navigate from *Site Map* to the Seller Central page), then choose the *What's Hot* link along the left-side column of links. In the next screen, select the *Hot Items by Category* text link to launch the Adobe Document Viewer (it's free from *www.adobe.com*, if you don't already have it on your computer); from here you can review the detailed statistics of what eBay itself has determined to be the most popular items recently sold on the site (see Figure 5-10).

With this data that eBay provides, you will have the final piece to the

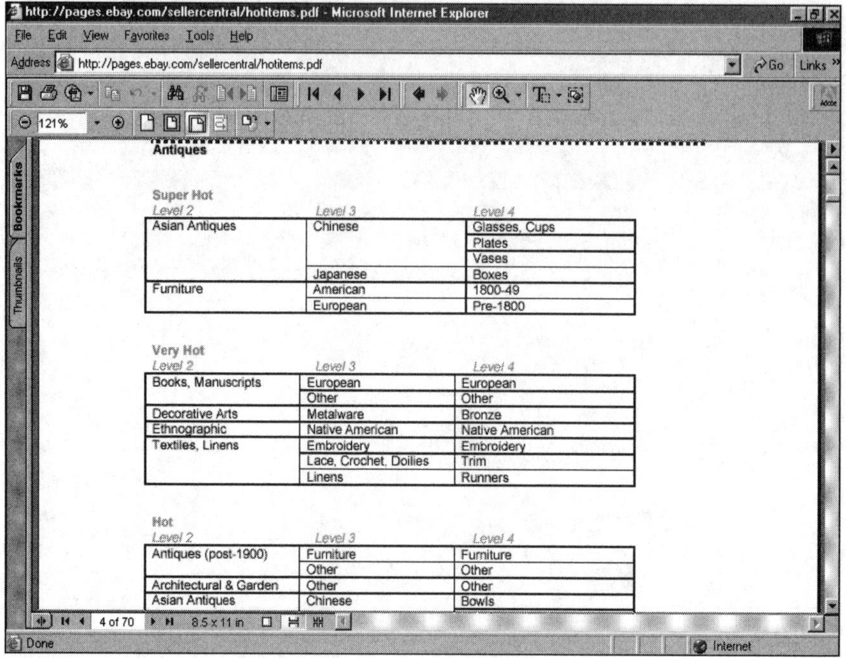

Antiques

Super Hot

Level 2	Level 3	Level 4
Asian Antiques	Chinese	Glasses, Cups
		Plates
		Vases
	Japanese	Boxes
Furniture	American	1800-49
	European	Pre-1800

Very Hot

Level 2	Level 3	Level 4
Books, Manuscripts	European	European
	Other	Other
Decorative Arts	Metalware	Bronze
Ethnographic	Native American	Native American
Textiles, Linens	Embroidery	Embroidery
	Lace, Crochet, Doilies	Trim
	Linens	Runners

Hot

Level 2	Level 3	Level 4
Antiques (post-1900)	Furniture	Furniture
	Other	Other
Architectural & Garden	Other	Other
Asian Antiques	Chinese	Bowls

Figure 5-10 eBay's Hot Item list is an Adobe (.pdf) document you can easily download and review from eBay's Seller Central area.

puzzle to help you confidently determine what goods are most active and potentially the most profitable to sell. In order to get the most complete and most accurate assessment of what's hot and what's not on eBay, it's in your best interest to compare, contrast, and combine the "hot items" statistics from multiple sources—within eBay and elsewhere—to be sure you're getting the most complete picture of what's selling at the big auction site.

TAGGING ALONG WITH eBAY'S MERCHANDISING CALENDAR

Now, if you looked carefully while navigating to the Hot Items by Category listing, you may have noticed another link on the What's Hot page: *Merchandising Calendar*. You'll notice that every time you visit eBay's home page at *www.ebay.com* the main theme changes to promote a different season or grouping of goods, such as "Dads and Grads" promotions during June, "Halloween Harvest" during October, and so on. What appears on the home page is driven by eBay's designated Merchandising Calendar; it's the site's promotional tool to reflect current trends or seasons and potentially inspire visitors in their searching and shopping experience. As a seller, you're well

served if you ride the coattails of this promotion. The key, of course, it to know in advance what eBay will be promoting and when and aligning your offerings to coincide with the overall theme or pitch of the day. Therefore, click on the *Merchandising Calendar* link from the What's Hot page to see what eBay has lined up for the coming weeks (see Figure 5-11).

Using eBay's Merchandising Calendar just makes good sense, because their marketing team has already analyzed the upcoming trends and events for you. You can easily identify and position appropriate goods to be available when shoppers visit the site, and they will likely be prompted by the main theme to explore further. Likewise, if you specialize in certain goods, you can get a bit of help from eBay regarding the best times to offer your goods and about how to make yourself and your business more visible during peak selling seasons.

CURRENT TRENDS: THE HIGH PRICE (AND VALUE) OF MEMORIES

While it makes good business sense to cater to the present-day mentality of online shoppers who want modern goods, remember how eBay established it-

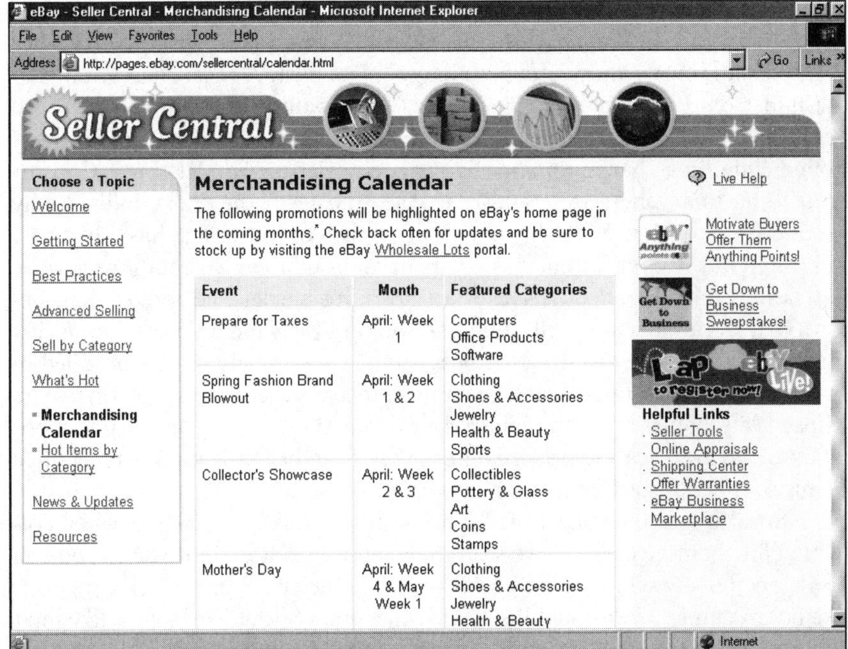

eBay - Seller Central - Merchandising Calendar - Microsoft Internet Explorer

http://pages.ebay.com/sellercentral/calendar.html

Seller Central

Choose a Topic
Welcome
Getting Started
Best Practices
Advanced Selling
Sell by Category
What's Hot
Merchandising Calendar
Hot Items by Category
News & Updates
Resources

Merchandising Calendar

The following promotions will be highlighted on eBay's home page in the coming months.* Check back often for updates and be sure to stock up by visiting the eBay Wholesale Lots portal.

Event	Month	Featured Categories
Prepare for Taxes	April: Week 1	Computers Office Products Software
Spring Fashion Brand Blowout	April: Week 1 & 2	Clothing Shoes & Accessories Jewelry Health & Beauty Sports
Collector's Showcase	April: Week 2 & 3	Collectibles Pottery & Glass Art Coins Stamps
Mother's Day	April: Week 4 & May Week 1	Clothing Shoes & Accessories Jewelry Health & Beauty

Live Help
Motivate Buyers Offer Them Anything Points!
Get Down to Business Sweepstakes!

Helpful Links
. Seller Tools
. Online Appraisals
. Shipping Center
. Offer Warranties
. eBay Business Marketplace

Figure 5-11 Use eBay's own Merchandising Calendar to help you prepare your own item promotions. Make plans to list goods that coincide with the home-page's themes.

self many years ago: in the collectibles market. The site became a boon for collectors who had been actively searching for just about anything, from old records to baby dolls to retro furnishings and decor. No longer bound by geography, online shoppers suddenly began turning up long-lost treasures with greater ease than ever before, thanks to the nationwide and now worldwide marketplace that increasingly filled with nostalgic notions from our collective past. And even though eBay has become a hub for everything else under the sun, be it practical goods or whatever, a large portion of its activity still caters to collectors—and so should you.

Even if you don't wish to "modernize" in your approach to eBay and you decide you're not very interested in selling everyday goods or chasing today's hot trend, you can do terrific business in selling the stuff of memories, the items collectors still seek and will continue to claw for. Although there was a time when people didn't want to own anything old—possessing such items was once an indication of substandard financial standing, that is, not being able to afford new items—today, almost everything that's old is commanding prices exponentially higher than original prices of 30 or more years ago. Collectors, eager to reclaim a piece of their past or attempt to freeze time with a whimsical item from years gone by, are paying big money for the ability to touch, feel, and smell the items of their youth.

Who are these collectors who are paying such big money for old junk? Clearly, the desire to collect childhood items is largely a baby-boom phenomenon. For whatever reason, this glorious generation (of which I'm a member in good standing) simply refuses to let go of its past. As this generation is in the midst of its prime collecting years (usually understood to be 20 to 40 years removed from its preteen pasts), nostalgia items like those already mentioned embody a charm, an appeal, and memories of simpler times. Considering that this generation is also in the midst of the most individually productive period in world history (that is, the computer age has effectively infiltrated our lives such that employers have raised their expectations and we individuals have found ourselves to be working harder and longer than before), baby boomers are, well, tired and looking for a mental vacation. Drifting off into one's past is often the best respite for so many of us embroiled in the computer age. Plus, as each generation reaches the prime collecting years (those 1980s babies are coming into theirs now) they're also coming into a position of greater earning potential and, therefore, have the money to indulge themselves in collectibles from their youth.

So who's selling collectibles? Thousands of folks who have enjoyed collecting for themselves and have seen the unending demand for such goods on eBay are actively selling these goods today. Some specialize in certain goods like board games or Barbie dolls, while others may specialize in *eras*, like mod 1960s items or funky 1970s stuff. I got my start as a seller and online auction analyst by collecting the nostalgia goodies I found on eBay, those that fed my hunger for baby-boomer toys and movie memorabilia. Thrilled whenever I'd

uncover a terrific item from my childhood, I'd typically bid, win, and revel in my acquisition. Afflicted with the collector's predisposition to seek out only the best of the best specimens (and I amassed a collection of toys in pristine *un*-played-with condition, which are notoriously difficult to obtain), I'd find myself buying numerous specimens until I had what I considered the best possible example of whatever it was I was on the lookout for. Soon, I had accumulated an inventory of these long-lost goods, which I could resell on eBay and, ultimately, recoup much if not all of my overall investment. If you're a collector, you probably have the same sort of "inventory" all around you and, as an expert in your area of collectibles, you're well-positioned to return the unwanted goods to the stream of collectibles that flows through eBay.

Look closely at eBay listings (current and completed) and you'll see that toys command a large share of the collectible market, and are sold in the greatest quantities to the boomer generation. Among the most popular items appear to be Mickey Mouse and Minnie Mouse paraphernalia (vintage Disney goods are always in high demand), G.I. Joe and Barbie dolls, robots, space toys, TV- and comic-related items, and early Star Wars items (from the late 1970s and early 1980s).

Beyond toys, aging generations are also interested in "period pieces," including furniture, decor, even kitchen utensils and condiment sets; anything that they either used in their own homes long ago or saw regularly in the homes of those fictitious families they saw on TV. Midcentury Modern furniture has become very popular, as have brightly colored Melmac and Melamine dinnerware, Formica featuring that classic amoeba design, vintage barware, old cookware (including those conversational fondue pots and even old coffee makers: I still have my folks' old CorningWare stove-top percolator and I love it). And don't forget one of the most obvious: the statistics show that more than 6000 lunchboxes are sold each month on eBay, too.

ANOTHER NEW TREND: HANDMADE GOODS FOR HOMEGROWN PROFITS

Many private artisans have also found eBay to be a lucrative showplace of sorts for their hand-crafted goods. Search eBay at any time and you'll find all kinds of handmade goods: latch rugs, pottery, paintings, wood crafts, and much more. eBay has offered these homegrown artists a worldwide stage for their exquisite creations, which had previously been relegated mostly to miniscule exposure at regional craft fairs and crafter's malls. Just as with collectibles and the fact that *old* no longer equates to *junk*, now *handcrafted* no longer bears the stigma of *unprofessional*. Artisans who offer their works, whether they consist of more common selections or truly unique one-of-a-kind pieces, are finding new status with their limited offerings. Today, many discriminating buyers prefer handcrafted goods to those mass produced out of factories both stateside and abroad. To their selective tastes, *handmade*

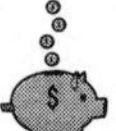

evokes high quality and limited availability, as in the case of offerings from top fashion designers. And, the more unique, the better.

Laura Henning of Smithtown, New York, has established a truly unique and quite successful niche in the handmade market, offering highly customized baby dolls she calls "reborns." Beginning from a nondescript vinyl doll that costs about $20 at any Kmart or Wal-Mart store, Henning adds her unique brand of artistry to give the doll an undeniably lifelike look. Hair and eyelashes are rerooted with mohair or, sometimes, real human hair. Mouths and noses are spliced open, eyes replaced. Bodies are actually filled with sand to simulate the actual weight of a real baby. Faces and limbs are tinted inside and out, then painted in countless layers to simulate a newborn's skin. The finished baby, appropriately, is given a name before being offered for "adoption" (see Figure 5-12). How well do these sometimes eerily lifelike reborns sell for? On eBay, they're fetching prices any where from $500 up to several thousand. This new cottage industry of reborns was launched and has found growing success because of eBay. If you're an artisan with a unique product to offer, use eBay to start up and advance the reach of your handcrafted venture.

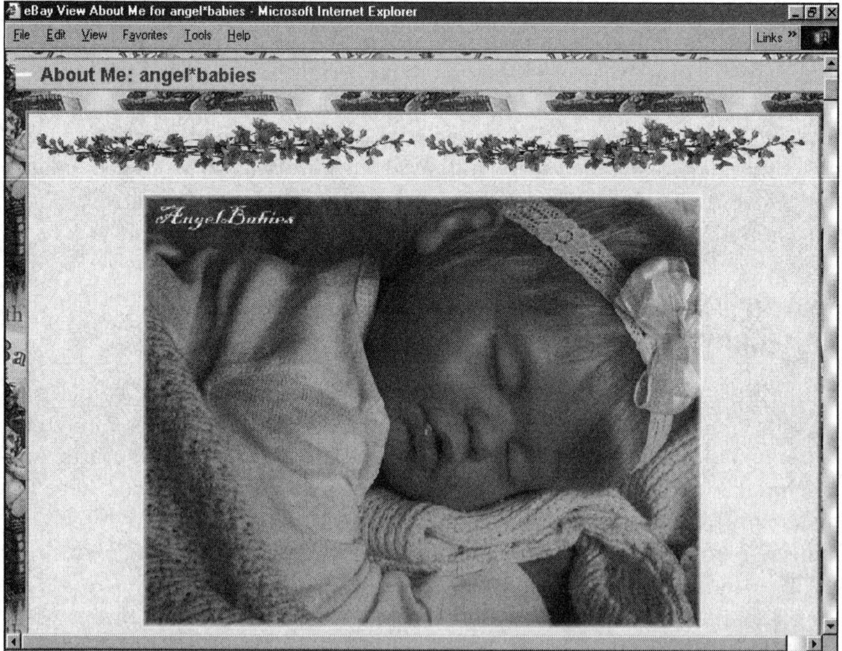

Figure 5-12 This incredible "reborn" created by Kimberly Angel demonstrates how artisans are using eBay to offer their unique works to a worldwide market.

DRIVING YOUR OWN TREND

Now that you have the requisite tools to acquire and analyze data about what's been selling on eBay, who's been selling it, and for how much, you're ready to apply what you've learned to your own selling efforts. Certainly, you would do well to emulate what you've seen and tap into selling the hot goods that seem to be selling successfully day in and day out. Of course, you should also consider taking the data you've pored over and *adapt* it to help you think outside of the box and deliver exciting new product offerings to the population of eBay buyers.

I have recently introduced an exciting new product to a highly impassioned niche audience of buyers. I've known there is a high demand for a series of model kits from 1971, *Monster Scenes*, shown in Figure 5-13. Having been an avid collector myself of these gruesome goodies, my research concluded that every time these items appear for bid on eBay, they routinely sell for at least $100 (not bad for items originally priced at about $2). The series was discontinued in 1972 just as two new kits, *The Animal Pit* and *The Dungeon*, were being prepared for release. When I acquired exclusive rights to the

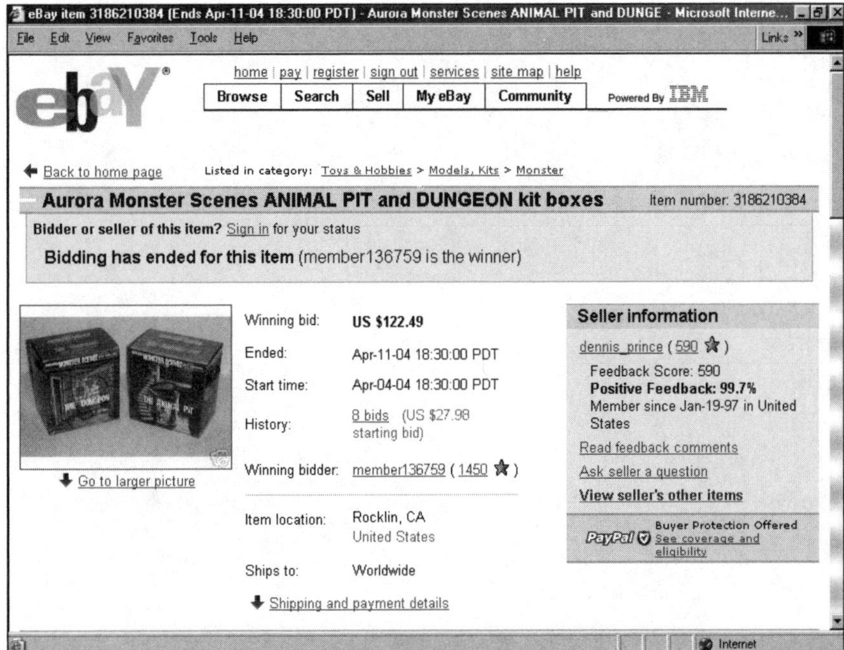

Figure 5-13 Aurora Monster Scenes *Animal Pit* and *Dungeon*. So rare they never existed, until I began offering them on eBay.

original box art paintings, those that were commissioned for use on the product packaging, I was determined to complete what the Aurora company didn't, and I developed the kit boxes that *would have been* had the series not been halted. Collectors in this niche have long known about these elusive "lost kits" and have expressed unwavering interest in any material associated with them. Using that knowledge, I began offering the finished boxes on eBay to overwhelming response. The final bid you see in Figure 5-13 upholds my decision to venture into this market (and this doesn't even account for the many other direct-sale inquiries I've since received).

The point is, study the eBay data well, then bend it, twist it, and apply it slightly differently to see if you can initiate a new trend of your own design.

6

Great Sales for Ordinary Goods

To wrap up this first section of the book and to give you just a bit more food for thought as you grasp how eBay is being used creatively today, what's selling, and what you'll ultimately sell, let's take a very *vanilla* look at perhaps some of the most, well, common items imaginable that can be found up for bid every day. As you read in Chapter 2, eBay has been harnessed by all sorts of buyers and sellers who have helped change the site from a place that mostly catered to collectibles into a whatever-you-need-whenever-you-need-it consumer hub. And while unique, rare, and collectible treasures and trinkets always do well at auction, as do high-priced, high-value specialty and luxury goods, you'll see here that even everyday, run-of-the-mill items can sometimes be just as popular with the millions of eBay shoppers. Before you deem those "boring old items" as unworthy of eBaying, read this and you may see those bland goods in a potentially profitable new light.

DAILY NEEDS

You run to your corner market or brave the often-crowded aisles of the local Wal-Mart to grab those routine items you want and need on a regular basis, but you can often find the same goods up for bid or Buy-It-Now on eBay. Savvy shoppers, bargain hunters, and those faced with stretching their budgets have found eBay to be a truly viable alternative for purchasing everyday items. The big retailers have already learned this, at least those that routinely offer their backlog of brand-name closeouts, excess inventory, and refurbished returns. Consider these numbers: 29,000 lawn and garden items and 2000 vacuums are sold every week. Nothing terribly exciting about these items, except for the fact that they're selling at a fast clip week in and week out.

Frugal Footwear

And what if the "baby needs a new pair of shoes?" No problem, because eBay has likewise become a fast-growing sector in footwear sales, with major retailers turning to the site to liquidate last year's styles and cost-conscious shoppers on the prowl for a better price than they find at the local shoe store. But this isn't a market just to be cornered by the authorized shoe dealers; some entrepreneurs have found staggering success in selling inventory acquired from stores, outlet malls, and wholesalers that have gone out of business. eBay Store Shoebacca, which claims to have the "best shoe deals in the galaxy," features more than 1000 listings for shoes and accessories every week (see Figure 6-1). The folks at eBay indicate that the shoe business is booming for Shoebacca and others and that roughly 72 percent of all athletic shoes listed sell within the first 10 days, a statistic that Shoebacca can readily endorse.

eBay for Babies?

Mothers are perhaps some of the most skilled bargain hunters, especially when it comes to providing for baby, and eBay lets them shop without the annoyance

Figure 6-1 Off and running, eBay Store Shoebacca is doing out-of-this-world business, serving the needs of eager shoppers who've grown tired of the Retail Empire's high prices.

of having to take the baby out of the house. Many have turned to eBay for their babies' needs, and many in-touch sellers have seen this need remain consistent within the auction place. Consider these numbers I came up with on a routine search for completed baby-related listings (covering two weeks of auctions):

- Baby formula: 1053 listings
- Diapers (cloth and disposable): 3119 listings
- Baby bottles: 981 listings
- Baby bedding: 970 listings
- Onesies (can't have enough of these easy-access baby garments): 2189

Here's to Your Health

Perhaps you fancy entering the field of fitness merchandising. If you do, enter eBay today, because the site is brimming with all manner of goods to help you look and feel better every day. You'll find everything from vitamins to protein powders to aerobic steps to instructional videos to the latest in top-quality exercise equipment. As the baby boomers continue to age, their interest in staying fit is getting them interested in shopping eBay for their health needs.

And what about body-care products: skin care, hair care, pampering baths, and so on? Here is another category of everyday goods that is thriving on eBay. Rather than spend premium prices at "body salons," eBay shoppers have found the auction to be the place to purchase their personal care items at a fraction of retail prices. For sellers, the body-care business is healthier than ever. Sue and Paul Stimers, owners and operators of BodyCare in Rocklin, California, are pleased and amazed at their level of eBay success. "We easily do around $7,000 worth of business each month on eBay, and that's above and beyond what our brick-and-mortar salon contributes to our operating profit."

Home Office Essentials

Don't forget the instruments of your online endeavor: your home office, your personal computer, and the various accessories and supplies. eBay has become a major outlet for buying and selling the kinds of goods you need, anything from ink cartridges, reams of printer paper, specialty papers, pens, pencils, desk lamps, office machinery, office furniture, and, of course, plenty of refurbished and remanufactured equipment that you can buy or sell to millions of active shoppers.

THE CLUTTER YOU KEEP

Now, to take you *all* the way back to the beginning, most eBay sellers got their start by selling the clutter they found around themselves in their daily lives. I've maintained that each of us easily has at least $3,000 worth of

"junk," "trash," and other such unwanted goods that, I can say with almost complete certainty, someone else would love to buy and own. This doesn't mean your clutter has to be collectible or any other sort of treasure; it can just be the stuff of your daily life, the accumulation of years of gathering, storing, and sidestepping. Although many eBay sellers have since migrated from selling their own goods to venturing into some of the merchandising areas I've discussed so far, many more are still selling clutter and carting the profits to the bank every week.

Appropriately, a story published March 2004 in England's *Birmingham Post* revealed the results of a survey that concluded local residents of Midland are collectively storing £1.7 billion of unwanted items. That averages out to about £187.96 (approximately $339.55 in U.S. dollars) per household, though I would argue that that number is far too low. Nevertheless, the survey went on to indicate that folks who answered the questionnaire never took the time to clear the clutter from their homes and lives, and 41 percent of respondents ashamedly admitted they hadn't partaken in the annual ritual of spring cleaning for the past five years. If you, too, are stepping around unwanted goods like old Disney VHS tapes, Vanilla Ice CDs, outdated decor, and retired computers and accessories, your start to an online business is at your feet, literally.

Don't worry whether your junk is worthy of an auction; everything's up for grabs on eBay when you deal in daily castoffs. Again, this is how I got my start back in 1995, and I'm still finding odds and ends that I've wrested from the dark corners of my living space and auctioned up on eBay.

If you still don't believe your everyday junk can be someone else's gems, check out John D. Freyer's book, *All My Life for Sale*, a chronicle of the Iowa art student's "online performance" in which he listed roughly 1000 of the lowest of low-brow items found within his own apartment. In the end, he earned roughly $3,000 (see?) by selling everything in sight, including an old manual typewriter, a kidney-shaped ashtray, still-wrapped Christmas gifts from his family, a brick, and even a canned ham. While Freyer's motivation was more artistic and cultural in nature, his "project" proved that just about anything can be sold (and usually does sell) if it's listed on eBay. But that's just a guy who sold goofy goods, not necessarily for profit but, rather, just as part of a sort of social experiment. So what about the guy who sells such odds and ends from our lifetimes *for his business*? Meet Joe (just "Joe"), proudly identified by his eBay ID, JoesCrap. Joe is doing some pretty swift business selling his . . . uh . . . stuff. A look at his daily listings will reveal that Joe sells just about anything and everything he finds within reach. Listings like "Vintage PISCES & LEO Astrology ASHTRAY, Set of 2," "Vintage 1950's?40's?30's? THE GAME OF INDIA Board Game," or "CHEAP SKATEBOARD WHEELS w/ trucks—buy em', ok?" are the sort of flotsam and jetsam that Joe sells—and sells well. So how did he get into this virtual

Sanford and Son junkyard business? Visit JoesCrap About Me page on eBay and you can read all about it in Joe's own words:

"If you're *really* bored continue on . . . Whats up with the name? (joescrap). Things have changed quite a bit since the early days of 'joescrap' and for eBay for that matter. It started primarily as an outlet to part with much of a life long collection of stuff, that included *everything* I've ever owned, in my entire life (not kidding; *very* close to it) of which it had always been referred to as 'crap' by most who had ever came across it. 'Useless' and 'worthless' (or so thought, by the masses) were words also used to describe the piles of items that I have stored across 3 different states, in buildings and storage units. Little did we know eBay would change all that. Now much of what I sell is . . . consignment of family and friends and friends of family. Many are very interesting personal items, though I continue to always slip some of my own stuff in here and there. Believe it or not, the name has truly proved to be a very popular and quite well respected in spite of what most would think."

Think what *stuff* you have that could be a valuable treasure for someone shopping on eBay.

THE HAULS OF HIGHER EDUCATION

Even if you're not an art student, if you're trudging the campuses of higher learning and finding that the cost of being a student is skyrocketing, here's a fast way to save big money or earn as much for yourself.

In my research, I found a recent statistic that concluded college students will spend around $300 every semester on textbooks. Long the predicament of students, campus bookstores have historically featured the most expensive texts known in the publishing world, those deemed *required*, in Draconian fashion, by the resident educators. Granted, most bookstores offered buy-back programs and, on opening day, college bookstores were summarily besieged by financially strapped students hopeful to grab a text at used-book prices. Today, though, students have turned to eBay and eBay's Half.com to buy their books, often at prices 50 to 80 percent lower than those of new books. With more than 90 million texts available at Half.com (not to mention the similar listings on eBay itself), struggling students have found new ways to save on up-front costs and recoup some of that cash after final exams (see Figure 6-2).

eBay TIP: According to a 2003 press release from Half.com, the average estimated price of a used textbook at a college campus bookstore is $60.17, while the average sales price of a textbook on Half.com is just $24.57—a savings of more than $35. This ain't rocket science.

Figure 6-2 Visit Half.com's Textbooks section to save big on college texts or turn yours into cash.

BUBBLES, BOXES, AND PEANUTS

Sometimes, the best business ideas come from the very things we eBayers scramble for—shipping supplies. If you've been selling on eBay for very long, you know how excited you get at the thought of bubble-wrap, packing peanuts, and a nice sturdy shipping box. Well, entrepreneur Karen Young saw it the same way, then set about in September 1997 to help other sellers get the shipping supplies they needed, at a fair price, within the very venue where they conducted business. A entrepreneur who embodies the "classic seller" story I've previously told, Young was a stay-at-home mom who turned to eBay to sell collectibles, trinkets, and knickknacks she found at local flea markets and garage sales. As her auctioning activity grew and she was pressed to actually hire an employee to help out with all the packing and shipping, Young realized she had a bona fide business on her hands and, like any good businessperson, began scrutinizing her profits and expenses. Naturally, the largest and most unwieldy expense of all was shipping supplies. Seeing the costs incurred each time she visited her local office supply store to stock up, she decided instead to shift her business focus, procure supplies direct from

the manufacturers, and ultimately launch ShippingSupply.com. She actively sells a wide range of packing supplies on eBay as well as at her own ShippingSupply.com site, items like bubble-wrap, self-sealing mailers, and shipping tape as fast as the 18-wheelers can deliver it. Young has expanded her business twice (it now occupies roughly 10,000 square feet of warehouse space) and has enlisted the services of employees, one of whom is her husband, who quit his "regular" job to assist in the bubble-wrap business.

DON'T FORGET ABOUT THE THINGS YOU *CAN'T* SELL ON eBAY

Yes, there's plenty you can sell on eBay and plenty that sells well, but remember that there are many items that the site prohibits. As you're carefully mulling over your niche in the online marketplace, don't forget to steer clear of these off-limits offerings:

- *Alcohol.* Alcohol is generally forbidden for auction because of the complex taxation, import, and licensing rules that govern it. Unless you're bidding through a licensed site and dealing with sellers licensed to deal in alcohol (such as at a site like WineBid.com), the rules generally state that alcohol auctions will be closed promptly by the site.
- *Firearms.* Though firearms are sometimes considered a sort of collectible (for period pieces), eBay has had to unequivocally forbid auctioning of any mechanism originally designed to fire some sort of projectile. There are, however, some sites that are properly licensed and specialize in auctioning such items, such as ArmsBay.com.
- *Fireworks.* These are illegal in many states and in other parts of the world. They are, therefore, not eligible for auctioning.
- *Drugs and drug paraphernalia.* Illegal goods, plain and simple.
- *Human parts and remains.* Yuck, right? On eBay, it started with the human kidney auction back in 1999. Since then, no body parts. However, on eBay, the rules do state that selling skulls and skeletons for educational purposes is allowed unless, of course, they're from hated relatives who, strangely enough, have been missing for some time.
- *Animals and Wildlife Products.* Excluding, perhaps, a warehouse find of vintage Sea Monkeys, dealing with the sale and shipping of live animals is typically left to the pros (animal handlers and such). Adhering to edicts set forth by the U.S. Fish & Wildlife Service, eBay does not allow the sale of live animals or animal parts unless expressly noted; for instance, sale of some taxidermic items, pelts, and so on might be allowed if strict conditions are adhered to. If you're

considering this sort of item, read the full disclosure of what's allowed—and what isn't—before you venture forward.

- *Stolen or counterfeit goods.* They're stolen. They're illegal. They aren't allowed for auctioning. This should be obvious.

Now that the most obvious items have been explained, here's the quick list of additional prohibitions and/or restricted items:

- Catalog and URL sales
- Counterfeit currency and stamps
- Credit cards
- Embargoed goods
- Government IDs and licenses
- Web links
- Lockpicking devices
- Lottery tickets
- Mailing lists and personal information
- Plants and seeds
- Postage meters
- Prescription drugs and devices
- Recalled items
- Satellite and cable TV descramblers
- Stocks and other securities
- Surveillance equipment
- Tobacco
- Travel (allowed but limited due to seller-verification and local-travel regulations)

If you disagree with the banning of these items or simply want to learn more about why they're disallowed, visit eBay's Site Map and click on the text link labeled *Is My Item Allowed on eBay?* There you'll find the most up-to-date list of prohibitions and restricted items, including full explanations of why these items are monitored and controlled by the site.

PART 2

BUILD A BETTER BUSINESS, eBAY STYLE

7

Your eBay Business Plan

Up to this point, I've given you plenty of compelling examples, statistics, and real-life stories about how eBay is being used every day to drive business creation and business growth. While it's exciting, encouraging, and even amusing to learn of the exploits and successes of others, it's all for naught if you don't apply it to your own efforts, your own business. Hopefully your mind has been whirring along in high gear as you've considered what you've read up to now and how you can borrow bits and pieces of what others have done for your own online venture. This chapter's goal, then, is to help you align all your terrific sales and marketing ideas and gather them into a comprehensive and sensible approach; that is, a *business plan.* Even if you're already in business and have been working from a plan you've previously enacted, this chapter will help you determine if refinement of that plan is in order to best harness the potential of adding eBay as a new sales channel. This is the critical juncture in your journey to establish or beef up your business; this is where you'll determine if a "business" is really what you want; this is where you can enable yourself to finally give your notice at your day job. If you're truly ready to raise your sail and venture into the seas of the self-employed, here's the place where you'll determine if your ideas are seaworthy (or is that *e-worthy*?) and if you're ready to chart your own course to independent employment. For many, this is the most exciting phase of going into business. Honest.

eBay TIP: Members of our community are evolving the way they utilize eBay, proving that our marketplace is just as relevant for small business use as it is for personal use.

—Meg Whitman, February 2004

YOUR BUSINESS PLAN WILL BE YOUR BEST FRIEND

A business plan?! Wait! Don't recoil in fear or dread, thinking that I've just sucked all the fun and fancy out of your entrepreneurial journey by suggesting you endure something that's about as welcome as a root canal. The fact is, your business plan might be your best friend (in business), practically a living companion in your venture. It may save you the countless hours and even money that you run the risk of wasting if you jump into the e-merchandising fray with plenty of enthusiasm but little vision. According to statistics from the Small Business Development Center in Madison, Wisconsin, roughly 80 percent of all small businesses fail within the first five years, largely because those behind the businesses failed to develop a concrete plan and execute it from the get-go. It's a scary statistic, I'll agree, but thanks to eBay and other potential online opportunities, you stand the best chance ever to start your business, grow your business, and keep your profits rolling in. And with a mortality rate of 80 percent, it's easy to see that the only ones who don't need a business plan these days are those who aren't going into business (yet, anyway).

Now, to soften the blow of that alarming failure statistic, a recent survey conducted by IBM revealed that about 2 in 10 American adults had plans to start a small business within 3 years and another 10 percent of those surveyed had already taken the leap. Of those entrepreneurially minded go-getters, two-thirds shared that they planned on using the Internet extensively in their business plans and recognized the power of cyberspace (including eBay) in enabling a lower-cost, higher-visibility existence. Like I said, this is perhaps one of the best times to be considering starting up an online business. Now, how about that plan?

THE PATH TO BUSINESS PLANNING

Like any task that may be somewhat overwhelming or seemingly unexciting, begin by breaking this key step of your auction business down to smaller, more manageable pieces. As you consider drafting your business plan, look at it as the red carpet that will lead you to realizing your business aspirations while simultaneously serving as the welcoming path to the customers who will likewise follow it to find, shop at, and buy from your virtual establishment. But, as energetic as you may be and as self-assured as you are that you're going to turn your passion into profit (most small business owners let their passions guide their entry into the business market), you might find yourself in panic mode when six months or a year down the road you find your expenses have skyrocketed, your sales have dropped off, and you're losing sleep wondering how you ever got into such a mess in the first place. The simple answer: don't let this happen to you because you can turn your passions

into profits with a sound business plan. Here are the ingredients for a successful plan.

What's Your Motivation to Go into Business?

How many times have you sat through a job interview and been asked the worn-out question, Where do you see yourself five years from now? Although you may have been bored at the thought of answering it, because you knew the intent was for a would-be employer to summarily assess your level of initiative, creativity, and ability to execute, as well as your plans to stay at the job if hired, ask *yourself* that question when you begin planning your business. This question becomes highly relevant as you begin to interview yourself, so to speak, to be sure that your dreams can be realized without risking your health, your home, and your financial solvency. Dare to dream, but then, as you ponder your five-year future, ask yourself these questions to determine your business goals:

- How impassioned am I about making this work?
- How much am I willing to sacrifice initially, in money, time, leisure, and so forth to ensure this comes to fruition?
- What will I do if this doesn't work out?
- Will I or can I do this alone or will I need to work with partners and hire employees?
- If I work with others, can I delegate tasks comfortably or will I feel the need to have my hands on all aspects of the business, every day?
- If I work with partners, am I open to complementary or contradictory opinions and ideas?
- How much can I reasonably expect to earn in my first year? my second year? my fifth year?
- For the market I want to enter, is it underserved or oversaturated, and can I compete?
- Will I specialize in my products and services, and how will I set myself apart from competitors?

That's quite a bit to consider, but it's important to do so, even if you had simple visions of leading the market in sales of psychedelic widgets. No matter what you want to do in your business, you need a plan, and by pondering these questions fully and answering them honestly, you can be sure your initial ideas will make for a reliable foundation upon which to launch your business.

What Do You Bring to the Business?

Before going any further, though, now is the time for true confessions: do you *really* have what it takes to run your own business? If the previous questions

raised a bit of concern in your mind or suddenly made you think, Hey, this is gonna be a lot of work, choose your next steps very carefully. While many among us want to be our own boss, want to choose our own work schedule, and want to improve our current standard of living, the fact is that running your own business can often consume significantly more hours than your current 9-to-5 drudgery. Personally, I put in at least 40 hours per week in my various ventures (author, film reviewer, product designer, and marketer) and that's on top of my 9-to-5 gig that actually runs more like 7-to-6. However, I've found incredible success and achievement in my extra-curricular endeavors, such that I've found it more than rewarding to busy myself in this way, especially as I continue to guide myself to a break-even point where I can leave my day job and chart my own entrepreneurial course. Hey, if it was going to be easy, everyone would be doing it, right?

So this is the critical "self-assessment" phase at which you'll need to decide if you're willing and able to support long hours and can find true reward (personally and financially) along the way and at the end of each day. With that said, here's another set of questions to consider:

- Are you a self-starter, able to motivate yourself whenever and wherever necessary to realize your self-employment goals?
- Do you get along well with others, especially business contacts (vendors, bankers, etc.) and clients (your valuable customers)?
- Can you make decisions, even difficult ones, quickly and confidently?
- Are you an organized person?
- Can you retain your resolve to succeed even in the face of intermittent setbacks and unexpected adversities?

Last but certainly not least on your self-assessment checklist is the need to consider and consult your family, friends, and anyone else who will be affected by your decision. Though you'll be starting your "own" business, you'll likely be involving many others around you. Of course, I believe that if I can do it, so can you—and your business plan will help you be sure you're making the right choices. At this point, if your resolve is unwavering and you're more eager than ever to make this work, onward we go.

DEFINING THE PIECES OF THE PLAN

Believe it or not, many small businesses have been proven to fail for the simple reason they lacked a business definition. If someone were to venture into an eBay business based on a definition as rudimentary as, "I wanna sell stuff online," they'll likely be challenged to maintain an active business when they run out of their as-yet undetermined inventory or, worse yet, may find themselves heavily invested in potential inventory that, for whatever reason, isn't

selling. A solid business definition up front can clarify the intent of the business and will immediately help the businessperson decide whether the products or services intended to be sold will be available and profit-bearing. So, to start, define your business in terms of its *structure*; that is, whether it will be a wholesale, retail, food service, manufacturing, or service-oriented venture.

The next step, and one which I already alluded to, regards defining the products or services that you'll market and sell. Whether it's going to be Patty's Party Goods, Ron's Rebuilt Radiators, or Edie's eBay Education Station, define what, exactly, you'll sell and how marketable your desired goods or services might be (and if your business will be founded and operated within eBay, remember to consider what the site prohibits from sale).

Next, consider the geography you'll serve. Will you sell and service only your homeland, or will you branch out to serve other countries around the world (a wise choice, by the way)? Consider how marketable your goods or services will be in other countries, and be especially sensitive to any cultural norms or standards that might run counter to your marketing plans.

eBay TIPS: During my days of studying marketing economics, I was fascinated by a story of a cake-mix manufacturer who was seeking to sell product in Japan. However, after learning that most people on this small island don't actually own conventional ovens, the manufacturer developed a breakthrough mix that could be prepared easily in a rice cooker, which is a common fixture in all Japanese homes. The only trouble was, in Japan, the rice cooker is *only* for rice, and to suggest preparing anything else in it was not only unwelcome, it was unthinkable. Oops. Consider carefully researching other cultures if you're considering doing significant business away from your homeland.

To help you in your cultural education, I heartily suggest you review the various books by Roger Axtell, including *Do's and Taboos around the World: A Guide to International Behavior* (1986, Wiley & Sons) and *Do's and Taboos of Using English around the World* (1995, Wiley & Sons).

If you plan to do significant business abroad, be sure you understand the costs and methods to ship your goods, and include that in your overall business definition. Shipping overseas is somewhat more complicated, costly, and time-consuming than shipping within your own continent. Be sure you have a well-thought-out plan for addressing the manner in which you'll receive funds from overseas and how you'll effectively ship goods to ensure safe and timely delivery to your customers (and look to Chapter 14 for more discussion about successfully selling to the international markets).

Lastly, your business definition should be clear about your profit potential, roughly speaking. Although there are other documents within a formal

business plan that capture the nitty-gritty financial details of your business, get a jump start by being clear about how you plan to turn a profit from your venture. This is tied to determining what you'll sell and being relatively assured that you *can* turn a profit doing so (remember your in-depth research of auction sales from Chapter 5).

But you just want to sell stuff on eBay, don't you? Of course you do, and if you'll create even the simplest business plan, you'll stand a better chance of achieving your goals and ensuring that your passion pays off and never becomes an unpleasant pain.

Getting to the Core of Your Plan

Depending on the complexity of your proposed business (and, again, if you plan to market goods on eBay and elsewhere on the Internet, you'll still need a plan to ensure that you can stay in business for years to come), your business plan can be anywhere from 1 to 100 pages long. At its core, your business plan should consist of two major sections, with details fleshed out as follows:

- *The Narrative*. This is the portion of the plan that covers some of what you've just read, including your *business objective* (why you're going into business, and how you expect the business to fare over the coming years), the *product or service summary* (a detailing of what you'll sell, where you'll sell it, and how your product offerings might expand or change), a *market analysis* (defining what market segment or niche you'll serve and how well-developed and demanding that market is), and your *product process* (clearly defining how you'll keep your "inventory" stocked and suitable to your target market).
- *The Financial Summary*. It all comes down to money, so this is where your business plan will detail exactly how your business will turn a profit. Often termed a *financial forecast*, this is where you'll describe your operating costs and revenues for your first year, your third year, on up to your fifth year in business. This is the most difficult part of the planning process, and it may likely give you fits as you attempt to devise a reasonably accurate profit prognosis. This is, however, the critical portion of the business plan that will help your business avoid becoming another tenant on the Island of Failed Ventures.

eBay TIP: No, I realize it isn't as easy as this and that a business plan will need to be far more detailed, potentially, than what I've shared here. If your business stands to be potentially complex, will require external financing (requiring a bank loan, for example), and carries a significant financial risk, I advise you to visit the Small Business Ad-

ministration Web site at *www.sba.gov* for even more detailed information about the variety of business plans possible and even some online tutoring to ensure that your plan, and therefore your business, will be successful.

WHO'S PLAYING ON YOUR TEAM?

During my extensive research, something I found most interesting was centered on how business owners select partners and employees and the significant impact those choices can have on a business's well-being. Before you tap your best friend or your dear Uncle Fred to join you in your auction business, give noted business consultant and industrial psychologist Brad Smart's book *Topgrading* (1999, Prentice-Hall) a good read. In his book, Smart takes what I consider a rather unbiased and unflinching look at the sorts of employees who have helped businesses thrive and those who have cost businesses dearly.

Speaking directly to small business owners, Smart's observations about the I-can-do-anything-and-everything-for-you employees are, surprisingly, most dangerous to the entrepreneur. Small business owners, he notes, need employees with very specialized skills, and these Jacks and Janes of all trades simply can't deliver the details most essential to small-business success. Dabblers will cost your business dollars, evidently. To counter this dilemma, Smart suggests small-business owners invest significant time and effort into finding—and grooming—employees when their business swells to levels where additional hands are needed. During this discussion, Smart singles out the highly respected CEO Jack Welch and relays that this retired chief of General Electric routinely spent 50 percent of his time hiring, coaching, and developing his team of employees. This, Smart concludes, is what makes for better employees: spending up-front investment in screening and selecting rather than hyping up a business to the extent it attracts all sorts of virtual cowboys and irreverent code-slingers.

I heartily recommend *Topgrading* as required reading before you consider turning to others to help run your business.

WHY SOME SMALL BUSINESSES FAIL

Without discouraging your motivation to start up your own business and without leading you to believe that writing a business plan is like walking into a bear trap, we need to shed some light upon why some businesses aren't as successful as others. We're talking about your eventual success here, so think of the phrase "The best defense is a strong offense." Here are 15 of the most common reasons small businesses fail (this particular list was gleaned from Action Business Partners, Inc.):

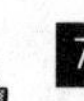

- Failure to use a business plan
- Lack of clear, attainable goals
- Not knowing what the customers want
- Underestimating the competition
- Inability to change
- Inefficient and inadequate systems and procedures
- Inadequate financial plan
- Not knowing the real costs of products and services that are being sold
- Not knowing the costs of hiring employees
- Lack of vision
- Lack of consistency
- Poor-quality service
- Low level of customer satisfaction
- Negative cash flow
- Excessive overhead

Of course, there are many other reasons for businesses to sputter, stall, or often cease to exist. The intent here is not to frighten you into inaction—far from it—but, rather, to warn you of some of the pitfalls that await when you decide to venture into the always exciting world of self-employment. Though it may seem that the odds are against you, take comfort in knowing that there are plenty of folks just like you who *are* succeeding, and they're doing it on eBay and elsewhere online (and offline, too) by taking careful and methodical measures.

YES, THERE IS A SILVER LINING

Whatever you do, don't let this blunt discussion give you cause to reconsider your business dreams and aspirations. While starting up a small business isn't for the fainthearted, it offers incredible amounts of self-satisfaction, drives personal and professional growth, and can reap some impressive financial results (recall some of the success stories shared in Chapters 2 and 6; those are just the tip of the iceberg of the millions of individuals who are happily self-employed on eBay and elsewhere). Ultimately, here's what you stand to gain by taking the leap into self-employment:

- You *will* be your own boss.
- Your hard work and long hours directly benefit *you*, not the profit statement of some other employer.
- Your personal earning potential is far greater than what you could achieve at a typical salaried occupation.

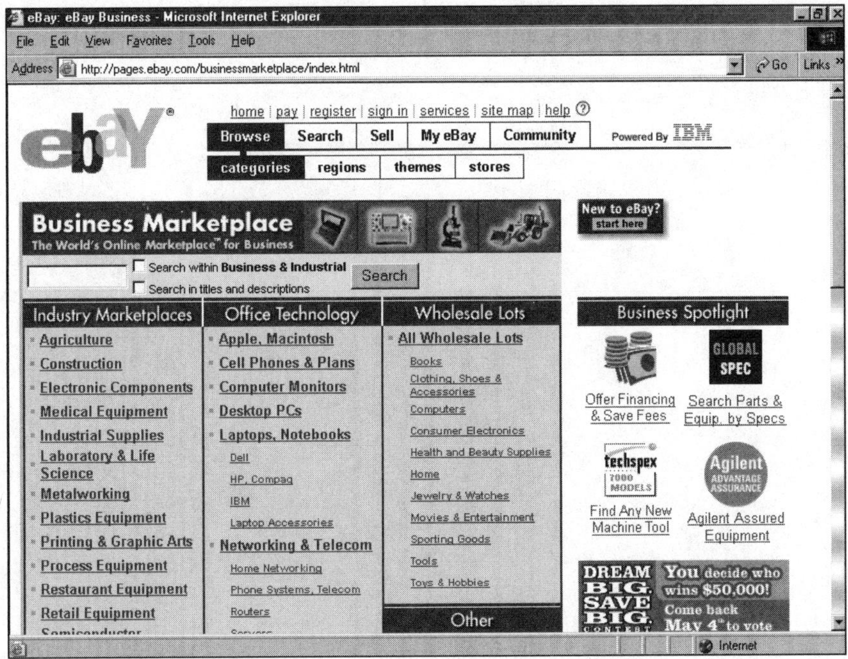

Figure 7-1 With the new eBay Business Marketplace, eBay shows its commitment to helping its business community thrive.

- Running your own business is as *exciting* as it is risky.
- Running a business allows you to fully explore and realize your personal potential and will drive you to grow and learn in ways you never before believed possible (and, who knows, you may even write a book or two about it someday).

By the way, don't forget to turn to eBay for help in your new or expanding business venture. eBay has committed itself to making its population of 430,000 full-time and part-time business sellers more successful by adding new features aimed at small-business success. Whether you're looking to purchase business-related goods, need to lease or finance equipment, or just want to share ideas with other eBay businesspeople, visit the site's new Business Marketplace at *www.ebaybusiness.com* (see Figure 7-1). If you've got the plan, eBay's got the platform.

8

eBay Industrialized: Machinery for Your Business

If you've studied world history, you're no doubt familiar with the era known as the Industrial Revolution, which began as far back as the late 1700s. It was a time when cottage industries, those that fashioned all manner of metalwork, woodwork, and textiles by use of cumbersome hand tools, came into being to deliver much-needed goods to the people of the day and served as the starting point of what we affectionately term the entrepreneurial spirit. Mechanization, however, was introduced to further the capabilities of industry and, though not immediately welcomed by many, it forged a new way to manufacture all manner of products and boost businesses by means of breakthrough inventions such as the steam engine, the cotton gin, the telegraph, and, of course, electricity.

In a way, you could also consider Internet and eBay as heading a new-age revolution—an economic revolution. As you've read up to now, eBay and the Internet have introduced dynamic and cost-effective ways to build businesses and bolster profitability. In its dynamism, eBay has also emerged as a different sort of business builder: many turn to eBay not necessarily to start an auction-based business but to purchase the various equipment needed to operate and profit in a non-eBay venture. When it comes to machinery, from office copiers to heavy-duty industrial machinery, eBay is revolutionizing the way businesses procure the often costly tools of their trade while allowing machinery manufacturers and distributors the ability to ramp up their sales in the active online marketplace.

BUILDING YOUR BUSINESS ON AN eBAY BUDGET

As I mentioned in the previous chapter, starting a business these days is a much easier endeavor than in decades past. And while it's not necessarily *easy* to own and operate your own business, getting started just got a whole lot simpler, especially when it comes to outfitting your new business headquarters. If you need to establish an office space, a warehouse, or a machine shop, turn to eBay as your first source for the goods you need.

Now with more than 110 subcategories in its *MRO (Maintenance, Repair, Operations) / Industrial Supply* category, including the categories *Electrical Distribution Equipment*, *Industrial Automation and Control*, *Electrical Tools and Supplies*, *Motors*, and *Lighting Products*, owners of small and large businesses alike can find practically everything their business needs. Whether the supplies and equipment are closeouts, refurbished, slightly used, or even new, they can all be found at dramatic savings over what the usual sources can offer. (Keep these categories in mind for potential items to sell for your own business.)

Office Essentials

If yours is a small business that wishes it could get the same volume discounts as bigger companies when establishing and outfitting office workspaces, turn to eBay for a new leveling of the office-space playing field. While you won't be getting volume discounts on factory- or distributor-direct equipment and supplies, you can still get the same high-volume pricing if you'll simply search around eBay. Now, if you're inclined to see eBay as a cost-effective alternative to shopping the retail outlets (and why shouldn't you?), you really stand a good chance of saving in your setup by shopping the daily offerings found on eBay (see Figure 8-1). Take, for example, the experiences of Tracey Kolpaczyk, co-owner of Mitchell Insurances Services and avid eBay hunter. I caught up with Tracey after I learned how she continually uses eBay to get the goods for her office without paying retail prices.

"We almost never buy something without at least looking on eBay first," said Kolpaczyk in an interview. By her figures, she comfortably estimates she's saved her business more than $60,000 a year since she began turning to eBay for her office needs as far back as 1997.

By her numbers, Kolpaczyk indicated she regularly saves between $40 and $60 off printer toner cartridges, buying them on eBay as opposed to purchasing at office-supply stores, some of which sell the same cartridges for upwards of $130. Along the way, she also uncovered a listing for a phone system that was the same as what was recently installed in her office. Seeing this as an inexpensive way to expand the office communications, she doubled the number of phones in her office at only half the price of the original installation. Truly, Kolpaczyk is a bargain hunter at heart, made even more evident when

Figure 8-1 Small businesses need to think big when searching for savings on office equipment and supplies. Start with the eBay Office Products page before you buy elsewhere.

she went so far as to purchase swanky leather portfolios on eBay. These gave her and her business partner a professional look during visits to customers and customers-to-be, who would never know that their big-company polish was supplied by eBay.

Food for Thought

If ever you dreamed of opening your own diner, malt shop, or any other such sort of enticing eatery, you might have lost your appetite for the venture quickly as you learned the cost of restaurant equipment and supplies. These days, turn to eBay first before you visit the traditional food-service suppliers. On eBay, sales of new and used restaurant equipment have been on the rise, with roughly $77 million worth of eatery equipment having changed hands on the site in 2003. Visit eBay's *Restaurant* subcategory within the *Business & Industrial* heading and you'll find well over 10,000 food-service items up for bid or sale at any given time. Whether you're looking for servingware in bulk, cooking equipment to fit any size establishment, or even an entire establishment ready to occupy (a businesswoman in Atlanta recently purchased an en-

Figure 8-2 Eliminate the pangs of despair by visiting eBay's restaurant-equipment listings to get a good price on your food-service needs.

tire ice cream shop on eBay, and fully-equipped concession trailers are always available for their next owner), eBay is seriously catering to food-service entrepreneurs (see Figure 8-2).

Test and Measurement

For those of you who are more prone to turn to a slide rule than a salad bar in your entrepreneurial exploits, do as Gregory Culkowski, chief technology officer at Transmitter Locator Systems of Burke, Virginia, did. As I continued to research how industry has been actively utilizing eBay as an alternate channel for equipment, I learned that Culkowski turned to the auction site when he needed new test and measurement equipment. Reportedly, he found a suitable analyzer he needed, one that would normally cost his firm $30,000; he got it for just $6,000. Apparently, Culkowski has since purchased more than $100,000 in high-end analytical equipment through eBay. "I've saved between 50 and 100 percent over list," Culkowski said in an interview. "The biggest savings have been on the scopes and analyzers."

Here again is yet another new sector that's rapidly growing within

eBay's business and industry category. A review of the test and measurement category showed more than 11,000 items at any given time, including analyzers, oscilloscopes, signal generators, and power supplies available for bid. And because bidders are actively seeking these precision tools, you'll now find many listings for high-end equipment direct from manufacturers like Agilent, Tektronix, and Anristu.

DOCTORS, DENTISTS, AND CHIROPRACTORS, TOO

Thomas Donahue III, a chiropractor in Chicago, had also turned to eBay to properly and cost-consciously outfit his new practice. The good news for him is that he found an X-ray machine, chiropractic tables, and physical therapy equipment on the auction site, all of which has helped him align his business goals with his start-up investment.

In a discussion, Donahue admitted he went to eBay on a whim, deciding to enter "chiropractic" as a search term, but he soon learned that the site was harboring the equipment his practice needed and at a price he couldn't pass up.

Figure 8-3 You needn't be a *mad* doctor to recognize the sanity of searching eBay for your health- and medical-equipment needs.

"I just thought, it's a bunch of junk on here, people trying to get rid of their Levi's," he had confessed. Now one of the converted, Donahue proudly proclaims he prefers to get used equipment instead of leasing new equipment, a shift, he estimates, that has saved him and his business more than $30,000.

If you take a look at the listings within the *Healthcare, Medical* subcategory you'll find thousands of listings for equipment and supplies, offered from a variety of sellers from all corners of the healthcare industry (see Figure 8-3).

Of course, with your senses appropriately piqued, you've likely come to see these listings as more than just goods that you can buy yourself but also as the indicators of business opportunities for you to join in the selling of. If you have access to this same sort of equipment and supplies, whether new, surplus, or gently used, look at the activity of the buyers I've mentioned here and recognize their willingness to purchase from sellers (maybe you) who can offer the sorts of goods they're actively pursuing.

WHY NOT GO WHOLESALE?

Visit the eBay Business section of the site and you'll see business and industrial goods for just about every trade imaginable: agriculture, construction, industrial supply, restaurant, electronic components, and more. A full 25 percent of eBay's business in 2003 was made up of business and industrial sales. Of that business, eBay category managers have indicated that the largest percentage of those purchases can be attributed to small businesses.

While I've alluded to the fact that many small businesses can save big money if they choose used or refurbished equipment, not all industrial items sold on eBay are necessarily previously owned (i.e., used). eBay has reported that as many as 40 percent of all business and industrial items sold within their virtual walls are new goods sold as excess inventory or in wholesale lots. Wholesale goods are so popular with buyers that eBay also included a *Wholesale Lots* subcategory within the eBay Business section (see Figure 8-4). While some buyers are purchasing wholesale goods for their own immediate use, many more are actively buying them for resale or for use within a manufacturing process.

BUYING ON eBAY MAKES LIGHT WORK OF HEAVY EQUIPMENT

If you're looking for anything from a Caterpillar to a Bobcat, you'll find a large cache of heavy equipment and other contractor tools available on eBay. Visit the *Construction* subcategory and you'll find still thousands more listings for all the equipment that construction firms and independent contractors use to operate their businesses. In fact, eBay account executives are

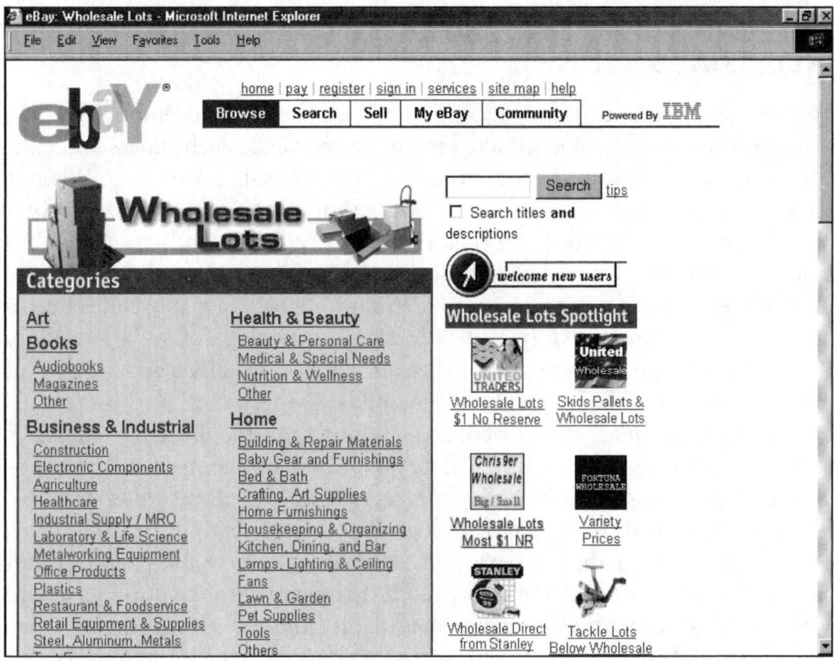

Figure 8-4 eBay's *Wholesale Lots* subcategory offers new goods at used prices, ready to serve immediate end use or as a means of supplying resale or manufacturing outfits.

reporting significant growth in its community of builders, contractors, and subcontractors, who are searching for the equipment they need within the eBay business marketplace.

eBay's first-quarter results in 2003 indicated that buyers of construction equipment, tools, and supplies accounted for more than $44 million in annualized gross margin sales at the site. The construction category alone accounted for a 220 percent increase over last year, making it yet another of eBay's fastest-growing categories. Because of the increased activity, eBay has since expanded the category from 17 to 54 subcategories, making it easier for equipment and tool buyers to find what they are looking for.

eBay TIP: The numbers are in, and it's clear that many contractors have added computer mice to their tool belts. There are more than 8000 new construction listings in the eBay Business section every week, ranging from heavy equipment to contractor tools. EBay reported that it sells 270 contractor tools per day in the construction category.

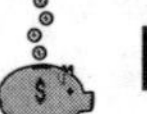

THE TRUTH BEHIND eBAY'S BUSINESS AND INDUSTRIAL SUCCESS

To the casual observer, it may seem that eBay is simply gifted enough to possess the Midas touch, able to take any realm or avenue of business and consumption and turn it into yet another area of unhampered growth. When it comes to the business and industrial commodities, though, eBay did have a bit of help. There's no denying that eBay has been and continues to be diligent in monitoring the activities of its sellers, matching those with the needs of its buyers, and then stepping in to help simplify or establish whatever categories or tools are necessary to better enable new areas of online trading. When it comes to business and industrial commerce, eBay was simply on hand to pick up the slack with the industry-specific B2B (business-to-business) when e-marketplaces collapsed along with the dot-com bubble. A look back to 1999 and 2000, the time when new online marketplaces proclaimed themselves to be the "eBay for electronics" or "eBay for agriculture," it was plain that those up-and-coming venues were ready to utilize eBay's business model then apply it beyond the realm of Beanie Babies and baseball cards. Most of those companies, however, dissipated with the dot-com crash. They failed to secure much-needed investment from the increasingly anxious venture capitalists of the day and weren't able to attract enough buyers and sellers to adequately populate their specialty marketplaces. After the demise of these eBay-wannabes, there was still a market for the buying and selling of business and industrial goods, and so that population of traders simply migrated their activity into eBay. Some sites have all the luck, I guess.

eBAY TEAMS WITH GLOBALSPEC TO BENEFIT YOUR BUSINESS

Going beyond sheer luck, eBay has made a significant investment in the success of its business and industrial segment, signing an agreement with GlobalSpec, Inc., a specialized search engine and online community that caters specifically to the needs of engineers and technical buyers. GlobalSpec has become a leading search destination for buyers of industrial equipment and supplies, thanks to its efficient way of searching for product information by manufacturer as well as by equipment specifications. Buyers simply type in specifications of the type of industrial supply or equipment they're looking for and GlobalSpec sends back product information results matching the search criteria. It's a sort of virtual industrial library *and* product catalog. Seeing that the market position of each company could be complementary to the other and that a partnership between the two could be of terrific value to users, GlobalSpec is now actively promoted on eBay's Business Marketplace pages, giving buyers quick and easy access to the product specifications

GlobalSpec has become known for. This information works to provide yet another seamless experience, allowing users easy access to necessary product information, which helps them in their purchase decisions. GlobalSpec, likewise, now promotes eBay as a viable source of equipment and is actively driving its audience of users to the auction site (which is *great* news if you're selling these sorts of goods).

eBay TIP: In case you're interested in GlobalSpec's numbers, its trademarked search technology—SpecSearch—allows users to search by specification more than 850,000 product families representing 45 million parts from more than 9500 supplier catalogs. If you want to know more about GlobalSpec, visit *www.globalspec.com.*

A BID FOR EASY EQUIPMENT FINANCING

So much has been said now about the tremendous savings you can expect when you shop eBay for the business and industrial equipment that your business, small or large, will need. Don't think I've forgotten, though, that while equipment purchased on eBay for $10,000 is an incredible bargain over paying $60,000 for it elsewhere, coming up with that $10,000 might still be a significant hurdle for your business to clear. If you're a bit light on investment capital yet aren't ready to throw in the towel on your small-business dreams, consider another new feature offered on eBay: equipment financing.

Equipment Financing for eBay, provided by Direct Capital Corp., makes it easier for business buyers to finance their industrial equipment purchases of $2,000 or more. Acting sort of like a combination escrow service and issue resolution provider (thus protecting *both* buyer and seller), equipment financing comes as a definite benefit to both parties. For starters, here's how buyers of equipment benefit from the program (as reported on eBay's site):

- *Buyer Security.* Direct Capital connects buyers with trusted sellers who have passed a screening process.
- *eBay Buyer Services Team.* A team of finance experts will focus on the details to assure that the transaction is completed smoothly, relieving buyers from worry over a high-value equipment transaction.
- Flexibility. Available finance options help buyers get the equipment they need with financing payments they can afford.
- *Preapproval.* Get preapproved for financing, and if there are currently no bids on a listing, buyers can ask sellers to switch the listing to "Buy It Now" and bid with a preapproved credit line.

- *Transferral of Credit Approval.* Ability to apply credit preapproval to other listings if a buyer doesn't win a particular item.
- *Worry-Free Transactions.* Sellers are not paid until buyers receive their purchased equipment (payments can be made via PayPal at no cost to the buyer or the seller).
- *Inclusion of Shipping Costs.* Shipping costs can be included in the financing agreement.

From my perspective, eBay has done their homework on this new program, building in mechanisms for security, verification, and smooth transaction completion up front (clearly leveraging from its many lessons learned in other auction business). This program, from the buyer's perspective, helps take the potential anxiety out of buying pricey industrial equipment on eBay. What about the seller, though? How does the Equipment Financing program serve those who offer up this great equipment? Here are the benefits eBay has built in for industrial equipment sellers:

- *No Final-Value Fee.* Pay no final-value fee when listings are financed on eBay. When a listing offers Equipment Financing, final-value fees will be reimbursed to the seller.
- *Payment in full.* Get paid in full once a listing is successfully financed. eBay will fund the seller's PayPal account for the winning price of the listing, plus the reimbursed Final Value Fee. Sellers need to have an active PayPal account to participate in Equipment Financing but won't be charged the usual PayPal commissions for these disbursements.
- *Easy Link for Buyers.* eBay provides simple HTML code to be added to equipment listings to allow the Equipment Financing logo and link for buyers to follow and get approved.
- *Flexibility.* Sellers have the option, if a listing does not have any bids, to change the listing to "Buy It Now" and immediately accept a purchase from a preapproved buyer.

This is a program that was built to assist businesspeople and their enterprises, whether they're buying or selling. And, it serves as tangible proof that eBay has come a long way in the development of its methods, mechanisms, and tools and programs that benefit the community of users.

eBay TIP: Yes, I have become one of the converted. There was a time when I found eBay to be too preoccupied with its own needs and earnings aspirations to effectively serve its community. In years past, eBay's longtime user base was regularly up in arms about anything

from unexpected site outages (remember the 22-hour fiasco in June 1999?) to increases in sellers' fees to loss of the warm-and-cozy cottage-industry feel. Having written extensively for years about eBay's shortcomings and lost opportunities, I've seen now that they've truly changed their style and have become more customer driven (the customer being the community of users, of course). So understand that I'm still here as an advocate for you, the user, and am not on the eBay payroll. Nevertheless, I must give credit where credit is due and, in the realm of the eBay business marketplace, I applaud the site's efforts and results.

A NEW VENUE FOR THE INDUSTRIOUS SELLER

To wrap this chapter up, let's discuss what this booming business marketplace has to offer to sellers in particular. Search any of the *Business & Industrial* subcategories and you'll find literally thousands of listings. Who's selling this stuff? Peeking into the *Electrical Equipment* subcategory, I found that not only are many of the listed items offered by sellers who are surplus dealers, they're also being sold by licensed electricians and other contractors who have likewise found profit in marketing their excess equipment. As I mentioned earlier, eBay's *Business & Industrial* pages are increasingly stocked with the goods from small distributors and professional contractors and installers, who've added the computer mouse to their box of essential tools. This is another example of eBay making it easy for a group of sellers who might not have the skills to create their own online presence to benefit from the 100-million-strong audience of registered users. Marketing, promotion, and visibility concerns have already been taken care of, and folks who wish to sell industrial goods to eager buyers—from around the corner to around the globe—can do so with relative ease.

As I wrapped up my explorations into selling industrial goods on eBay, I discovered the successes of Art Lazarus of Machinery Values, Inc., and how eBay's business marketplace saved his 34-year-old business from vanishing completely. "We were in a lot of trouble. It was like somebody turned a switch and our industry died," Art shared. Not selling enough industrial equipment to cover overhead costs, the company, which was founded back in 1971, was forced to cut staff and reduce office space. Still, that wasn't enough. The usual sales channels of catalog and trade publications no longer delivered the necessary level of sales to support Machinery Values's operation of acquiring, refurbishing, and reselling large industrial machines. The business was at a crossroads.

Art admits he was familiar with eBay and had used it to buy personal items for himself for a few years. Call it an act of desperation or a divine revelation, but Art got the notion to offer the company's swelling stockpile of

machines and various spare parts on eBay. Great idea! Although initial sales were slow, the items Art listed were selling. Suddenly, Machinery Values began earning up to $5,000 a week on eBay-listed items. That, of course, blossomed into even more listings and more sales, literally rescuing Machinery Values from the scrap heap. "That $250,000 a year we were getting from eBay was the difference between us making a small profit and losing money," Art said. "It saved us; it really saved us."

Instead of publishing and mailing equipment catalogs throughout the year, Art has eliminated that cost from his operating budget, electing to use eBay as Machinery Values' main advertising mechanism. Today, Art happily reports he's selling about $4.5 million worth of machines on eBay every year.

9

The Feedback on Feedback

When it comes to your business, a reputation is indeed a fragile thing. Recall the earlier discussion about how Pierre Omidyar conceived eBay with the purest of altruistic motives then positioned its community of users to grow organically through the open and interactive Feedback Forum. Some may have scoffed at Pierre's original vision, and his beloved Feedback Forum has had a few bumps and bruises along the way. Nevertheless, his vision *has* worked, and while eBay hobbyists of the past found their positive feedback ratings (their overall "scores" that communicate their success in doing good and honest business online) to provide a certain warm and fuzzy feeling, eBay business people have since learned how important a positive online reputation can be in attracting and retaining customers within the sea of buyers. In this chapter, I'll revisit the principles of eBay's Feedback Forum, show you a few new features in online feedback, and discuss how big-time business analysts have come to recognize the high value for high marks in the cyber-marketplace.

FOUNDING OF A FORUM

There was a time when feedback was Greek to eBay newcomers. In eBay's early days, feedback was utilized to nurture community spirit, involvement, and responsibility and to take some of the chill out of transacting with virtual strangers in the vastness of cyberspace. Way back when, Pierre's Feedback Forum at eBay helped forge friendships and foster the notion that "we're all in this together; we can make it sail or we can make it sink by our behaviors." It sounded all very Pollyannish at the time, but feedback has definitely worked for longtime eBayers . . . well, mostly.

Originally, it was all about trust and community values—Pierre deliv-

ered it and it was good. By developing this public online referral system of sorts, eBay users were afforded the ability to praise or discipline others with whom they traded. Other online sites, auction or otherwise, recognized the power of Pierre's virtual kiosk and quickly embraced and emulated eBay's innovative self-policing solution. At its outset, it appeared to be a system above reproach. Well, not exactly. As the community grew in numbers, so did the proliferation of feedback abuse. Many community members complained that others among them were illicitly contracting with friends and relatives to artificially pad positive-feedback ratings; that is, any user could have his best friend, his mom, or his sweet Aunt Pat visit the Feedback Forum and deposit ten or twenty positive notes, thereby artificially boosting the cumulative feedback rating number (the net result of +1 positive comments, –1 negative comments, and inconsequential neutral notes). Worse yet was the outright abomination of feedback "bombing," the merciless inundation of venomous posts, which were intended to slur a seller and sabotage his, her, or its overall rating and reputation. Suddenly, the results could be skewed favorably or unfavorably, and something funny was going on at the Forum.

In response, eBay implemented a couple of stopgaps aimed at blocking unearned praise and, at the other extreme, halting the more vitriolic character assassins, thereby restoring order to the person-to-person report-card repository. First, eBay limited the ability to post feedback comments only to those actually engaged in a transaction; only the seller and the winning bidder of a successful auction could post comments for one another. Unless sweet Aunt Pat was a covert hacker of some sort, her days of padding her dear nephew's feedback rating were at an end. As for the more vicious vagrants, eBay instituted a response feature, thereby granting the transactor accused of engaging in bad business their day in court, so to speak. (There are, after all, two sides to every story.) A good idea, to be sure, and certain to curtail any future feedback fallout.

Again, not exactly. After a couple of years in use, the revised and restricted neg policy has still been impotent to prevent a verbal volley between a buyer and seller who either refuse to play by the rules or suffer from communication breakdown and throw caution to the wind when they lob the often colorful and contrived assessments of their new-found foe. In my estimation, these are by and large the behavior of the casual eBayers; those engaged in bona fide business activities (whether buying or selling; usually a combination of both) elect to take the high road at every opportunity, working diligently to iron out any misunderstandings quickly and compassionately.

THE NEW VALUE OF A STELLAR REPUTATION

Is an eBay feedback rating really so valuable? The short answer: yes. As eBay has evolved to become the business Mecca that I've witnessed and described, the Feedback Forum has become the foundation for an eBay business's po-

tential success and ability to attract online patrons. It all comes down to trust and, if you ask any active businessperson or business analyst, trust is the underpinning of a business's health.

I found it best put by MIT Sloan Professor of Management Chrysanthos Dellarocas when he succinctly deemed the communicating of online opinions as "word of mouse." This captures how business reputations, which are so important to eBay's unrivaled growth and the growth potential for its legions of sellers, can be just a click away from elevation or ruin.

"Word-of-mouth, which is one of the most ancient mechanisms in the history of human society, is given new significance by the unique properties of the Internet," Dellarocas proclaimed to those in attendance at the first-ever Interdisciplinary Symposium on Online Reputation Mechanisms, co-hosted by MIT Sloan and the National Science Foundation. "Feedback from consumers on the Web is global, instant, and persistent." So true.

As Dellarocas explains, the reason an online reputation has become of such importance to anyone interested in doing business online is its immediacy, what with conceivably thousands of feedback comments being posted on eBay every hour of every day. Many emerging small businesses made their start on eBay, and they often wish to refer back to their feedback ratings as a point of referral, especially as they venture outside of eBay to further their business reach. To have mismanaged or ignored the value of eBay feedback would have been foolish in hindsight. Moreover, just as you and I find ease in doing business throughout the global community, thanks to eBay (I've sold to customers in 23 countries and counting), international customers enjoy equal ease in reviewing our virtual business report card. So it's easy to see how feedback not only enables eBay users to make sound choices before engaging in a transaction, it affords every customer the ability to actually *influence* millions of other potential customers, positively or negatively, through the power of their ultimate feedback comments posted.

So, how much is feedback worth to your business?

eBay TIP: In 2003, Richard Zeckhauser, economist at the University of Michigan, studied eBay's feedback function and concluded that sellers with positive reputations actually sold more merchandise at higher prices than others. His results also indicated that more than 90 percent of eBay users actively leave feedback at the conclusion of a transaction.

IT'S STILL ALL ABOUT TRUST

When it comes to your business, your ability to bolster your earnings can be directly associated with your ability to instill trust in your active and prospec-

tive customers. Undoubtedly, the foundation for successful transactions is *trust*, for practically any and all personal and economic exchanges. Consider your need to trust your employer, your credit card issuer, or the smiling fellow who insists you'll look fabulous in that new car. If you trust the person on the opposite side of the table, you'll likely do business. As that person on the other side of the table, you have to ensure you *are* trustworthy if you hope to make the sale. And *trustworthiness*, in this context, may be defined as the ability of two people engaged in a potential transaction to conduct themselves in a cooperative and mutually beneficial manner. The benefits of perceived trustworthiness for you, the seller, are that it makes attracting new customers easier and that you'll instill loyalty in those who've done business with you before. When you can operate in a manner of mutual trust, your transactions can be completed quicker and with less hand-holding or follow-up. If your customers feel anxious or unsure about dealing with you, it will cost *you* more time and effort to continually assure and reassure them throughout a transaction; that's time you should be spending elsewhere in your business. However, if you have a good reputation, one you'll proudly post on your virtual office wall, customers will feel immediately at ease in doing business with you and make it easier for you to make sale after sale after sale. And you just wanted to sell some junk on eBay, huh? Well, if you're in it for the long haul you can see that reputation and feedback have become highly important to those seriously interested in establishing an online business.

THE COST OF NEGATIVE ENERGY

When a seller or buyer does you wrong on eBay—failing to ship, pay, or generally conduct themselves to your expectations—many in the community have stood poised and ready to let their anger be expressed in the Feedback Forum. Bad behavior deserves to be publicly exposed, right? Therefore, when bad deeds are done or business practices aren't what they should be (in somebody's subjective estimation) negative feedback (or "negs" as the long-timers say) should be promptly posted.

Maybe.

Along my virtual travels, I was surprised to learn there was something other than sniping (the practice of last-second stealth bidding) that could stir up the embers of opposing viewpoints within the online auction forum. We've all heard of fee avoidance in the online auction places, but how about this: feedback avoidance.

I found that many folks preferred *not* to post negative feedback on eBay even though it might be well within their right (and encouraged by eBay itself) to do so. In many cases (and I'll attest to this from my own experiences), eBay users and business people are purposely skirting their opportunity (some call it a duty) of posting negative feedback against other online buyers

and sellers with whom they've had difficulties. Why? Well, what has many looking the other way in times of online injustice isn't indifference necessarily but an aversion to receive a retaliatory "neg" in return. *That* won't look good on a feedback record, will it?

The underlying motivation to avoid posting, and then potentially receiving, negative feedback is flatly pragmatic: negative feedback is bad for business. Just like that, eBay's feedback mechanism was again challenged in its ability to accurately capture and reflect all that goes on at the auction site. For your consideration, here's the meat of the debate as it was told to me (users' identities have been protected):

- *From Camp A.* "It's on account of [sellers who don't neg] that people are ripping us off left and right. I can't see that a certain bidder has received a non-paying bidder warning but I *can* see feedback from another seller saying he or she didn't get paid. I could have avoided [that bidder] if it weren't for other sellers' cowardly business practices."
- *From Camp B.* "I've left negs in the past but gave it up as a bad habit. Potential bidders don't take the time to scroll through umpteen hundred pages of feedback [to read the actual neg and response]. Some bidders simply see several red marks [from negs] and decide not to bid or buy. Why risk losing even *one* potential buyer because of a retaliatory negative comment in response to one I might post? Leaving negs does nothing to improve my business."
- *From Camp A.* Camp A says, "Let 'em have it" while Camp B retorts, "To what end?" One side says the only way to ensure that the deadbeats and other dregs of the auction society will be flushed out is to shine the spotlight on their spotty exploits. After enough negs have been levied, the unsavory element will be effectively NARU'd (removed from the site and deemed Not A Registered User).
- *From Camp B.* The other side says the problem lies in the fact that, to buyers, a neg is of little consequence, especially given that a banished user can easily rejoin under a new identity. To the seller, however, the building up of a large feedback profile is tantamount to attracting business and even a few negs might quickly tarnish an otherwise unblemished reputation.

This polarization is the fuel that feeds the fire of this philosophical standoff and has many within the community pointing fingers at one another over accusations of unnecessary brashness and selfish abandon of community values. Of course, there's always the group aligned in the middle of the road that has learned to neg very judiciously and after all other avenues of contact and resolution have duly exercised. This no-surprises approach seems

to be favored by most who engage in the discussion, citing that, of the negs they do ultimately post, it's not often that a retaliatory follows.

eBay TIP: Is reputation a fragile thing? Seems so by this user's comment: "So far, I have yet to [receive] a retaliatory neg and know I have left at least 20+ after thousands of transactions. I say this knowing that at any moment that could change."

There is no right or wrong answer here. For the budding business owner, this need to establish and maintain a reputation for being above reproach might just be the reasoning behind the not-always-accurate sentiment "The customer is always right." I won't decide for you how you should respond when the opportunity to post a negative comment presents itself. You certainly don't want to feel you're being restrained from posting your honest thoughts when its appropriate and justified, but be sure you're prepared to receive the reciprocal effect. My advice: try to work it out with the other person to the best of your ability, and if that effort fails, sleep on it before you act.

THE LEGAL REPERCUSSIONS

Just so you know, posting your opinions online could have a greater impact than you think, possibly far beyond what you intend. Sure, it's the Internet, and the Bill of Rights ensures that we can all speak freely, but in the land of free speech, some of us aren't as enlightened as others about the costs and consequences of exercising our rights in unbridled fashion. Yes, it's a legal thing that will protect citizens from unfounded character defamation, incriminating diatribe, and other such written verbal assault more affectionately known as libel.

From *www.findlaw.com*:

> Libel is a false . . . publication by writing . . . which exposes any person to hatred, contempt, ridicule, or obloquy, or which causes him to be shunned or avoided, or which has a tendency to injure him in his occupation.

Basically, all the stuff that has made angry negative feedback feel so satisfying at the height of passion is the same caustic fare that can be actionable by law. Pleading ignorance of the law, of course, is no excuse. Therefore, with the law backing them up, an eBay feedback moderator will counsel posters to stick to the facts: unemotional, uncontrived, and strictly nonthreatening. Before posting a neg, we're all cautioned, we must allow for a cooling-off period so we don't stray onto the path of injurious embellishment (hence my advice

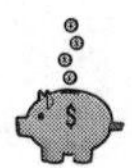

to sleep on it first). And, again, how will it really serve your business? That's up to you to decide.

CHANGES TO eBAY'S NEGATIVE FEEDBACK POLICY

Often, in the heat of passion and while cooler heads were not prevailing, eBay users have found themselves in a virtual spat and resorted to lobbing negative feedback bombs at one another. Sometimes, though, after the smoke clears, these adversaries have found common ground, understanding, and reconciliation. Still, their feedback ratings have borne the scars of their moment of anger and persisted regardless of the fact that wounds had since healed and broken fences mended.

Feedback posted on eBay is permanent. However, eBay has heard the cries of its community, particularly those who sometimes lashed out at one another in moments of discord or miscommunication. In 2003, eBay responded to users' requests and introduced the Mutual Feedback Withdrawal option. While the comments made would not be removed, the negative tally and the effect the negative point had on a user's overall rating can now be nullified. The key, of course, is in the word *mutual.* In order for a negative comment's undesirable effect to be rescinded, both parties would need to agree that it could be. And, even though the original remark would still remain visible, reconciled transactors can easily apply responses to the comments, verifying for the rest of the community that the source of their former feud has since been resolved peaceably and to both parties' satisfaction.

Finding this Mutual Feedback Withdrawal function is a bit of a hunt, however. Your best bet, if you find yourself in the situation of needing it, is to click on the *Help* text link above the eBay main tool bar. In the next screen you see, type in "Mutual Feedback Withdrawal" in the *Search Help* field. You'll see that hidden within the FAQ (Frequently Asked Questions) is a tiny text link to an online form to initiate a feedback withdrawal (see Figure 9-1).

eBay TIP: Honestly, I've scoured the Site Map and the Services pages to find easier access to this *Mutual Feedback Withdrawal* form, and I simply can't find it. I won't infer what this might or might not mean in regard to eBay's desire (or lack thereof) to engage in feedback nullification, but it seems strange.

Next, you'll find a new page in which you can enter the item number that was the source of the feedback fallout (see Figure 9-2). Click on the "Continue" button and review the feedback for which you wish withdrawal. Remember, this is to be a mutual agreement before feedback is withdrawn,

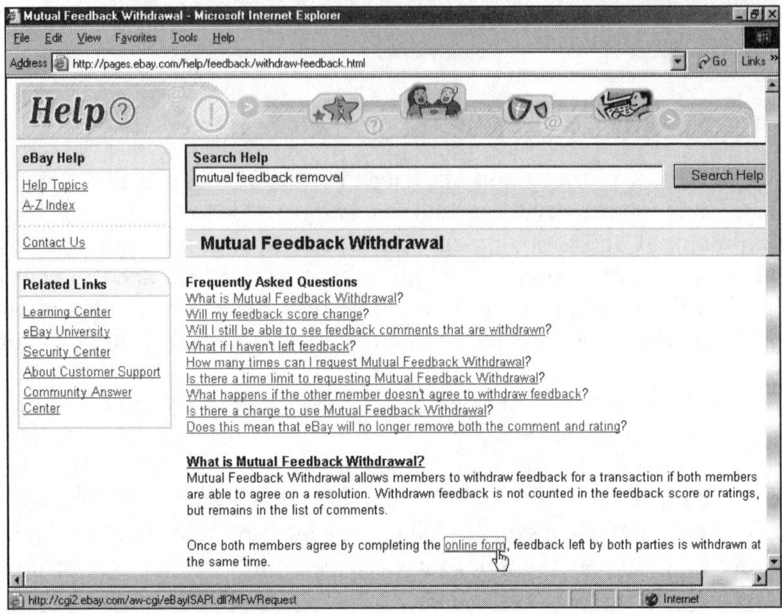

Figure 9-1 Access to the Mutual Feedback Withdrawal request form is curiously hidden within eBay's Help suite.

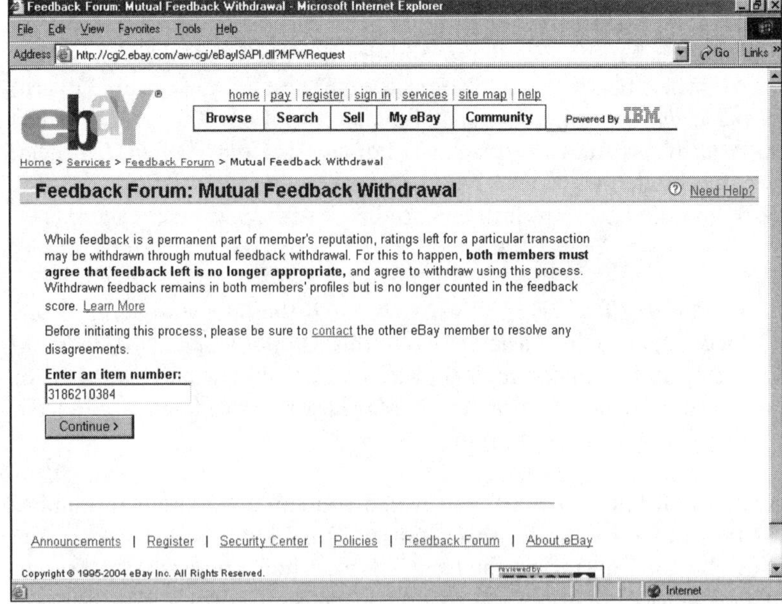

Figure 9-2 Once at the request form, enter the item number for which feedback is to be withdrawn.

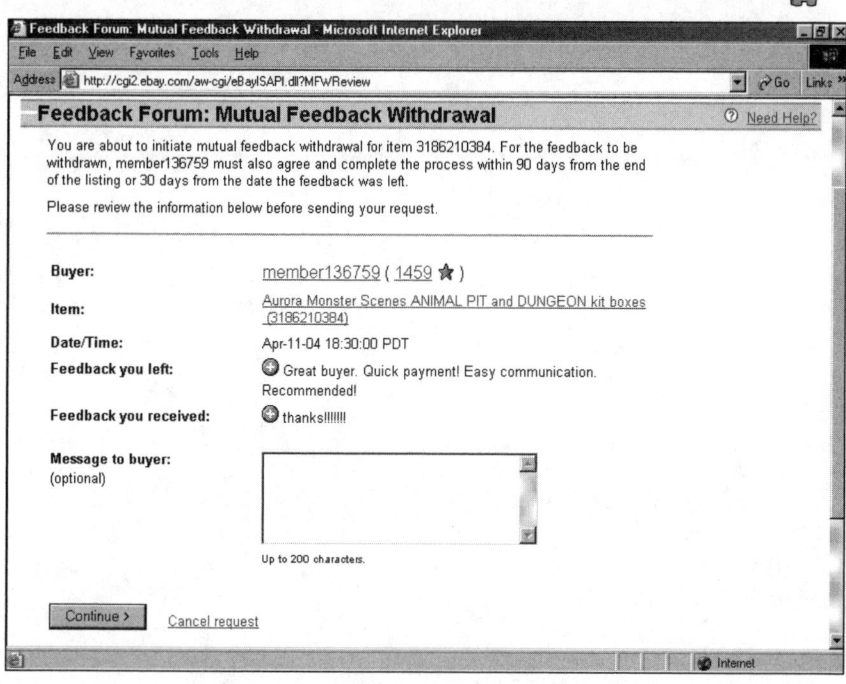

Feedback Forum: Mutual Feedback Withdrawal - Microsoft Internet Explorer

File Edit View Favorites Tools Help

Address http://cgi2.ebay.com/aw-cgi/eBayISAPI.dll?MFWReview

Feedback Forum: Mutual Feedback Withdrawal Need Help?

You are about to initiate mutual feedback withdrawal for item 3186210384. For the feedback to be withdrawn, member136759 must also agree and complete the process within 90 days from the end of the listing or 30 days from the date the feedback was left.

Please review the information below before sending your request.

Buyer:	member136759 (1459)
Item:	Aurora Monster Scenes ANIMAL PIT and DUNGEON kit boxes (3186210384)
Date/Time:	Apr-11-04 18:30:00 PDT
Feedback you left:	Great buyer. Quick payment! Easy communication. Recommended!
Feedback you received:	thanks!!!!!!
Message to buyer: (optional)	Up to 200 characters.

Continue > Cancel request

Internet

Figure 9-3 At this time, I don't have negative feedback to withdraw but this is a sample of the form you would see if you wished a feedback nullification.

thus, eBay will notify the other party of your request for feedback withdrawal, and that person has up to 90 days to agree and accept your request (of course, you would have already established this agreement prior to launching the request). See Figure 9-3 for a look at the form to submit.

So is this recent Feedback Forum significant? Yes and no. eBay still stands by its contention that all users should be responsible for their feedback comments and their effects *before* posting. And, in order to preserve the history, eBay has chosen to retain the comments, viewable by all, regardless of whether two parties worked out their prior differences. Here again is another reason to treat feedback with the utmost care and nurturing; your reputation will precede you in everything you do on eBay. Most often, that's good news for conscientious businesspeople.

10

Still a Fee-sible Endeavor?

An eBay business is a pay-as-you-go proposition and, if you're serious about your online endeavors, you'll need to understand clearly and objectively exactly what you might expect to pay when you decide to go with eBay as your sales platform. eBay is making some hefty profits, thanks to the fees they collect from each of us who has chosen to list and sell goods at the mammoth auction site. While it would hardly be controversial to say that it does indeed "take money to make money," seasoned entrepreneurs also know that in order to make a fortune, you must likewise *save* a fortune. Long a topic of sometimes heated debate, eBay's own fee structure has been and still is fertile fuel for lengthy discussions regarding sellers' ability to truly earn a profit and maintain (and grow) a business.

This chapter revisits the whole matter of eBay fees: what they are, what they cost, and how to control them to better ensure that your business is running squarely in the black at all times. Most importantly to the overall discussion at hand of growing your business and unleashing the power of eBay, this chapter will focus on how eBay's fee changes (both current and any others in the future) affect sellers and what you can do to counter their potentially profit-stealing effect.

A LOOK AT eBAY FEES TODAY

Make no mistake: the profit potential on eBay is still very much alive and well and ready to be tapped. eBay, though, being a business like any other, may be expected to incur additional costs or set incremental goals for its own bottom-line earnings. As with any other landlord who leases business space, sellers like you and I will be on the receiving end of rent increases, so to speak.

In February 2004, eBay announced widespread changes to its fee structure. In some cases, fees were actually lowered, but in most cases they were raised. Before going any further with a discussion of what these fee changes might mean to your business's bottom line, take a look at what eBay is charging your business. Because it is of use to understand what fees used to cost in order to assess the new fee structure, I'll present the before and after look as a source for comparison and ensuing discussion.

Insertion Fees

First up is the inescapable insertion fee. This is the cost levied when you list an item, either for auction or fixed-price sale (see Figure 10-1). This fee is nonrefundable; you will be charged even if your item *does not* sell.

Look closely at Figure 10-1 and you'll see that eBay raised insertion fees slightly (from 5 cents on up), but it also redefined the fee break points. They introduced two new insertion-fee break points: one at the lowest level (from $0.01–$0.99) and another at the high end ($500 and up). At first glance, it pretty much looks like eBay has added roughly 10 to 20 cents on average to the fee for a single item. Notice that the insertion fee increases are progres-

Insertion Fees: eBay.com and eBay Motors Parts & Accessories

Item Starting Price	Previous Fee
$0.01–$9.99	$0.30
$10.00–$24.99	$0.55
$25.00–$49.99	$1.10
$50.00–$199.99	$2.20
$200.00 and up	$3.30

Item Starting Price	Fee as of February 2, 2004
$0.01 - $0.99	$0.30
$1.00 - $9.99	$0.35
$10.00 - $24.99	$0.60
$25.00 - $49.99	$1.20
$50.00 - $199.99	$2.40
$200.00 - $499.99	$3.60
$500 and up	$4.80

Figure 10-1 Schedule of eBay insertion fees.

sively greater as the value of the starting bid increases. Immediately, longtime sellers felt they were about to become nickeled and dimed to death. These fee increases were of little consequence if only a few items were listed, but to those who list hundreds or thousands of items each month as their business requires, the calculated impact of these fees becomes far more significant. However, there is a turnabout tactic savvy sellers use to protect themselves from the potentially negative effect of the raised rates. Before discussing tactics, let's look at the other fee changes.

Reserve Price Fees

Reserve Prices are those designations you make when listing items on eBay to determine a price that your auction must reach during bidding if you are going to sell. If you're concerned you might not recoup your original investment on an auction (and reserve prices are typically used in cases of collectibles, one-of-a-kinds, or other such "one-off" items), the reserve price allows you to protect your investment and prevent you from having to sell on the cheap (and at a loss) if the bidders fail to bring you a price you can live with. Figure 10-2 presents the before and after look at the fee levied to use this seller's protective device.

Reserve price fees have doubled! This one really had sellers grumbling at being "robbed" at twice the cost just so they could provide a little insurance for their auction sales. I agreed that this one was a bit harder to swallow but, again, there is a counteroffensive to this fee hike. More on that later.

Reserve Price Fees: eBay.com and eBay Motors Parts & Accessories

Reserve Price	Current Fee
$0.01–$24.99	$0.50
$25.00–$99.99	$1.00
$100 and up	1% of reserve price (with a maximum of $100.00)
Reserve Price	**Fee as of February 2, 2004**
$0.01–$49.99	$1.00
$50.00–$199.99	$2.00
$200 and up	1% of reserve price (with a maximum of $100.00)

Figure 10-2 Schedule of eBay reserve price fees.

eBay Stores Insertion Fees

Sidestepping the auction parlor for a moment, changes were also made to the fees levied to sellers electing to open an eBay Store and offer items on a fixed-price basis (see Figure 10-3).

Look at Figure 10-3! Fees went down in the eBay Stores arena. That's great news, right? Sure it is, although Stores listings are not made as visible to eBay shoppers. Hit lists that show the different listings that match a buyer's search do not include items listed in eBay Stores; buyers would need to search Stores discretely in order to find those items offered for fixed-price sale and that match a keyword search. Good or bad? Again, there's an opportunity here that I'll share momentarily.

A Few Other Fee Changes

A few more fees changed as of February 2004, as shown Figures 10-4 and 10-5.

Figure 10-4 shows another fee that was reduced, significantly I might add; yet it was never what I considered to be a worthwhile expense for sellers anyway. Look at the home page featured items and, sadly, most of what you will find are weight-loss come-ons and other such infomercial products.

I found it curious that eBay would choose to double the cost of this listing upgrade, unless it was a quasi-psychological attempt to dissuade use. After all, the longer a listing lasts on eBay, the more precious database space it consumes. I've never been a fan of the 10-day listing. Bidders simply don't like to wait that long for an auction to end, and sellers risk having another similar or superior item be listed by a competitor.

As I have mentioned, these fee changes can be deftly navigated in a way that they won't significantly impact your bottom line.

Store Inventory Insertion Fees

Duration	Current Fee	Fee as of February 2, 2004
30 days	$0.05	$0.02
60 days	$0.05 plus .05 surcharge	$0.02 plus .02 surcharge
90 days	$0.05 plus .10 surcharge	$0.02 plus .04 surcharge
120 days	$0.05 plus .15 surcharge	$0.02 plus .06 surcharge
*GTC	$0.05 plus $.05 per 30 days	$0.02 plus .02 per 30 days

(*Good 'Til Cancelled)

Figure 10-3 Schedule of eBay Store inventory insertion fees.

Home Page Featured Fee: eBay.com	
Current Fee	**Fee Effective January 31, 2004**
$99.95 for single item	$39.95 for single item
$199.95 for multiple items	$79.95

Figure 10-4 Schedule of eBay home page featured fees.

10-Day Listing Fee: eBay.com and eBay Motors Parts & Accessories	
Current Fee	**Fee as of February 2, 2004**
$0.10	$0.20

Figure 10-5 The eBay 10-day listing fee.

COUNTERING THE FEE INCREASES

Naturally, the most concerning of these fee changes regards the insertion fees; let's understand how to corral those first. Look very closely at the insertion-fee break points (see Figure 10-1) and you'll notice what many other sellers have already embraced: fees jump dramatically between the levels of the most popular midrange break points. While some sellers have knee-jerked into a reaction of outrage that the cost of insertion doubles from 60 cents ($10.00–$24.99) to $1.20 ($25.00–$49.99), savvy sellers have simply dropped their opening bid amounts by a single penny and have been able to avoid that 60-cent jump by choosing $24.99 over $25.00. It's just a penny to you, but it can save you half the insertion fee in one fell swoop. Look carefully at the other insertion-fee break points and you'll see the same opportunity. Play the break points and you'll save big on the cost of inserting new listings.

The Reserve Price fees (see Figure 10-2) have doubled, yet you can work the single break points there to reduce that add-on fee (it's levied *in addition* to the basic insertion fee if you choose to use it). Some have told me a reserve price of only $24.99 is hardly worthwhile, and I agree; usually a reserve price would be set much higher if a seller feels the need to protect the value (which is usually high) for an item being listed for bid. The best and simplest countermeasure, then, to the rather costly $2 reserve price fee or incur the 1 percent take for higher-value reserve prices is this: don't use a reserve price. This tactic goes back to your market research and understanding of what you

can sell and at what prices (recall the discussion from Chapter 7 and how this research was tied into the creation of your business plan), and use that to help you determine what you might expect to earn from the current marketplace. Perhaps you might set your opening bid higher and let that help you protect your investment. Bidders can then decide if they'll offer that opening bid and how much more they might be willing to ante up for what you're offering. All the while you'll still be protecting your investment value through the higher starting bid price.

eBay TIP: I recognize the previous statement flies in the face of my long-held belief that lower opening bid values are required to inspire bidding. That's still true but, for the individual who truly feels a need to protect the value of a particular item, it might be a better strategy to raise the bid amount at the outset. Remember that bidders still tend to shy away from reserve-price auctions, not always liking that a preset selling value has been instituted, thereby quashing the true spirit of open bidding. Again, know the value of what you want to sell, understand what the current market is offering, and then decide if this is the right time for your item to be put up on the auction block. If the current prices don't support what you want to earn for your item(s), then listing and incurring *any* fees, reserve price or otherwise, probably isn't in the best interest of your profits.

The good news in this discussion is that eBay Store insertion fees have dropped, clearly a signal from eBay that it wants to attract more fixed-price selling into the venue. That's actually good news, because now it's less expensive to list inventoried items for direct sale at the same time that eBay buyers are discovering that offerings are increasing from eBay Store owners. Don't worry about the search-results issue I mentioned earlier: stock your eBay Store, but also keep a few items available in the auction space (either for bid or fixed-price; you can choose either) to help your goods appear on more buyers' search lists while acting as a beacon to your store. If you're clear in your auction listings that you have more terrific goods available within your store, you'll see that bidders will be visiting your virtual aisles with increased regularity.

eBay TIP: Lest I forget, there is a fee for maintaining an eBay Store: subscription rates are $9.95 per month, $49.95 per month, and $499.95 per month. That's quite a jump from one level to the next. eBay Store subscription rates differ due to different features available at each subscription level. I'll cover the breakdown of cost-per-features in Chapter 13.

A PHILOSOPHICAL LOOK AT FEES AND YOUR PROFIT ON eBAY

Perhaps one of the biggest early challenges that faced Pierre Omidyar came when he reluctantly began charging final value fees (the percentage of fee levied based on the final selling price of an auctioned item) in order to keep up with the growing costs he was incurring to keep eBay (then AuctionWeb) active on his ISP's server, which was rapidly being consumed by the growing auction site. As eBay has evolved, so, too, has its fee structure. The costs rise to offset eBay's maintenance and infrastructure costs and to bolster eBay's profits. This was a tough pill for the early sellers at the site to swallow, because they had been weaned on the grass-roots tenet that the Internet was free. Many other such Web sites that started up as free services then migrated to fee-based models have since dried up, evidently unable to prove that their offerings were worth paying for. eBay, has been different in this regard, because the sellers and buyers have never abandoned the site. Even though the community has sometimes become enraged and threatened a boycott or virtual picket, business on eBay has grown steadily year by year. Some have said that eBay is exploiting its community, knowing they'll continue to pay in order to have access to the huge consumer audience it hosts. Others, though, have realized that to leave eBay would be to essentially "cut off the nose" from their business. eBay is good for businesses, and when costs rise, businesses must adjust. It's a harsh truth, but it is the reality of consumer economics.

So what's my point? Your business will be faced with fees, costs, and other such expenditures that you'll need to control to the best of your ability, causing you to be in perpetual tune-up mode. Longtime business owners know this and for that reason often state that owning and operating a business is hardly for the faint of heart. However, with up-front planning (that business plan), constant awareness of the market and trends, and unrelenting dedication to carefully controlling your costs, your business can also withstand changes and increases in operating fees, even those on eBay.

A SMALL PRICE TO PAY

To close this update regarding eBay fees, consider what you get for your money when you list on eBay. Just as the realtor says that "location, location, location" is what matters most in a home investment, the same can be said for where you decide to establish your business. When it comes to online business, eBay is the Bel Air of cybershopping hubs. More importantly, eBay is practically a business-on-demand that's easy to use and ready to apply. Consider what you gain when you choose eBay as a foundation for your business:

- No overhead or up-front costs to launch your business (sell from your garage immediately)
- No sales staff or distributors to manage at the outset
- No Web site of your own to develop, manage, and pay for
- No initial investment beyond insertion fees to begin marketing your product to a vast audience of buyers

You likewise profit from the fact that eBay leads the online auction industry, with a more than 60 percent share of the market, while its closest competitor (if you can call it that), Yahoo! Auctions, is only half its size. Amazon.com Auctions follows at a distant third. eBay has dominated the online auction and fixed-price market for years now and is only getting bigger. That translates into stability and security to virtual shopkeepers who are looking for firm ground upon which to build their own empires.

11

Fighting Fraud

While good business is booming on eBay, "bad business" is likewise active and in the mix. If you've been around eBay for very long or if you've even casually monitored business- and Internet-related news from the past few years, you'll know that online fraud has been afflicting some of us who do business on eBay and elsewhere online. eBay still contends that less than 100th of 1 percent of its auctions are tainted by fraudulent doings or other such misdeeds yet, as the number of active auctions continues to rise each month, so too, it would appear, do bidding schemes.

I'm very pro-eBay in regard to starting and expanding a business, but I have to be honest about what I hear and read regarding online auction fraud. And, though I don't wish to scare you off by revealing the realities of fraud on eBay, I feel you'll be better equipped to spot and avoid such problems with a little precaution. This chapter, then, offers a current look at fraud on eBay and elsewhere online, giving you scoop on what's new in auction affronts and how you can continue to arm yourself with vital information to stop scammers in their tracks.

THE CURRENT STATISTICS

While I remain unmoved in my belief that you can conduct safe and successful business on eBay without a pervasive fear of being snared in a fraud, the official statistics show that fraud at the online auction house is still alive and well. As reported by the Internet Fraud Watch (IFW) program, online auctions accounted for 89 percent of consumer complaints in 2003. That led to online auctions once again earning the dubious distinction of being the number-one area of consumer-reported frauds. Here's how 2003's top-ten fraud list rounded out:

- Fraudulent auctions
- General merchandise sales scams
- Off-shore money offers (false laundering scams)
- Information/adult services
- Fraudulent internet access services
- Fraudulent or stolen computer equipment/software sales
- Work-at-home plans
- Lotteries
- Fake checks
- Advance-fee loan swindles

Unfortunately, there is now plenty of data available to further distill the impact of online auction fraud (I say *unfortunately* because more data means more fraud). In 2003, the National Consumer League (NCL) was able to calculate the actual number of fraud victims relative to the populations of the states where they live. Here's what the NCL concluded:

- Alaska was number one, with 60 complaints per 100,000 residents
- Hawaii came in at 21 complaints per 100,000 residents

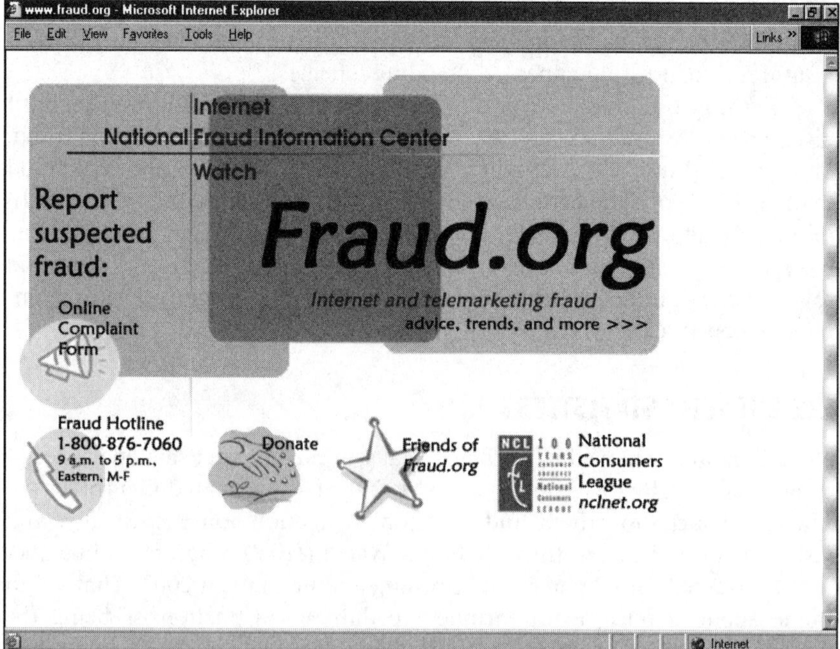

Figure 11-1 The IFW's Fraud.org site offers current information on frauds and fraudsters and tips to avoid getting scammed.

- Washington, Wyoming, and Rhode Island each had 15 complaints per 100,000 residents

While it's unfortunate that consumer watch groups have so much data on these dastardly deeds, on the positive side, they can provide a good amount of education and information to help you steer clear of the next bum deal (see Figure 11-1). Make it a point to check in regularly (at least once a month) at the Web sites of the NCL, Federal Trade Commission (FTC), and IFW. The information you find there is always up to date and always useful.

UNDERSTANDING "PHISHING" AND "SPOOFING"

Perhaps the most prevalent new scam is one that's actually been around for many years yet is finding an alarming heightened level of effectiveness: phishing. Also referred to as spoofing or carding, this scam is running quite rampant these days in the form of e-mail messages that appear to be legitimate company-issued alerts and warnings instructing recipients to update their account information via an Internet link embedded within the body of the message (see Figure 11-2).

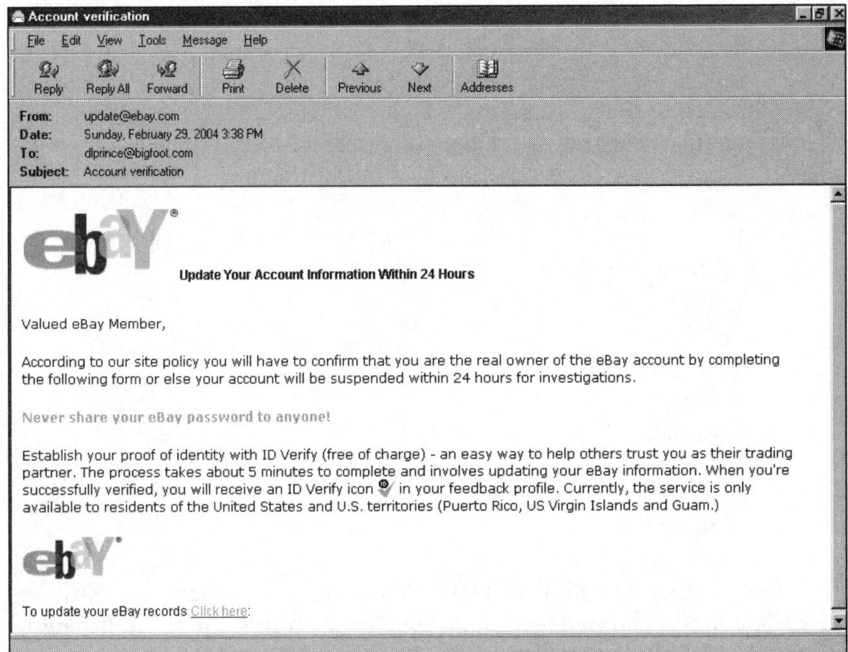

Figure 11-2 According to eBay (or so I'm led to believe), I have 24 hours to click on the embedded link and update my account information. If I fall for it, *spoof*, I've been had.

Phish scammers are using all sorts of warnings, alerts, and "we just want to be sure your account is updated" come-ons to illicitly cull your sensitive bank information, credit card numbers, user account names and passwords, social security numbers, and other such "identity" information. Recipients are instructed, via the spoof e-mail, to follow a link within the message and then enter their information on the subsequent and seemingly authentic Web page. Look out! If you fall for it, the information you provide will be used to hijack your account or other such data and be used for purposes of withdrawing funds or using your online accounts to conduct any manner of larcenous deeds. By incorporating the use of well-known company brands, names, and logos, phishers have actually been successful in fooling about 5 percent of phish recipients. One moment you think you're updating your eBay account, the next moment your user ID is at use listing phony goods, without your knowledge.

Phishers actively try to fool registered users (using sophisticated Web bots and crawlers to illegally pluck user e-mail addresses) wherever they have online accounts. While eBay is the number-one target of phishers (according to *www.antiphishing.org*), other industries being targeted include:

- Financial services
- Retail
- Internet service providers (ISPs)
- Miscellaneous others

Within these business sectors, which brands might you see hijacked to act as a front for a phish attack? Here are the most widely targeted companies in order of phish attacks, as reported by AntiPhishing.org:

- eBay
- CitiBank
- PayPal
- Fleet Bank
- Barclays
- AOL
- Westpac
- Visa
- BankOne
- Earthlink

The list goes on and, if you haven't already, you probably soon will receive a spoof e-mail trying to surreptitiously snatch your online information.

eBay TIP: According to a student attending my eBay seminar, he registered for eBay one evening prior to attending my class and reported receiving a suspicious e-mail the next day indicating that his account required updating. Thankfully, he'd heard of phishing and decided to wait until the seminar to determine if the message was legitimate. It wasn't.

Ensuring You Don't Become Phish-Bait

So how do you protect *yourself* from phish attacks? As with any other fraud, know the criminal's approach and you'll be more likely to avoid being duped. When it comes to spoof e-mails, most are rather poorly constructed, with bad grammar and punctuation offering the first clue that something is amiss. Consider the text of this spoof email I received:

> As a part of our ongoing commitment to provide the "Best Possible" service to all our Members, we are now requiring each Member to validate their accounts once per year.
>
> https://validate.ebay.com
>
> Click this link, and go to validate server
>
> Now, when you enter all information needed,you account will be validated.
>
> These security measures are necessary to protect the integrity of your account. We apologize for any inconvenience this may cause you now, we know that in the long run this added security measure will help to keep your accounts protected at all times.

Even a quick read-through of the above example reveals misspelling, improper grammar, and grade-school punctuation errors.

Some phish emails aren't text messages at all, as in the case of the mock CitiBank notice shown in Figure 11-3, which is actually a graphic file in the .gif format. Notice the rather choppy-looking logo and the oddly stretched text throughout. The entire image is linked to a bogus Web site that would illicitly harvest information from unsuspecting users. My immediate clue that this was a ruse: I'm not a CitiBank customer.

An added wrinkle to the CitiBank scam was the manner in which the phishers constructed the target Web site, one that looked like an official account-maintenance form for the online banking arm of the institution.

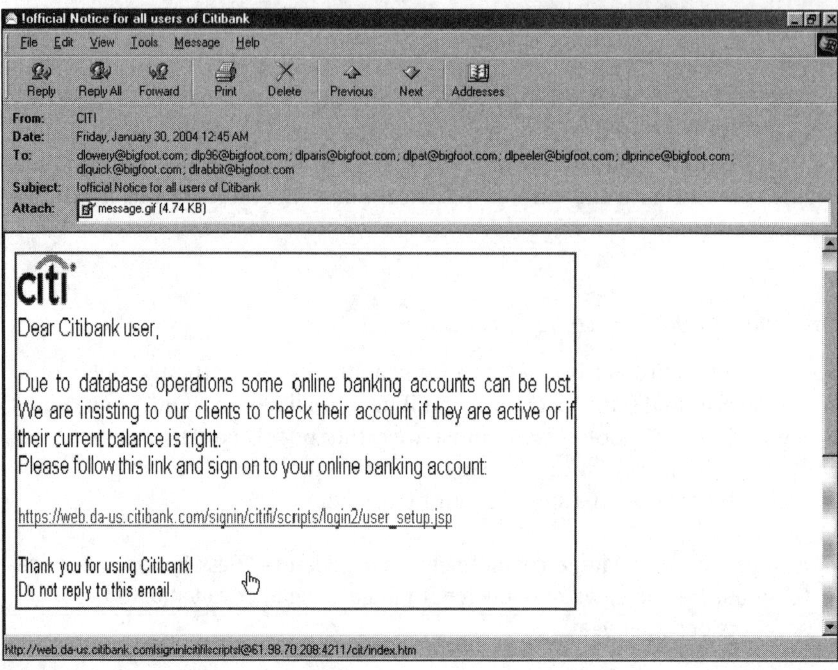

Figure 11-3 This phony CitiBank message wasn't a text message at all. The entire image is a graphic file that, if clicked anywhere within the outlining box, will redirect the recipient to a bogus Web site.

While many phishers construct relatively convincing Web pages, using actual company site designs to fool scammees, it's usually the Web page address that gives the scam away. Most phish messages will provide a forged link, such as *security@eBay.com*, and also include forged "from" addresses in the e-mail message. The resultant Web destination usually shows an odd ISP address that blows the whole cover. In the case of the CitiBank fraud, the phishers utilized very sophisticated Java code to mask (that is, cover up) the actual Web site address with a "painted over" address that showed CitiBank's real Web address (see Figure 11-4).

Certainly, phishing is becoming quite sophisticated in its attempts to defraud unwary Netizens. To help you spot a phish, look for the following in an e-mail message:

- Unexpected notifications to act quickly to prevent service disruption or account suspension.
- Messages requesting that you divulge any account numbers, names, passwords, or any other such unique information, either to be pro-

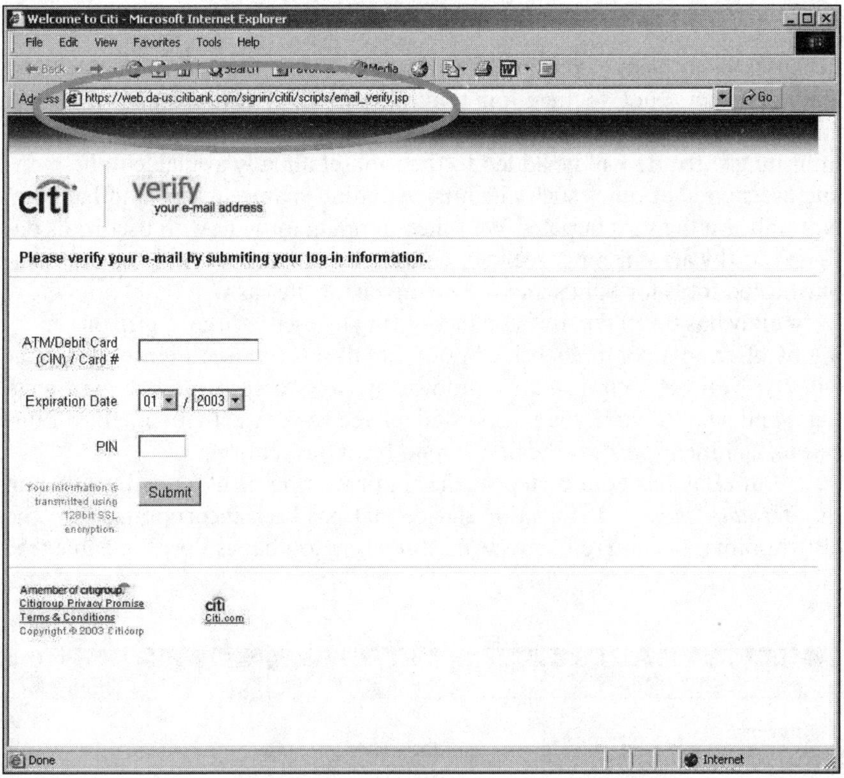

Figure 11-4 A look at the bogus CitiBank Web site that utilized a masked address window to conceal the site's real Web address.

vided in direct response to the message or to be entered and collected in a follow-up Web site.

- Generally, poor grammar, spelling, and punctuation.

Most important of all, *never* utilize active links embedded within suspicious e-mails. If you receive a message, say, posing as PayPal and indicating that your account requires updating, *don't click on any embedded links*. Instead, open a new Web browser window, navigate directly to the Web site from there, and check your account status in that manner. In all spoof e-mails I have received, my direct navigation to my accounts has shown me that my data is current and in good standing.

Who's Helping You Avoid Phish?

Because the problem of phishing is growing and affecting more and more online consumers, not to mention tainting the otherwise upstanding brand names that are being held up as the front for this fraudulent activity, antiphishing software will be added to the tool set already available to help online users combat other such affronts, including spam, viruses, and hacking. Not only are the sites targeted Web sites stepping forward with user tools designed to thwart phishing, security companies are also working to build sophisticated tools for banks and online merchant sites as well.

eBay has taken the first step in assisting its user base get a grip on phishing by offering a comprehensive Spoof Email tutorial (see Figure 11-5) that will give you the soup-to-nuts rundown on how to spot spoof e-mail messages and what to do if you receive one related to your activity on eBay. Education, as I mentioned, is the first step in fraud prevention.

But eBay has gone a step further in protecting its users by introducing the *Account Guard,* a verification device that has been incorporated into the eBay toolbar. As you're likely aware, the eBay toolbar is downloadable free

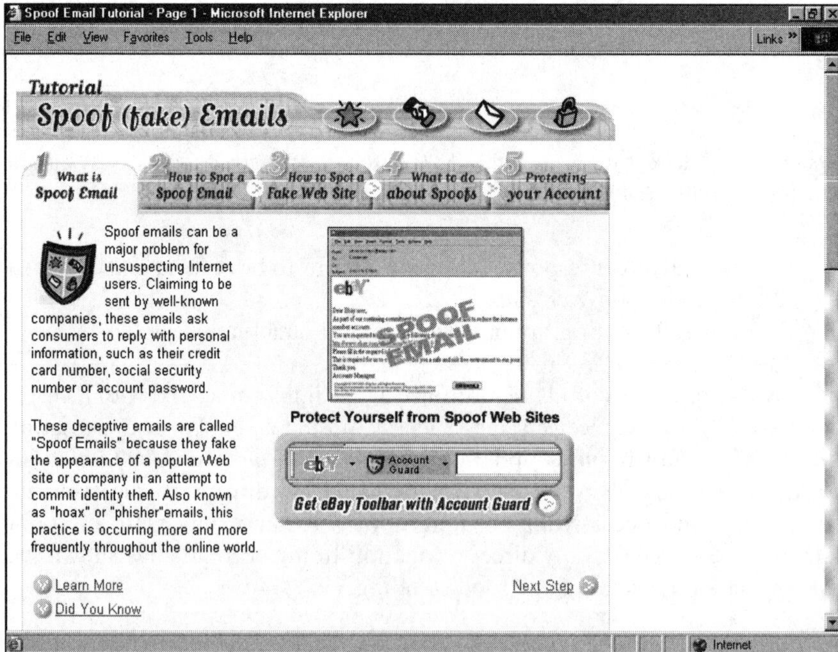

Figure 11-5 If you're new to spoof e-mails and would like to understand more about them in regard to your eBay activity, visit eBay's tutorial page.

from eBay and adds an eBay-specific bar of functions that will be incorporated into your Web browser software. The toolbar was created to allow eBay users constant access to eBay, even when not at the site, to search for items, watch items, and be alerted to bid on items about to close. While before the toolbar was mainly a function of convenience, now with the Account Guard feature added (see Figure 11-6), it alerts users if a site they've navigated is a spoof version of eBay or PayPal. The Account Guard area of the eBay toolbar will indicate "green," "gray," or "red" as it monitors the eBay site you're visiting. While on a valid eBay site (including Half.com or PayPal.com) the Account Guard will display green. If you're on a non-eBay site, legitimate as it may be, the Account Guard will display gray. (Account Guard only monitors eBay-related sites.) If, however, you accidentally follow a link that lands you on a spoof eBay, Half.com, or PayPal site, the Account Guard will display red and warn you that the site you're visiting is bogus. To learn more about eBay's Account Guard, visit the eBay Account Guard tutorial on eBay.

Beyond eBay, look for other major sites and companies, including Yahoo! Earthlink, and Microsoft to implement toolbars and other such mechanisms to help online users and businesses ensure that the sites they visit are valid.

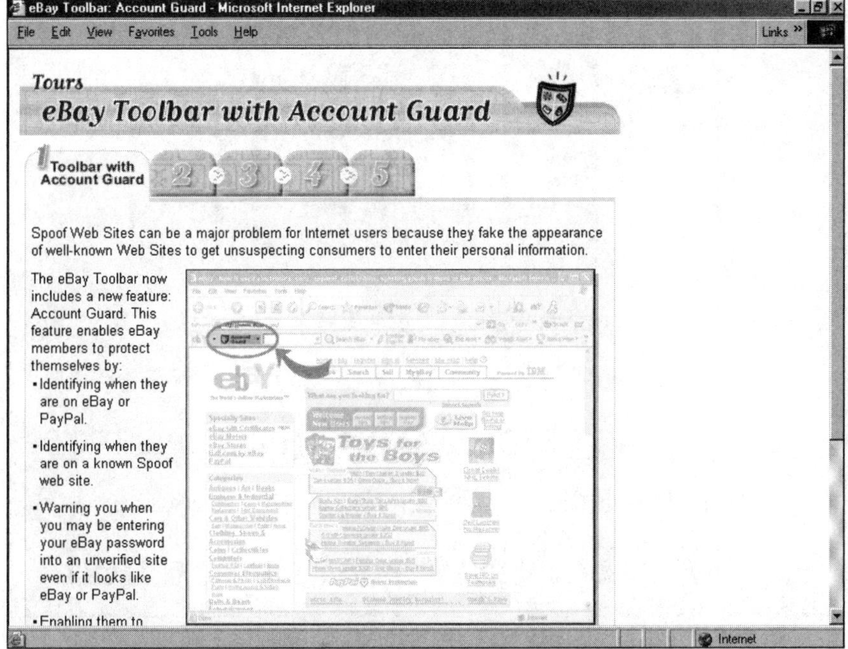

Figure 11-6 Use eBay's Account Guard feature on the eBay toolbar for safe surfing.

A NEW PLACE FOR AN OLD FRAUD

Of course, phishing isn't the only fraud that has emerged from the online auction realm to scam the unwary. The old-fashioned pyramid scheme, also known as multilevel marketing plans, has arrived on eBay in full force with a modern-day look and hook.

Pyramid, multilevel, or "network" marketing plans are a way of selling goods or services through distributors. The hook to these plans is some sort of promise that if you sign up as a distributor, you'll receive commissions, either in the form of cash or goods. The catch is that, in order to receive such compensation, you'll need to recruit more people into the plan. Some of these plans ask for your cash investment (anywhere from $5 to $5,000) or pressure you to purchase marketing literature, e-books, or other such "success materials" upon joining. Some multilevel plans are legitimate and legal, but most are not; specifically, those that pay commissions only on the number of additional distributors recruited and not on the basis of any sort of actual product sales. These schemes usually only benefit the few who got in early and who now sit back and wait for *their* recruits to recruit more individuals

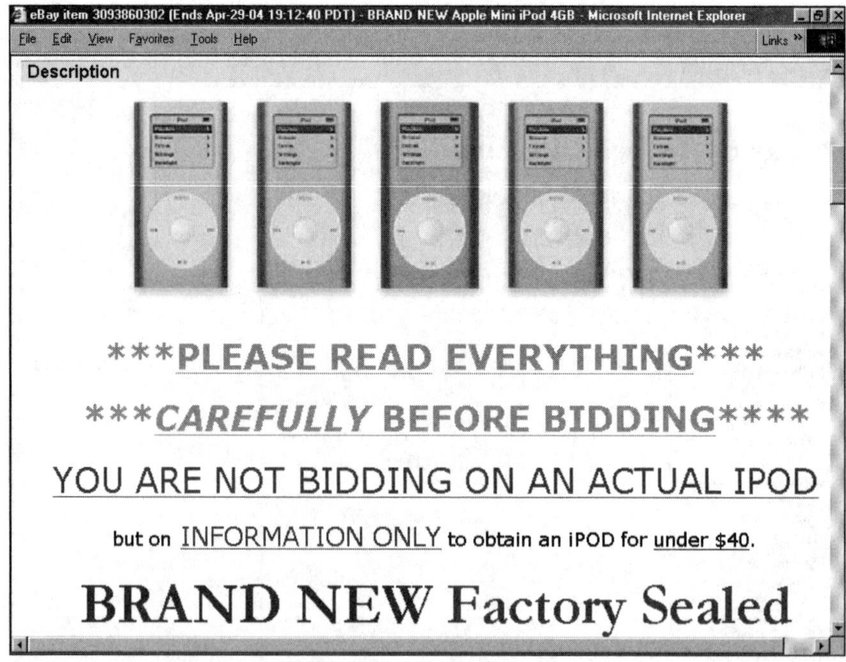

Figure 11-7 Here's an example of a pyramid scheme hiding behind an iPod auction.

down the line. Ultimately, the scheme cannot attract more inductees and it eventually collapses, usually leaving those lower recruits with no compensation for their investment.

So what does this have to do with fraud on eBay? Recently, numerous listings for the popular Apple Computer iPod (the music-playing device) have been used as a front for a new take on the old pyramid sham (see Figure 11-7). Hundreds of these listings appear to be offerings for the digital music players but are actually inducements to join pyramid-style scams. Potential bidders are encouraged not to bid but to rustle up recruits to get into the "buying club," the reward being iPods or accessories or laptops or whatever. eBay has been actively scouring its listings for these illegal come-ons and is shutting them down upon detection. Given the fact that pyramid schemes rely on person-to-person networking to succeed, eBay is a fertile recruiting ground for such a scam.

A PATSY FOR EMPLOYMENT

Back in the 1930s, crime bosses were always on the lookout for a "patsy." Not wanting to risk getting caught in illegal actions like money laundering, moonshining, or any other kind of illicit exchanges, criminals made it common practice to enlist the services of another individual: a dupe or a fall guy. Decades later, patsies are still being farmed by criminals, those who have now turned to eBay to turn an unlawful profit.

In recent news, a person in Holland was "sent up the river" after admitting to selling fake Rolex watches on eBay. Promised he could get rich quick, the malleable Dutchman bought into the scheme of peddling the phony timepieces on eBay—and he got caught. Duped into setting up an eBay account with his own name, address, and bank account, the patsy complied and proceeded to mislead buyers that they were bidding on and purchasing authentic Rolex watches. While it's nothing new to hear of knockoffs being peddled on eBay, criminals are now enlisting the services of the unenlightened to carry out the crime.

Beyond the stories of the usual fall guy being hooked into peddling stolen or counterfeit goods, there have been other reports coming from Eastern Europe about some criminals now using job-listing sites to attract unsuspecting victims into eBay scams. The popular auction help site, AuctionBytes, reported a story from a reader stating that he had shown interest in a job opening for an employer seeking sales representatives, as posted on CareerBuilder.com. As it turned out, the "employer" was a Taiwan-based operation seeking individuals to sell plasma TVs on eBay. As the reader told AuctionBytes, "I was told that [company name] was new to the U.S. market and in the process of opening U.S. bank and PayPal accounts. Until then, all payments

for items were to be wired to an account in Latvia." Purportedly, the individual hired for the position would receive $2,150 per month provided at least one TV was successfully sold. The company assured would-be representatives that it would ship the TVs direct to the buyer. What's wrong with this plasma picture?

HOW eBAY FRAUD AFFECTS YOUR BUSINESS

Certainly, if you're tempted to step over to the dark side and actively participate in fraud, you're already in bad business. However, knowing that you're an honest, hard-working, ethical businessperson, does the fraud going on at eBay and elsewhere online affect your upstanding efforts? Absolutely. The fact is, the fraud factor is what has kept millions of would-be shoppers away from eBay and other consumer sites on the Web. For those who have hesitated to venture into cyberspace to shop, they're usually timid about making purchases, engaging in e-conversations with merchants, and reticent to offer up any reasonable transaction information (credit card info for PayPal purchases, for example). In that way, fraud *does* affect your ability to conduct business online.

eBay, the FTC, the NCL, and federal and local law enforcement agencies are actively battling online crime and auction fraud; their efforts will help provide a reasonable level of safety and security for Internet bidders and buyers. Is there anything you and your business can do to help the effort while helping your business grow too? As an eBay business owner, your first step is to keep current the various online frauds and the latest trends in Internet racketeering. Not only will this provide you protection as you buy and sell online, it also puts you in a position to *assist* your customers in their efforts to avoid being scammed. These days, bidders and buyers are looking for the safe havens where they can shop without fear of being defrauded. By understanding the means and methods of online fraud (especially on eBay) you can take steps in your business to avoid having any of your activities misconstrued as anything less than honorable. For example, knowing how phishing is conducted, you'll be sure never to include active links in any e-mail correspondence you use, especially those messages that seek to inform customers of a commercial Web site you might be hosting. When you offer items for bid on eBay, you might be wise to make use of a tool like eBay's Shipping Calculator to allow bidders and buyers to see up front what the additional costs will be, then use those exacts costs at the close of the deal; this helps your customers see that you're not in the practice of improperly hiking up such costs to sneak out a little extra profit. The more you know about eBay scams, the more antifraud practices you can build into your own business processes, letting customers know you're here to earn an honest day's pay.

eBay TIP: Don't overlook the fact that some customers might engage you in some conversation about frauds, hoping to learn more about mischievous online deeds and how to avoid them. If you're an expert in the bad deals that sometimes go down, you can also emerge as a fount of information to potentially wary shoppers, providing a high-value intangible service that builds confidence in those who bid on your items and shop with you.

12

Simplifying Shipping

When it comes to your online auction business, great products are only part of the solution for success. Once you've made the sale, it comes time to ship the goods. For many casual auction-sellers, this has been the step of drudgery, a time-consuming, sometimes clumsy effort to get that great item securely packaged and safely delivered to the waiting customer. Of special concern are those larger items (such as pianos, perhaps, or pinball machines, maybe) that simply defy being dropped in a tidy box and sent on their way. As you further define your niche in the eBay marketplace, you'll need to consider shipping concerns *before* you invest in inventory or begin advertising the goods you want to sell but maybe aren't yet clear about how you'll deliver them. Packing and shipping don't have to be a chore and a time-intensive, costly, or even prohibitive endeavor. Here's a look at some of the latest tools and techniques that will help your business soar when it comes time to ship your terrific goods, whether they're bigger than a bread box or not.

PACKAGING SUPPLIES AT YOUR FINGERTIPS

It all starts with having the right packing supplies for the job without having the cost of your supplies mercilessly chew into your ultimate profits. Before you embark on any selling venture, be sure you have the right supplies, in the right amount, and at the right time so you can ship goods as soon as the sales start rolling in. Here's a review of some of the supply depots that have been available for some time, plus a look a some newer packing supplies that might help you specialize in goods you might never have thought you could ship.

Free Supplies Just a Mouse-Click Away

If you've been shipping nominal-sized goods for even a short time, you might well know that the majority of appropriate packing supplies you need are free; if you weren't aware, this is the sort of news you want to hear as you build your business. The boom of eBay has brought along with it a boom in the shipping of packages. Recognizing how online trade has increased the need for services and supplies, major package carriers have responded by offering shipping boxes, envelopes, and even tape and labels free to customers. Whether you like to ship via the United States Postal Services (USPS), United Parcel Service (UPS), Federal Express (FedEx), or other carrier services, you'll be pleased to know that each provides sturdy packing goods to help you send goods to your customers.

To get free supplies, you can visit any carrier's office or drop-off station near you, but you'll save time and effort if you'll simply visit their online destinations. Beginning with the USPS, visit *www.usps.com* then, from the home page, navigate to All Products and Services and find the *Shipping Supplies* link. Once at the Postal Store page (see Figure 12-1), select the "Shipping Supplies" then "Business Use" buttons.

In the following screen, you can choose from an impressive selection of boxes, envelopes, tubes, tape, labels, and forms for almost every delivery method the USPS offers. Best of all, this stuff is free. Simply make your selections, add them to your shopping cart, and notice that there is no cost. The post office will even deliver them to your doorstep, all free of charge. The only catch, of course, is you use this packaging *only for the delivery method implied.* No problem, right?

eBay TIP: Many clever businesspeople have made it a practice to turn the free USPS supplies inside-out, resulting in a nondescript brown box, in order to utilize cheaper shipping methods (for example, media mail or First Class delivery). The USPS has gotten wise to this unwanted activity and now prints *inside* the boxes to clearly indicate a reversed package. In many cases, the USPS will not deliver such packages, so take care.

The USPS isn't the only place to get free packaging. If you prefer to ship via UPS, visit their site at *www.ups.com* to get free supplies there, too. Unfortunately, FedEx and DHL don't offer online supply ordering at this time.

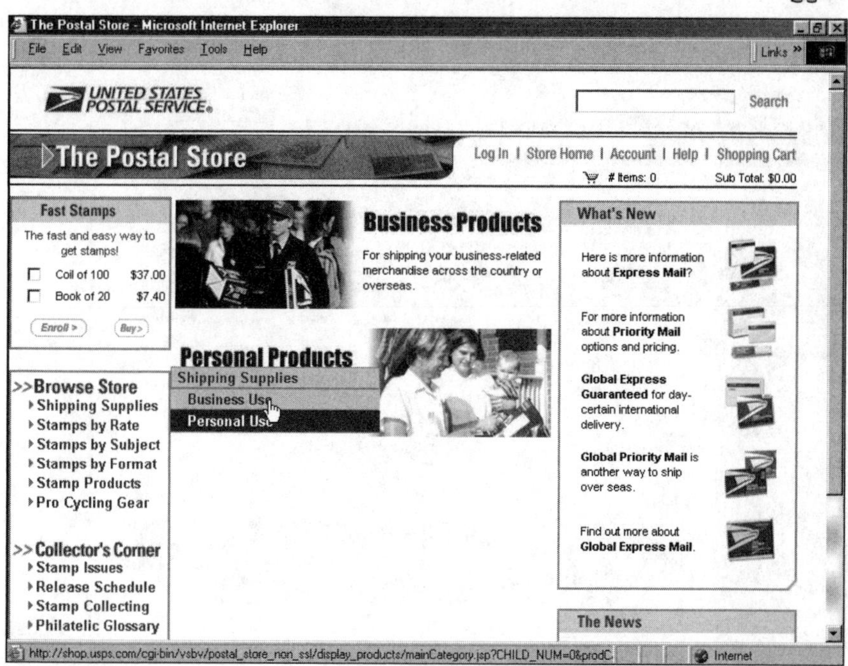

Figure 12-1 Visit the Postal Store at *www.usps.com* to get free supplies to pack and ship your goods.

Cushioning the Journey

With free boxes at the ready, your packing problems are largely solved. Now you'll need to consider what is perhaps the second most important aspect of safe and secure delivery, the interior of your sturdy shipping carton. Naturally, packing peanuts (those fun little foam curls) are perfect but they will cost you (the carriers don't offer these for free, unfortunately). However, if you receive many packages yourself, you'll likely find plenty of peanuts you can reuse; just store them in a large garbage bag or clean trash can for easy use. If you do purchase them, head to a wholesaler and buy them in the large, large bags (see Figure 12-2).

Bursting the Bubble

Although bubble wrap is great for wrapping delicate items, not to mention the therapeutic, stress-reducing qualities it offers to those who choose to sit and pop the air pockets, it's expensive to purchase. Usually costing around $25 to $35 for a large roll, it's probably not the material you'll want to use exclusively for interior cushioning. By all means, you should have it on hand,

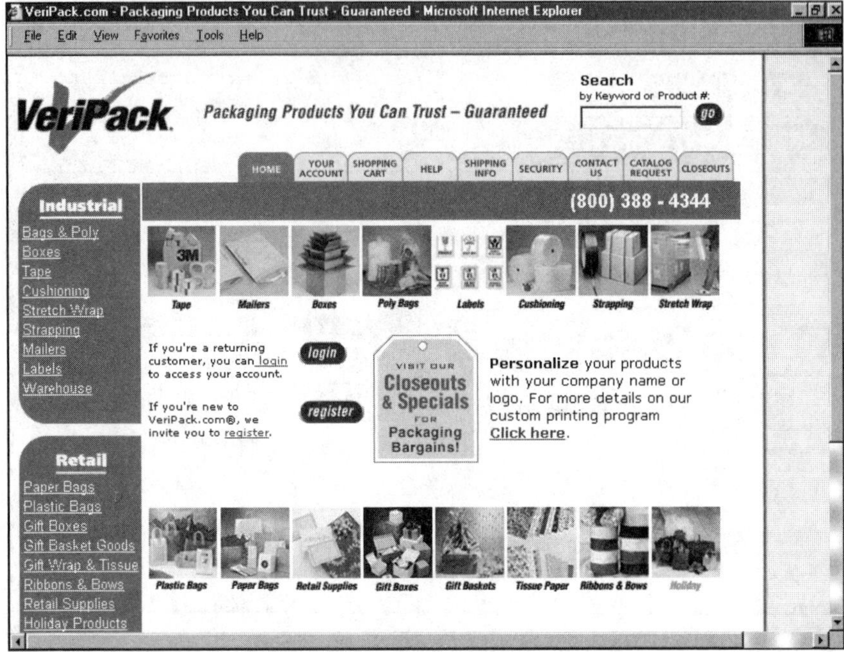

Figure 12-2 Looking for interior cushioning? Check out *www.veripack.com* for some great wholesale prices on the packing goods you need.

but use it only to wrap the item you're shipping, then position that within a box full of the equally cushioning but less expensive packing peanuts. Using the two materials together will make sure the item you ship is well protected without costing you your profits in the process.

Foam in Place

One of the most interesting innovations in interior packing material is called foam in place. You've likely seen it used in some items you've purchased (especially sculpture, pottery, or other delicate goods): a form-fitting, expandable foam wrapped in a thin sheet of plastic. Foam in Place machines utilize a two-part liquid foam compound that, when combined, will slowly expand to effectively fill the gaps around an item. Plastic is put in a box, the foam compound is squirted in, and as the foam begins to expand, a sheet of plastic is placed over the foam, and the item to be shipped is pressed into the expanding foam under the protective plastic. Another plastic sheet is placed over the item, more foam added, then one more plastic sheet before the box is closed. The result is practically a mold of the item made inside the box and one that effectively protects the item like a glove protects your hand.

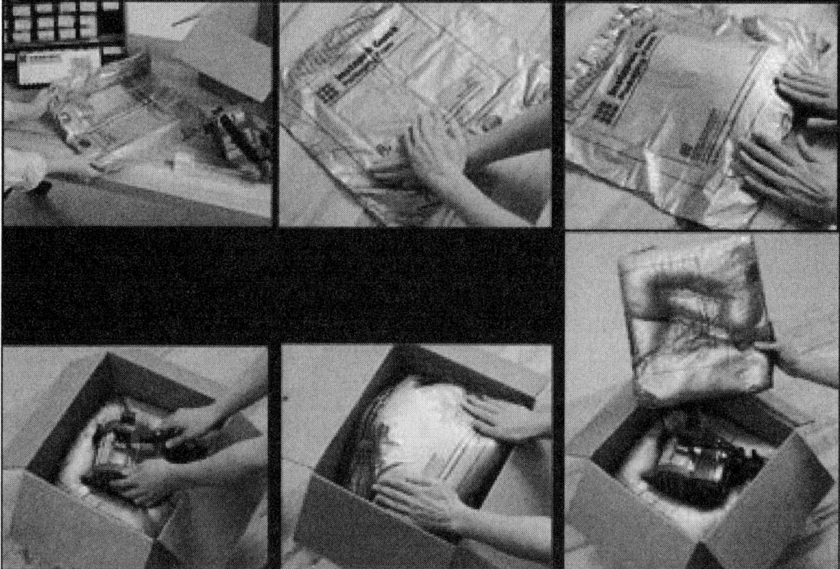

Figure 12-3 How easy is Foam in Place? This series of images shows how the InstaPak product makes formfitting packaging a snap.

Though this is a more expensive proposition to invest in up front (the machinery described will cost about $3,000, but be sure to search eBay for even better deals from time to time), there is a lower-cost startup alternative that provides the same formfitting protection: Foam in Place InstaPaks (also known as Foam in Bag) provide the same contoured protection in the convenience of easy-to-use sealed bags. By simply activating the compounds sealed within a protective bag, you can initiate the foam expansion inside a box, insert the item to ship, then add another activated foam bag on top to create the same high-quality, high protection cushioning without the expensive machinery (see Figure 12-3). InstaPaks cost about $2 a bag (available in different sizes and sold by the case), and a room's worth of expanded packing cushion comes neatly stored in a single carton, ready for use when you need it. That's what I call *unleashing the power of packing*.

Supplies to Avoid

It bears mentioning that not all packing supplies are good for your business. While you should always look to reduce costs wherever possible, sometimes cutting corners can cut the appearance of your products and your business. When it comes to packing supplies, here are some of the things you'll want to avoid before customers begin avoiding you:

- *Worn-Out Boxes.* Recycling is great, but boxes do have something of a life expectancy. Typically, a box or carton can be used two or three times safely before its structural and protective qualities start to break down. Besides, what customer wants to receive an item in a banged up, overused carton? It doesn't look very professional, either.
- *Foam Sheets.* While lining a box with sheets of foam may be useful if properly applied, most often these act more like a stiff piece of pressboard, not providing the sort of flexible cushioning that packing peanuts offers. One smack on a box tightly packed with foam sheets and, *crash*, something inside just broke.
- *Newspaper.* Loosely twisted or shredded newspaper can be useful if it doesn't come in direct contact with an item, but too much can add weight to a package, driving up the shipping cost unnecessarily. Don't forget, too, that the newsprint ink rubs off easily and can be pretty messy for your customer. Again, it doesn't look as professional as peanuts or bubble wrap.

Remember, recycling and reusing are good for the environment and good for your business. However, these tenets can be taken too far, so be sure not to *overuse* your packing supplies.

HEAVY-DUTY SHIPPING

This discussion has been all well and good for the shipment of nominally sized items, but what about those who want to sell and ship larger items such as antique furniture, vending machines, or perhaps a pool table? Just because these items are large is no reason to immediately dismiss the business opportunity at hand when selling on eBay. On the contrary, eBay is a target venue for buyers looking to purchase *any* items, no matter how big or how small. When it comes to selling big items, you'll just need to find a shipper that can manage the task. The good news: there are plenty of services to help you satisfy your big-item customers.

Finding a Crew for the Task

Right away, the USPS is out when it comes to large items, because they won't handle anything that exceeds a weight of 70 pounds. Scratch UPS and FedEx, as well, because they won't touch anything that weighs more than 150 pounds or is larger than a combined length and girth of 130 inches. Don't give up, though; just give a call to the large-item experts.

If you want to sell items like furniture or perhaps vintage arcade games

(a *very* hot commodity these days), look to carriers that solve your problem through a variety of services. If cost is of utmost concern, look to Forward Air (*www.forwardair.com*); they have the best prices on large-item transit, but they will require you to crate items yourself. Forward Air provides freight-forwarding services, arranging to deliver or receive large items transported via sea or air. Located near 80 major airports nationwide, the company will receive deferred air-freight shipments and will transport those to its nearest company terminal. Although Forward Air doesn't offer local pickup or delivery services (sellers and buyers need to arrange to travel to the company terminals for drop off or pick up), it conversely doesn't impose any size or weight restrictions on the items it will manage. If you don't mind rolling up your sleeves a bit, Forward Air might be the most cost-effective solution to the large-item problem. Of course, comparison shopping is a must when assessing the costs and services of large-item shippers, so also take a look at the following:

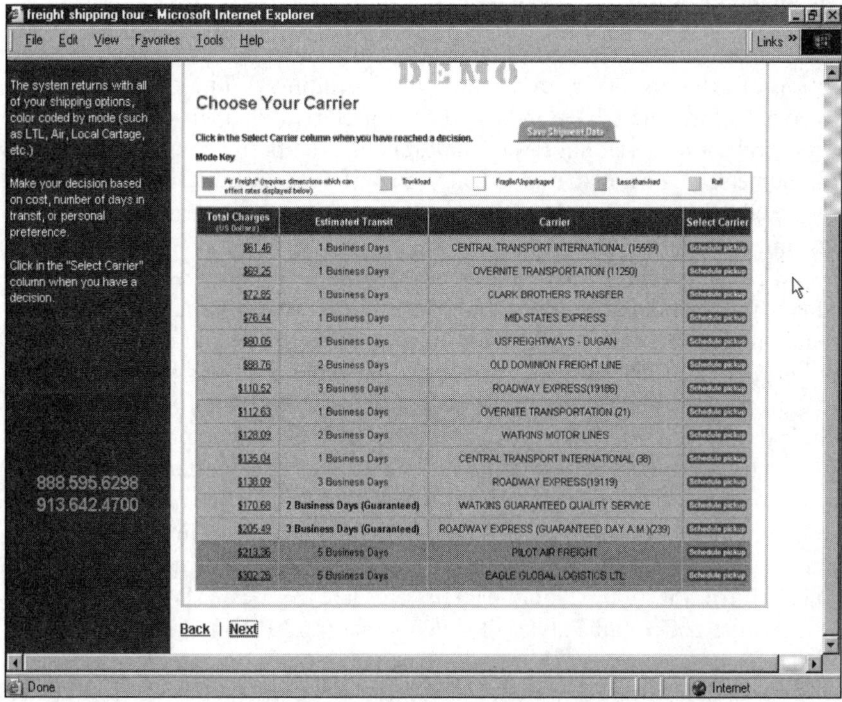

Figure 12-4 For easy cost comparison and simplified pickup scheduling, check out Freight Quote online.

- *YellowFreight* (*www.myyellow.com*). You crate it, but they'll pick it up when you schedule a pickup. Shipping rates are always available via their RateQuote system online.
- *Freightquote.com* (*www.freightquote.com*). Sort of an online broker of freight carriers, this site allows you to declare freight specifications then view a comparative table of freighters who can manage the task for you (see Figure 12-4). The information you enter online will be used to complete a printable bill of lading for your item; FreightQuote, in the process, has already contacted the selected carrier to pick up your item.
- *Craters and Freighters* (*www.cratersandfreighters.com*). This company has seen the potential of servicing the online auction market by offering a tool that allows sellers of large items to establish a shipping quote calculator for bidders to use prior to placing bids. These folks also offer crating and door-to-door delivery services. They're a bit more expensive, but they have more features, too.

Considering Crating

When it comes to large items like video games or restaurant machinery, the notion of packing takes on a whole new meaning. While crating isn't for eveyone, some sellers have indicated they prefer to do their own crating or hire a crating professional rather than rely on a shipping company to do the job. Some sellers want the added assurance that the job of crating has been done well before the item heads across the country or overseas to the waiting customer.

Crating can be done by the noncarpenter, and there are plenty of local lumber yards that can help you with the process (once you have it down, you merely repeat the process while you increase your speed and efficiency at it). Online, there are also plenty of help sites that explain step-by-step the process of crating large items. The nice thing about crating is that you can do the whole thing from scratch or you can prepurchase fabricated portions (such as the palette upon which an item might be bolted). One of the most thorough online tutorials I found comes from Appolo's Arcade (*www.appolo.com*), an online company that deals in buying, restoring, and selling arcade video games. With plenty of materials lists and step-by-step instructions, you can quickly learn how to box or crate large items like a Ms. PacMan upright game or a Popeye coffee-table-style, sit-down game (and the methods can be employed for use in crating other similarly sized items).

Of course, if you'd rather not get into crate construction yourself, there are plenty of professional crating services that will do the job for you, giving you a securely boxed large item ready for the carrier. Begin with your local

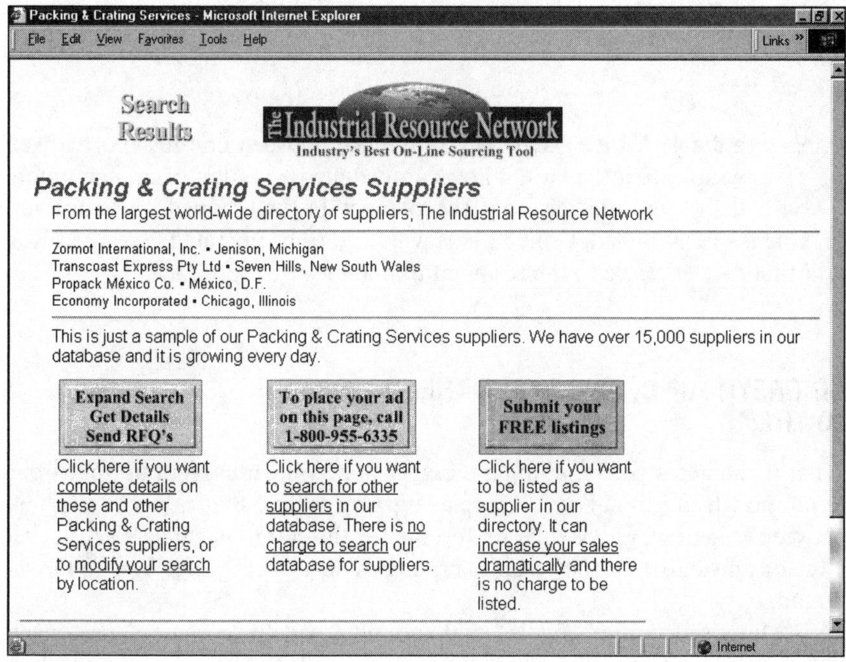

Figure 12-5 If you need to find a crating service, consider using the Industrial Resource Network online.

telephone directory to locate a crating service near you or visit the Industrial Resource Network online at *www.powersourcing.com* (see Figure 12.5) for a convenient directory of crating services available near you.

Using the Blanket Approach

If crating sounds overwhelming or seems like overkill for shipping the items you'll sell, the lower-cost alternative is called blanket wrap. If ever you've hired or rented a moving van when you've relocated, you likely saw those comfy, quilted blankets used to protect items stacked next to or on top of one another; that's blanket wrap. When it comes to shipping merchandise, most carriers who offer blanket wrap also utilize specialized trucks and trailers designed for the securing of blanket-wrapped items. Items are wrapped and then strapped to van walls to prevent shifting. In addition, some carriers install interior decking that surrounds the blanketed item and acts like a temporary crate but without the cost and construction of an actual crate. If you'll be shipping many large items in a single pickup (and for the sake of your business, I hope you will) this method is also

preferable because of its superior ability utilize the interior area of a truck or trailer.

eBay TIP: One key difference between crating and blanket wrap is that the latter allows immediate inspection of an item upon delivery, requiring only the blanket be unwrapped once interior decking is disassembled. Crated items will need to be uncrated first, usually a task that carriers leave to the recipient to manage.

GO GREYHOUND, AND LEAVE THE SHIPPING TO THEM

What if the items you're selling are bigger than a breadbasket but not as big as an industrial ice-maker? Is there a shipping service that caters to the "in-between" big item, goods that are too big for the common carriers yet not so large or unwieldy that they require crating or special carrying? Yes, go Greyhound.

Many sellers don't realize that the most widely recognized passenger bus service is also in the courier business as well. It's true. Greyhound bus lines offers their own Greyhound Package Express (GPX) service designed especially for shipping items that weigh less than 100 pounds but are too bulky to be shipped via the USPS, UPS, or FedEx. If you're dealing in reclaimed auto parts like car bumpers, seats, or side panels, Greyhound might be your best shipping alternative. Greyhound provides an online rate calculator on their Web site, *www.shipgreyhound.com*, where you can determine if your not-that-large-of-an-item product is a candidate for GPX transit and what the cost might be. Understand that the GPX service is terminal-to-terminal, not door-to-door, so be clear with your buyer that they'll need to travel to their local terminal to retrieve the item. Next, be sure the item you're shipping is sturdy enough or packed sturdily enough to make the trip safely, understanding that it won't be receiving the same "gentle care" as a true freight company might offer. For this reason, you might also consider using insurance. And, there's also a Priority GPX service available if it makes sense to get the item delivered quickly and without having the package transferred from bus to bus using the standard delivery method.

The Costs of Big-Item Business

While specializing or dabbling frequently in the selling of large items poses some shipping challenges different from the shipment of smaller goods, it's

still a decent pursuit if you can understand the methods available to you and the costs those will incur (which you'll likely pass along to your customers). These shipping costs can vary depending on the size and weight of the item, the distance the item will travel to the ultimate delivery point, the method of item packing (crating, blanket wrap, or boxing) and whether the item will be carried from door-to-door or merely terminal to terminal. Carefully review the different services each carrier and package preparer offers, the costs of those services, the needs of your items for a safe journey, and, ultimately, how this will affect your customer's final price and satisfaction. In the end, that's what it's all about.

RESTATING YOUR SHIPPING POLICIES

No matter if you ship large or small items, your key to success when establishing your shipping methods and costs is the clear and concise communication of shipping details to your bidders and buyers. Many buyers are somewhat wary about shipping costs, knowing that their winning bid or fixed-price purchase amount will ultimately have the additional transport charge tacked on; successful sellers communicate either the exact costs or provide a user-friendly shipping calculator so customers can assess that additional charge *before* they bid or buy.

If ever you've had a bidder or buyer ask the always precarious question, "How did you come up with that cost for shipping and handling?" that's your indicator that your shipping policy needs to be clarified and brought front and center right away.

As you approach creating or revising your shipping policy, understand that many buyers who do not also actively sell online are likely unaware of the nuances of shipping. If you target this type of buyer as your audience, you'll find you can develop a much more deliberate and comprehensive shipping policy. Most importantly, you need to be sure your customers actually *read* your policy. Policies in small print or that are difficult to locate (maybe tucked away on a Web page you link from within your auctions or fixed-price listings) usually lead to questions or misunderstandings in the minds of your customers.

eBay TIP: I don't like to rely solely on the shipping-policy selections eBay offers, those that you merely check during an item listing. EBay communicates the details of those selections in smaller print and tucked somewhat deeper into the listing (especially considering the Bid Now or Buy It Now buttons are prominently positioned *before* the item description). Because of this, make it a point to draw out the details clearly in

your item descriptions, either in a bold or different colored text or, if you're using HTML, in an otherwise highlighted area that ensures the details will be seen, read, and understood.

As I said before, try to offer buyers the ability to calculate shipping costs themselves, thus giving them more control and greater understanding of the additional costs to be charged. Use eBay's Shipping Calculator in all of your listings, use a third-party calculator (as shown earlier in this chapter to calculate large item freight costs), or clearly specify a flat-rate charge if that's what you choose to do. With the exception of international shipments, you can avoid questions, conflicts, or endless negotiation with your buyers if you state your shipping costs *up front*. International shipments will typically require after-the-sale shipping calculation because costs will vary based on shipping methods and final destination; be clear about this up front as well if you accept international sales (and why wouldn't you?) by indicating something to the effect of, "International shipping charges will be calculated after the auction has ended." So how about a shipping-policy checklist? Good idea. Be sure your policy includes the following:

- Where will you ship goods: domestic only or international as well?
- What shipping methods, services, or specific carriers do you use to ship?
- When will you ship (upon payment received or just at certain times each week)?
- Will you offer any shipping discounts (such as combining multiple items into a single shipment)?
- Do you offer special services such as insurance, tracking, and delivery confirmation, and at what additional costs, if any?

Recall that an ambiguous shipping-cost policy is one of those scams that unscrupulous sellers try to inflict on unsuspecting buyers, hoping to eke out a few extra dollars. Avoid misunderstanding or mischaracterization of your intent by clearly stating your policy and clearly posting it so it can be read and understood by all of your customers.

eBay TIP: Although you may post a very clear and straightforward shipping policy, remain open to buyer questions. Be especially attentive to repeated concerns raised or suggestions made, coming from different customers, which could indicate to you that either your policy is not clear enough or your items may sell better if you adjust your policy to suit your customers. You don't want to get into the mode of bending over every which way to satisfy the specific needs or whimsical wants of *every*

buyer, but if you hear the same feedback on several occasions or more, that might be a clear signal that your policy could stand some revising.

One last point: be sure to check eBay's own stated policy regarding the seller's responsibilities and restrictions in stating shipping charges. Visit *pages.ebay.com/help/policies/listing-shipping.html* to be sure your policy doesn't collide with eBay's.

13

Developing Your Marketing Strategy

At this point, you have most of the pieces in place to start or grow your business on eBay and elsewhere online. However, if you just plop your products out there for bid or sale without much fanfare or strategy, you could unwittingly rob yourself of establishing a firm business persona and etching your business's name into the minds of customers. What you need now is, you guessed it, a marketing plan. Different from the business plan, which helped you establish the groundwork for developing and launching your enterprise, the marketing plan is the next phase, where you'll develop various means and methods to essentially "get the word out" that your business is open and that you're offering tantalizing goods or services for bid or sale. Therefore, it's back to the think tank again to develop a strategy that ensures all your hard work up to this point pays off in the most lucrative way possible.

THE KEY INGREDIENTS OF A MARKETING PLAN

Creating a marketing plan is actually quite exciting and enlightening; it drives you another step further toward becoming a successful business and a savvy businessperson. Since your ultimate goal is to sell products and grow your business, this portion of your business assessment can be the most revealing step in helping you reach your goal. So let's begin at a somewhat high level to see what sorts of information make up a good business plan.

In a nutshell, your marketing plan should include:

- Data gathered from your market research; that is, much of what you did during the business plan phase
- Your business's location (online and off)
- The target market you'll serve; that is, the kinds of customers you expect will be interested in buying what you offer

- Your competition in the market
- Your method of presenting or "positioning" your products
- Your pricing plan
- Your advertising approach and promotion plan

I'll look at each of these elements in more detail throughout this chapter, but first let's revisit the definition of your "market."

IDENTIFYING AND UNDERSTANDING YOUR TARGET MARKET

Oftentimes, entrepreneurs who strive to set up shop on eBay confidently proclaim, "eBay is my market." Bzzt! Wrong! The first thing to understand is that *market* actually refers to people, not a place. That is, your market is the group of consumers to whom you'll sell your goods. Some first-time small-business owners tend to focus solely on the products they'll sell and the profit they intend to make without giving enough thought and consideration to *who* will be buying the products, why they'll want to buy them from you, and how much they'll be willing to pay to help you earn your profit. Therefore, your target market is actually the concentration or grouping of consumers who, by your careful market research, will step forward to purchase products from you because you identified what they want to buy and have presented it in the *way* they want to buy it.

eBay TIP: Immediately, think of those eBay buyers who perhaps don't want to engage in a bidding battle to get the item they seek. Good sellers have researched their market well enough to understand whether buyers are inclined to endure the run of an auction or would prefer to purchase quickly in a fixed-price scenario, which eliminates the fear of being outbid. When you set up shop on eBay, this will be one of the first things to find out about the mood of your target market.

So if *market* refers to people, your goal in defining your target market is to identify the characteristics (that is, the buying tendencies) of the people that allows them to be grouped, if you will, into the target area of your marketing plan. To do this, you'll need to gather statistics on that market of buyers to help you develop a strategy or plan to appeal to their consumer tastes. Immediately, you can visit eBay and, in watching how items similar to those you'll offer are selling, look at the behaviors of the different bidders and buyers who showed interest in the items. From there you can search eBay for what other items those folks have bid on and possibly won, how much they bid or spent to get the item, and possibly what differences there might be be-

tween offerings that were bid on or bought versus similar or identical items that may have been offered simultaneously but not bid on (remember the value of searching by bidder on eBay to learn more about the buying tendencies of the individuals within your target market).

eBay TIP: As you research your market's buying habits, you can simultaneously research the manner in which your competition is presenting items and what differences exist that may have made one item listing more appealing than another. I said it before and I'll say it again: study your competition and emulate their best methods and techniques.

Now, as you study the trends and tendencies of buyers—on eBay's site but also through reading other market research papers and findings about the market you hope to serve—look carefully for commonalities that can be defined as segments; these are key market characteristics that will help you identify your market more easily. For example, perhaps young adults aged 18 to 25 are primarily interested in the products you might offer. Or, perhaps you'll find that professional women are interested in your items. Essentially, you need to clearly describe the consumers you'll be marketing to by identifying them in terms of age, sex, income level, marital status, hobbies, and so forth. Maybe you'll even discover that there is strong demand for what you'll offer with specific consumers overseas. These groupings will help you define your target market in segments identified by market demographics, drawing out physical, social, or geographic similarities; that's called a demographic segment (see Figure 13-1). You also want to draw out information that will point you toward the motivations that drive a target market to buy an item; that is, their psychographics. Here you'll study characteristics of the people who purchase items because it suits their lifestyle, will solve a problem of theirs, meet a specific need, or provide a unique form of satisfaction. When you can confidently make these identifications, you have yet more critical information to help you develop a plan that will serve the "identity" of that target market.

eBay TIP: One of the best books I've read regarding target markets and understanding what about both content and presentation motivates consumers to buy certain products over others is Paco Underhill's incredibly compelling *Why We Buy: The Science of Shopping* (2000, Simon & Schuster). If you're going to read just one book about target marketing, be sure Underhill's book is it. It's fascinating.

All this hubbub over identifying your target market is well founded, rest assured. You'll find it easier to price, distribute, promote, and position your

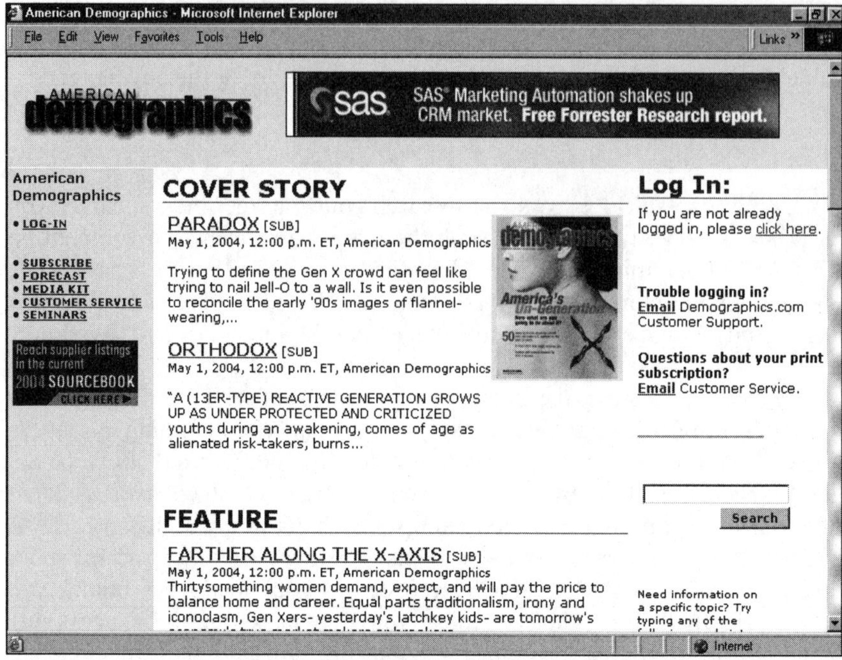

Figure 13-1 When identifying your target market, be sure to visit *www.demographics.com* (the Web companion to *American Demographics* magazine), where you'll find plenty of useful information about markets, trends, and consumer segments.

products (not to mention design or source *new* products) if you understand what your audience of buyers is looking for. In the long run, you'll also find you stand a better opportunity to sell more products and recognize when your target audience's tastes, needs, or desires are changing. No crystal balls are required, just a good understanding of who's buying what you're selling.

UNDERSTANDING THE ELEMENTS OF A MARKETING PLAN

Now that you're settled on the target market you'll serve, it's time to put together the body of your marketing plan. Much like the business plan you created, the marketing plan typically includes key elements of information that will help you define how you'll market your goods and how you'll know if you're doing so successfully.

eBay TIP: It was put to me, as I was about to begin a marketing plan, that I needed to be very clear with myself regarding what I truly wanted to accomplish with my business; ask yourself the very same question at the outset. Do you aspire to manage large volumes of sales? Are you looking to redefine the personality of your existing business (maybe bring it up to date with the eBay and Internet age)? Do you want to find new ways to bring customers to know your existing brick-and-mortar store? Do you want to close up your brick-and-mortar store and deal primarily on the Web? Or do you want to create an entirely new market that you believe is underserved? Ask yourself what your intent is and you'll find it easier to develop a marketing plan that will meet your needs.

The elements you should develop in your marketing plan include:

- *Executive Summary.* Although this will be the first element of your marketing plan, it should be the last you'll actually write. As its name indicates, this is a *summary*, sort of a thumbnail sketch, of your overall marketing plan. It will allude to some of the details that you'll be spelling out through the rest of the plan and, therefore, it's appropriate to write this *after* you've fleshed out those details. The purpose of this element is to provide a quick overview of your plan, either for your own review or, more importantly, for those who may be working with you or for you or possibly for those from whom you may be seeking financial investment.
- *Current Situation.* Before you describe where you're going, you first need to be clear about where you currently are, businesswise. This element of the plan covers details of your business status now, whether you're already in business and eager to expand or you're new on the block and ready to open shop. Here you'll want to draw out specifics regarding your business's current or proposed location (be it online or off, eBay only or with companion Web sites). Is your business easy to recognize and interpret or is it somewhat unique and eclectic and therefore requiring some effort in order to define its personality and appeal to your target market? What is your business's philosophy: how does it intend to serve customers in a way that other similar businesses don't, either in terms of products or services or both? What do you perceive as your business's strengths and what have you identified as its weaknesses?
- *Competition.* Since you seek to attract customers to *your* business and potentially away from others, define competitors who offer the same or similar products, either within eBay, at other Web sites, or

even in the brick-and-mortar world. What are those products they provide? What do you perceive as your competitors' strengths and weaknesses? Can you determine your competitors' strategies to gain market share (that is, more customers than *their* competitors)?

- *Marketing Objectives.* Here's where the rubber hits the road. Your marketing objectives should be very clear, concise, and measurable. That last point is crucial: each objective you state should have a calculable result associated with it such that you can determine by level of sales whether the objective is being met (there are no guesses here). If you determine you want to sell on eBay in order to net, say, $5,000 in sales per month, calculate your results to see if your goal can be met. If you're extending your existing brick-and-mortar business into eBay to increase your sales by 15 percent, be sure your eBay results fulfill that objective. In addition, your objectives should be governed by established time frames; that is, a measurable period by which the objective should be met (for instance, that you want to increase your profits by 15 percent within six months).
- *Marketing Strategies.* To meet your marketing objectives, you need strategies from which to work. In this element of your plan, you again refer to the products you'll offer and how they'll be seen as preferable to those of competitors. Whether your product will be superior in quality, usability, price-friendliness, or ease of acquisition (either via streamlined distribution methods [think eBay] or fast and easy to find), detail all of this in your strategies to seize the marketplace and meet your stated objectives.
- *Action Plan.* The plan's almost done, and you have some great market analysis, objectives, and strategies in the bag. Now you need a definitive action plan by which you'll take actual steps to implement your strategy. Whether you'll be launching a series of eBay listings, opening an eBay Store, introducing an exciting new Web site, or visiting trade shows to show off your business and products, this is where you construct your "to do" list to get the plan off paper and in front of the eyes of your customers, again, with measurable results (tasks completed) and established milestones (dates upon which each task is to be completed).
- *Budget.* Sure, it would be great to have a blimp circle the next Super Bowl with your business's logo vibrantly emblazoned across it, but that might cost a bit too much (for the moment, anyway). At this stage, you'll need to lay out the costs to launch your marketing plan, including cost of eBay listings, costs to host a Web site, promotional giveaways, advertising space, and any other costs associated with the elements of your marketing plan. There's no hard and fast rule that

I've found about *what* this cost should or shouldn't be, so begin by allocating anywhere from 5 to 10 percent of your business's expected gross revenue, and use that for an initial marketing budget.

Sure, it's a bit of work and it's not always immediately profit bearing, spending so much effort *planning* when you'd rather be *selling*. Agreed, but you'll stand a better chance of selling more if you commit to planning more before you lift a finger or spend a dime on your business.

eBay TIP: Although the considerations I've covered are not all the detail you'll want to know or read regarding the finer details of creating a stellar marketing plan, hopefully I've demonstrated the need and reason for constructing a plan and you're ready to begin yours. If you want more information about marketing plans (and you probably do), visit the United States Small Business Administration's (SBA) Web site at *www.sba.gov* for a tremendous amount of additional information, as well as some sample plans you can learn from.

Figure 13-2 Visit *www.sba.com* for more about marketing plans and details for successfully launching and growing your business.

GETTING THE WORD OUT THROUGH GREAT ADVERTISING

Finally, it comes down to promoting your business, heralding the great products or services you have to offer, then smiling from ear to ear as hordes of eager customers come by to shop, shop, and shop some more. No, this isn't a fantasy notion, provided you advertise as carefully as you have planned.

Your job now is clear: you must communicate your message, showcase your offerings, and create an overall awareness of your business and its products in a way that motivates customers to buy your goods and tell their friends about the magnificence of your establishment. Again, advertising is driven by *strategies*, those clear and measurable methods that will enable you to understand if you're reaching the target audience you previously defined and are properly meeting and exceeding their expectations.

Whenever you engage in advertising efforts, you're attempting to reach this common goal: to attract customers and improve sales. To do this, you need to rely on your careful research and findings regarding your target market and use that information to reach those customers who are ready, willing, and able to purchase the goods you're selling. If you haven't defined your target market by this point, you'll waste time, effort, and money in a hit-and-miss promotional scheme that likely won't produce the results you want. But with your target market well defined and understood, your advertising approach can effectively include the following list of typical advertising objectives:

- Creating new customers
- Establishing customer demand for your products
- Increasing order size and rate of return-customer business
- Promoting replacement or upgrade of similar products already owned
- Establishing and improving your brand or business name in consumers' minds
- Generating customer inquiries for additional products that would be purchased
- Generating word-of-mouth referral from existing customers to generate new customers

Essentially, you want your advertising campaign—the collective methods you'll use to get the word out about your business—to create an undeniable buzz about your business, your products, and your services. Think long and hard about this step, because it can get costly if you're not careful, purchasing, for example, promotional goodies and ad space without that ever-important target market squarely in mind.

eBay TIP: Whenever I think I've devised the next great promotional idea I stop and ask myself, Would that encourage *me* to shop or buy? As business owner, you're also in position to pose as your most difficult customer to sway. Try to be as objective as possible here to see if you'd be convinced to stop, look, and buy. At the same time, take note of other businesses' promotions that you'll encounter and, when something catches your eye or motivates you to purchase, quickly ask yourself, Why? Those are the real-life examples you may want to emulate.

So when it comes to advertising your business, eBay provides a real two-for-one opportunity. First, the site is always buzzing with ready shoppers and can almost guarantee you'll make a sale to at least one of the 100 million sets of eyes scouring the site for great items. More importantly, though, many (like myself) have found eBay an effective and inexpensive place to "float a test balloon," if you will; that is, to see if you're really on target with your product and your approach. With its real-time market qualities, you'll quickly find out if your product has appeal, if your prices are compelling, and whether the competition is alive and well and challenging you for customer attention. In a few short weeks, you can revise your approach, refine your delivery, and even re-launch your strategy (if needed) at probably the lowest cost imaginable.

THE CORE PIECES OF AN ADVERTISING CAMPAIGN

By way of brief review, here's what your good advertising campaign should include. This campaign draws from your overall marketing plan and will ensure that your campaign touches on all the necessary points to boost your business:

- Remind customers and potential customers about the benefits of your product or service.
- Effectively identify you and your business as the source for superior products and services.
- Enhance your business's reputation (see point above).
- Motivate existing customers to buy more of what you sell.
- Attract new customers and replace any lost ones.
- Increase sales and thereby increase your operating profit.

Advertising campaigns are highly effective, the reason why big businesses spend billions of dollars each year on their own campaigns. And while

good advertising campaigns are crucial to foster business success and growth, recognize that there are some things an advertising campaign *can't* do for your business. Just to keep you grounded in reality and your expectations reasonable, you *shouldn't* expect an advertising campaign to:

- Establish an immediate base of customers
- Result in an overnight flood of sales
- Quickly resolve debt problems incurred previously by the business
- Mask the harmful effects of poor sales or customer service
- Generate demand for genuinely useless or undesirable products

No advertising campaigns are cure-alls for businesses, so keep these caveats in mind so your expectations remain on the realistic side.

SOME IMMEDIATE MARKETING AND ADVERTISING IDEAS TO EMPLOY

I've already mentioned how hosting eBay auctions or listing items for sale in an eBay Store can provide quick sales and telling information about your products and the way in which you are presenting them. Working from that, here are a few more things you should consider to try to jump-start your business and explore potential new opportunities.

Concurrent and Complementary eBay Auctions

It practically goes without saying (but I'll say it anyway) that you should always host simultaneous auctions or fixed-price listings when you list on eBay. Just as a shopper rarely ventures into a store that only has one product on display, you need to offer multiple items for bidders to peruse when you list goods on eBay. In this way, bidders and buyers will learn more about your product specialty—your niche—and your expertise will likewise be apparent when they see the items you are focused on marketing. To this end, it makes sense to offer a concurrent offering of complementary *goods*; that is, goods that go hand in hand with one another and that buyers, if they buy an item from one category, might also want or need one or more from one of the other categories to go with it. For example, if you'll be selling photographic equipment, you might be selling a terrific selection of cameras, ranging in features and price to satisfy shoppers' varying wants and needs, then you might also want to offer the complementary goods like flash equipment, tripods, and so forth. This is the same approach the giant retailers use when they present products for sale (think about the eye-catching window displays or endcaps that you see when you shop the brick-and-mortar world).

eBay TIP: By the way, using concurrent listings works fine for sellers who offer odds and ends in their business (remember JoesCrap?) in that it shows buyers you are a purveyor of eclectic goods and are likely harboring truly unique and interesting items at all times, listings that are surely not to be missed.

One last point here: you may also consider offering packages of complementary items, such as a listing that includes a camera, flash unit, tripod, and camera bag. In these cases, you may be able to offer a slightly lower price than if the items were purchased separately which, by the way, is another excellent approach to generating customer excitement.

E-mail Lists, Newsletters, and Questionnaires

Please don't accuse me of proliferating the undeniable problem of spam (that flood of unwanted e-mail that clogs our electronic in-trays to almost criminal proportions), but building and maintaining an e-mail customer list is proving to be one of the most effective ways to keep in touch with your customers (those who've shown interest in your products already, not an unwary population of recipients who would certainly feel harassed if bombarded by repetitive and unsolicited appeals). As you receive sales and other inquiries about your products, keep the contact information of these folks in a customer folder somewhere on your computer (typically in a spot within your e-mail application). E-mail promotion is probably the most cost-effective way to reach your customers and inform them of new products or services, and if done properly, it can surely help you build awareness of your business name or product brand.

eBay TIP: Aren't the e-mail messages you might send to your customers just fodder for immediate deletion? Actually, recent statistics have shown that the response rate to e-mail promotions is quite high, up to 35 percent of those contacted. That's a good number and can be great for developing your business.

Beyond merely informing customers of your products and services, sales or specials, e-mail marketing is one the easiest ways to gain that all-important demographic information about your target market. Consider including a very simple questionnaire with your e-mail messages, perhaps inquiring about what other products your customers might be interested in,

what suggestions they might have about your current products or services, and what details they might share (in general terms) regarding their age, income, gender, and special interests. This is the sort of data that will also help you track the changing wants, needs, and attitudes of your target market, all easily attainable from a simple and discreet e-mail message. Of course, be absolutely clear that your e-mail messages are not intended as spam and, therefore, ask recipients if they'd like to "opt in" to receive future correspondence; otherwise, leave them off your mailing list. When creating a promotional e-mail message or, better yet, when developing a company newsletter that keeps your customers regularly informed about your products and services, consider the following:

- *HTML may be preferable to plain text.* Recent studies I've reviewed have indicated the response rates for HTML-designed newsletters are generally far higher than plain text, allowing you to judiciously insert your company logo, colors, and product images in a way that will make the publications look far more professional and immediately appealing. Take note of the word *judiciously*; too many graphics will make your publication take too long to download and can actually discourage customers from doing business with you.
- *Offer an incentive to subscribe to your newsletters or mailing list.* Advertise that your newsletters will include more than just product information, communicating the additional benefits of subscribing. Including special coupons, useful information, and even early product-release information (especially in regard to limited goods) can be a real incentive for customers to respond Yes! when you ask if they'd like to subscribe to your communications.
- *Do more than just sell.* Many studies suggest that e-mail newsletters are read far more carefully when they offer information that is useful to your customers' lives rather than merely selling products and services. Helpful tips, engaging content, and even a bit of humor are often expected to accompany e-mail newsletters.

Remember, e-mail promotion can be truly effective both in terms of cost-conscious marketing and results-oriented objectives. Just as you steer your business and products to appeal to the tastes and needs of your target market, so too should you carefully tailor your e-mail marketing to keep your messages useful and desirable and to be sure they're never construed as spam.

Trade Shows Are *Still Fashionable*

Long before the days of eBay, it was trade shows that served as the platform for entrepreneurs to launch their businesses and make their wares more visi-

ble to a large gathering of customers. When the Internet, e-mail, and eBay came on the scene, many believed the days of the trade shows' effectiveness were numbered. Although the virtual world is a more preferable platform upon which to float test balloons and launch business ideas, trade shows still have a high level of appeal and remain quite effective in spreading the word to a target audience.

Remember that the original benefit of trade shows was their ability to let entrepreneurs meet and interact with a large number of potential customers in a brief but effective period of time. Better yet, the costs of attending and exhibiting at a trade show is relatively inexpensive.

Much like using eBay itself, trade shows work to level the playing field for smaller businesses, given that booth rental is generally quite affordable (still around $15 per square foot with a typical booth covering about 100 square feet) and that low-cost but highly attractive displays can be created without depleting the marketing and advertising budget. Actually, with some creative insight, you can present your small company on a rather large scale with an eye-catching and interactive display, perhaps making your operation appear larger than it might be at present (and larger in your customers' eyes, too).

Trade shows generally take place at a single location, run for just a limited time of about one to three days, and bring together thousands of exhibitors and potential customers in a very concentrated and powerful marketing forum.

Even though online marketing is hugely responsible for enabling more small businesses than ever to start and grow their entrepreneurial enterprises, trade shows still give business owners the opportunity to meet and interact with a large audience of important clients, suppliers, and an overall sampling of your target audience. Specifically, by visiting trade shows, you can quickly and cost-effectively accomplish the following:

- Generate sales leads.
- Generate actual sales at the show.
- Establish your business's image and enhance its visibility.
- Reach your target audience in face-to-face fashion.
- Announce and establish your business's presence in the marketplace.
- Assess and improve the effectiveness and efficiency of your marketing and advertising efforts.
- Personally meet your customers, competitors, and suppliers.
- Attract and solicit new customers.
- Unveil new products and services.
- Provide actual product demonstrations in ways not possible by other means.
- Recruit distributors, suppliers, and dealer channels where appropriate.

TRACKING TRENDS TO IMPROVE MARKETING RESULTS

With all this talk about marketing plans and advertising campaigns, don't overlook one of the best indicators of the success of your marketing efforts: tracking consumer trends and attitudes. We all know that, as consumers, we're easily distracted or diverted in our wants (and sometimes needs) when it comes to buying goods. While it's obvious that you'll have trouble selling fireplace tools in the summertime, other buying habits aren't as obvious. You'll also have to track what consumers are buying and feed that information into your overall marketing and advertising strategy to ensure your efforts gain the best possible results for the moment. Here are some tips to help you navigate the ever-changing sea of consumer trends and use your marketing plan to deliver the best goods at the best times.

Online Sales Mining

It's back to the market research, only this time you'll want to be identifying current trends in consumer purchases. Use eBay's Completed Item search capabilities to see what's been selling recently, as well as the What's Hot list I showed to you previously; that will give you an indication of what consumers seem to be the most interested in at the moment and will help you position the best goods in the best way to take advantage of the current buying mood. Go back and study the particulars of auction and fixed-price sales on eBay, identifying what seems to be selling and, of those items, which seem to be selling best. Again, this is where your study of the actions of other sellers will help you see firsthand how buyers are responding to different sales techniques, the sort you'll want to consider incorporating, and what improvements you'll want to make to your own sales efforts.

eBay TIP: When analyzing final sales prices for items on eBay, try to determine if prices are holding steady or are experiencing either upward or downward trends. Be particularly attentive to listings that seem to appear as spikes in the market (with a final price being either unusually high or low); these are the listings to closely scrutinize as you seek to determine what contributed to the spike (was the item the center of a two-person bidding war, resulting in an unusually high price, or was it priced too high at the outset or poorly presented, thus resulting in an unusually low price?). Sometimes you have to "peel the layers of the onion" to get to the real heart of the story, and those are the kinds of detailed and telling sales statistics you'll want to uncover for your marketing efforts.

Mine Your Own Business

While you're actively sifting through the offerings of others around you, don't forget to carefully examine your own offerings as well. Keep close track of *your* sales history, determining where your items sell best, when they seem to be in greatest demand, and which transactions encouraged a customer to make a return visit. By carefully tracking your own sales results while regularly watching the sales of others, you'll have the conclusive data that will help you successfully navigate the ever-changing online marketplace and make the best decisions for which goods you'll continue to offer.

Distrust Your Own Bias

One of the biggest challenges to small-business owners is determining which items are truly popular in buyers' minds as opposed to what you, the seller, are most interested in. To develop a truly astute understanding of marketing and merchandising trends, you need to be able to see everything that seems to be selling, not just those items that interest *you* the most. So many times, sellers will look right past popular items that hold little interest for them. Buyers, however, may be buying up those goods fast and furious. To be successful in detecting trends, sellers need to develop a wider scope of vision, being able to recognize *anything* that appears in demand, regardless of the seller's own personal view of the goods.

A FINAL NOTE

Even though all this talk of a marketing plan and advertising campaign leads to new and inventive ways to promote and sell your products, both online and off, don't overlook some of the most obvious and immediate-response methods to get the word out about your products. Yes, it's a lot to consider, all this marketing and advertising, but with the proper effort and up-front planning, you'll see results you might otherwise miss without this deliberate and well-thought out approach.

14

Going International

Following the topic of the previous chapter, one more thing to consider seriously is the international market and its function in helping you reach new factions of your target customer base while growing your business's bottom line. If you wonder about the difficulty of breaking into the international market, don't. Although many sellers are likewise wary about venturing overseas to conduct business, doing business online makes serving international customers just about as easy as selling to a customer in your own hometown. Sure, there are some differences in selling abroad, but this chapter will show you how even these differences are practically insignificant as you get ready to roll out the red carpet to a whole new audience of overseas buyers. Get ready: you're about to go global.

WHAT'S REALLY DIFFERENT ABOUT INTERNATIONAL SALES?

Generally speaking, there's very little difference to selling internationally. Often, listings you post on eBay will attract the attention of bidders and buyers from other countries and you never have to lift a finger to attract overseas attention. Recall that when you list an item for bid or sale it goes up to be viewed by eBay's worldwide registered community of users. These users will review your listing just as anyone else and will bid (often in earnest) to win and purchase what you're offering. Besides receiving e-mail inquiries about your goods and perhaps a potential buyer confirming you'll ship internationally, the only true differences you'll encounter when dealing with international customers typically come *after* the sale. Receiving payment and shipping goods sometimes requires a couple of extra steps, but they're certainly nothing of such significance that you should shy away from selling globally.

eBay TIP: Recall that when you list items for bid or sale, you have the option to specify whether you'll ship internationally. Some sellers have determined that they *won't* sell to international buyers because of issues of difficulty, but I've found bids from people abroad to be just as valid and their money to be as green as that of my local customers. Moreover, you'll often find that international bidders bid higher for items they can't get in their home country. To date, I've successfully collected payment from and shipped goods to great customers in 15 different countries. When it comes to selling internationally, my virtual borders are always open. Hopefully, by the time you finish with this chapter, yours will be, too. And don't forget that sometimes when you're buying, you might be looking to purchase from an overseas seller yourself. Hopefully that seller will accept your international bids, right?

To further explain more of the differences you'll encounter in international selling and to see they're hardly obstacles to selling outside your home country with ease, read on.

FIRST THINGS FIRST: ESTABLISHING YOUR INTERNATIONAL SALES POLICIES

Your first policy in selling to international customers is letting them know you gladly welcome their bids, purchases, and any questions they may have about purchasing from you. Therefore, be sure to click on the checkbox in your item listings that indicates you'll ship worldwide, thus beginning your international sales adventures.

eBay TIP: Take note that eBay allows you to specify exactly which countries you'll ship to, in case you want to enter global selling slowly or you have other reasons for restricting shipment of goods to certain areas of the world.

As I discussed previously in this book, it's up to you to establish your sales and shipping policies clearly and completely so bidders and buyers know what sorts of services they can expect when buying from you. When you add international shipping to that equation, you'll need to add a few more points of explanation to help foreign customers understand what they

can expect when buying from you. To that end, be sure to answer the following questions for your international bidders and buyers:

- Are there any countries serviced by eBay to which you will not ship?
- Do you make any special arrangements to list in ways that suit bidders and buyers in different time zones?
- What forms of payment will you accept from international buyers?
- What will be the shipping charges to ship to a particular country, and will you provide actual international shipping charges *after* the auction has ended or the purchase has been made? (Hint: this is an excellent time to be sure you're using the Shipping Calculator in your listings so international bidders and buyers can calculate the rates for themselves. See the full treatment of this subject in Chapter 3.)
- Will there be any additional packaging or handling charges in preparing an item for international shipment?
- Are there any special shipping methods you use for shipping internationally, and will there be any delay in actually shipping an item that will require such services?
- Do you have special policies, instructions, or restrictions in managing potential returns from international customers? Be *very* clear about this most important point right from the beginning.

Well, that's the high-level look at international shipping considerations. Now let's look deeper into each issue to help you skillfully navigate the nuances of each.

ACCOMMODATING YOUR INTERNATIONAL AUDIENCE

For years I've advocated the importance of the time at which you launch (and thereby close) your auctions, catering to the hours at which most bidders will be available to participate in your auction before it closes. Most of that discussion has been directed to domestic eBay bidders, but if you find your business offers products that have specific international appeal, you have a perfect opportunity to shift your listings to coincide with the availability of customers in another country and, hence, in another time zone. This is a simple matter really, because all you need to do is determine the time difference between where you are and where your international customers are. eBay has been good enough to recognize this opportunity, too, by providing an easy-to-use time-zone chart to help you in this effort (see Figure 14-1).

Just visit *pages.ebay.com/internationaltrading/timezones.html* and you'll

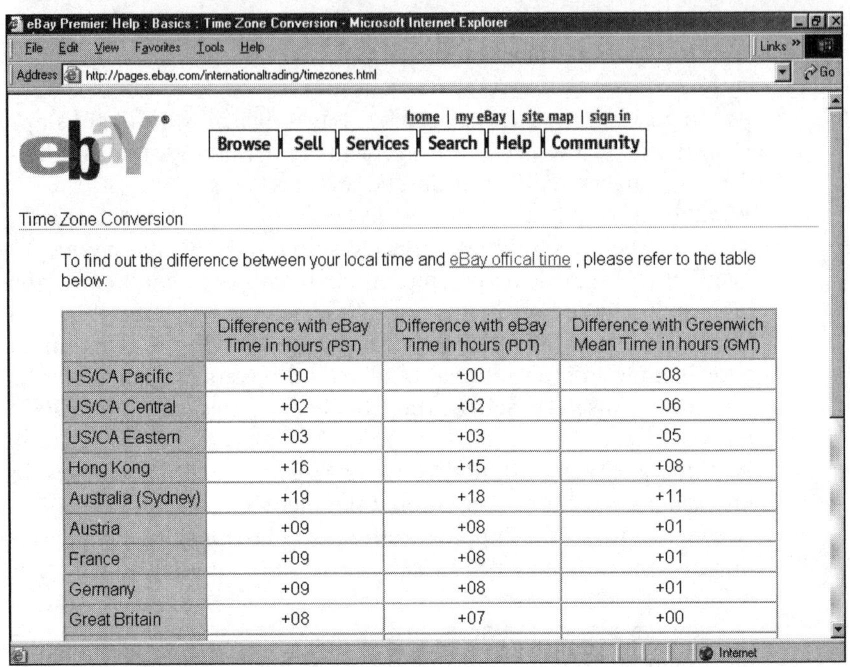

	Difference with eBay Time in hours (PST)	Difference with eBay Time in hours (PDT)	Difference with Greenwich Mean Time in hours (GMT)
US/CA Pacific	+00	+00	-08
US/CA Central	+02	+02	-06
US/CA Eastern	+03	+03	-05
Hong Kong	+16	+15	+08
Australia (Sydney)	+19	+18	+11
Austria	+09	+08	+01
France	+09	+08	+01
Germany	+09	+08	+01
Great Britain	+08	+07	+00

Figure 14-1 eBay's Time Zone Conversion chart is useful in helping you launch your auction at a time that best suits your international customers.

find a chart that tells you the hour difference between eBay (always synchronized to Pacific time in the United States) and that of the country where you'll be listing for its population of bidders. Although you may think it is of little consequence to list items to align with the time in other countries, this is another part of identifying that all-important target market and positioning your products in a way that will appeal to that audience of customers (and auction timing is a big deal to bidders in other lands).

eBay TIP: Wait! If you list items to align to foreign hours, won't that mean you'll be awake at odd hours listing goods? Not at all. Create your item listings and then employ the auction start date and time function within the listing to launch the auction so it caters to international customers without requiring you to lurk around like a bat at your computer late into the night.

On a final point, don't forget that dealing with customers in different time zones will also have an effect on the response time for communication

between the two of you. Expect that it may take 12 hours or more to get a response from your buyer, who may be located halfway around the world.

ACCEPTING INTERNATIONAL PAYMENTS

Long considered the most unwieldy bugaboo about dealing with customers in other countries, accepting international payment is now an absolute breeze. Here's a rundown of the different ways you can elect to receive payment from your customers abroad.

Online Payment

As online payment methods have improved markedly to meet the needs of both buyers and sellers, they have become the preferred method of payment when transacting on eBay. Of the different online payment services available today, PayPal gets highest marks from me for simplifying payment for buyers and sellers all over the world. With your PayPal account, you can easily receive credit card payments from buyers in over 35 countries without the headache of having to calculate and manage foreign-currency exchange rates. PayPal supports and automatically converts payments made and payments received in Canadian dollars, euro, pounds sterling, and yen. When a buyer from, say, Canada pays you from their PayPal account using Canadian dollars, the payment you receive in your U.S. account is automatically converted to U.S. dollars at the current rate of exchange. Just like that, you're receiving foreign payments with zero hassle while your buyer is likewise afforded an easy way to make their purchase. There are more options available to you, though, regarding accepting PayPal payments from foreign customers:

- You can accept payments that will be converted automatically to your local currency as noted.
- You can accept the payment in the buyer's currency, thus holding a foreign-currency balance in your PayPal account.
- You can deny the payment outright if you choose not to receive international payments (but again, why would you limit your sales in this way?).

That second point above bears a bit more explanation, because it uncovers an interesting option available to you when accepting credit card payments from international customers. When you accept a payment in a currency different than that which you set as the default for your PayPal account (for example, U.S. dollars), PayPal automatically opens a new currency balance in your account to maintain the foreign payment you've accepted. This way, you can easily receive foreign payments in a specific currency and

then utilize that balance to easily make international purchases for yourself or your business in the international market. For example, assume you've found an excellent source of goods located in Japan and the seller of those goods accepts PayPal payments. You make your purchase for the new inventory from the source (with PayPal automatically making the dollars to yen conversion for you), and then you begin to vigorously sell those goods to Japanese customers who pay *you* via PayPal in yen. You can keep that yen balance in your PayPal account and apply it directly to future inventory purchases from your Japan source. All of these steps used to take considerable effort and often required involvement from banks and others to manage the various exchanges. With the PayPal solution, it's as simple as clicking the mouse on your computer.

eBay TIP: Any time you wish to convert any currency balance you hold in your account, you can easily choose PayPal's Transfer Funds function to make an immediate conversion at the current conversion rate at no extra cost.

International Money Orders, Bank Checks, or Cashier's Checks

If online payment won't be used, most sellers then prefer payment via international money orders (IMOs). Just like domestic money orders, these are purchased by buyers at their local postal centers or other authorized issuers and are as good as cash when received by a seller. Most sellers agree to ship goods immediately upon receiving IMOs because they are just like money in the bank.

Next down the list of preferred payment methods are certified bank or cashier's checks. Again, just like money orders, these are like cash in hand. The only caveat for sellers here—and something to specify in an international selling policy—is that such checks need to be drawn to the normal currency you deal with in your homeland (for example, U.S. dollars). If you don't make this specification and receive a payment drawn in another currency, your bank may charge you conversion fees.

Wire Transfers

Although not as common in the United States as it is in other parts of the world, and often feared as a common means for fraudulent dealing (which, unfortunately, it is), a wire transfer is a fast and convenient way to quickly issue payment in international transactions. Personally, I've only accepted wire transfer payments on a couple of occasions, and I was required to provide my bank account information to the buyer, who then authorized his bank to

transfer the agreed payment amount to my account. Of course, I made sure I was confident in dealing with my buyer before providing my bank information for the payment and likewise checked with my bank to ensure there were safeguards in place to protect my account information (there were). Wire transfers usually involve a charge, which the buyer will incur, to initiate the transaction; sellers are typically not required by their bank to pay any such fees. Again, this is not a very commonly used payment method, because of the availability and ease of use of other methods.

eBay TIP: If you do decide to accept a wire transfer to your bank account but are fearful that your account information could be used inappropriately, rest easy that the details you'll provide to the sender—you bank account and routing numbers—is the same information that can be identified from the personal checks you may have. Funds can only be withdrawn from your account (the reverse process of what we're discussing here) via wire transfer if you have authorized your bank to do so. Again, check with your bank to fully understand their methods and safeguards when it comes to managing wire transfers, either into or out of your account.

Cash Payments

And then there's cash. Few sellers proclaim a preference for receiving cash payments from international customers, and for obvious reasons: cash can easily be intercepted and stolen in transit, and it cannot be tracked or recovered. If cash is lost in transit, it potentially puts the seller in the position of being accused of dishonesty about having received it, and the buyer might be accused of not actually having sent payment at all, thereby significantly complicating matters between buyer and seller.

This isn't to say you *can't* accept cash payments, especially if it's the only way for an international buyer to pay you. If you decide you'll accept cash payments, be sure to add the following specifications:

- The payment needs to be sent by registered or otherwise traceable mail delivery.
- The cash will be properly concealed in a dark envelope or wrapped in paper inside the envelope.
- All cash payments will be sent at the buyer's own risk.

Really, collecting international payments isn't so different or terribly difficult when compared to collecting domestically. Actually, you'll likely be surprised to find that many international buyers will be quite eager to pay

quickly and conveniently in a way that suits your needs just fine. Many are as concerned as you are to ensure a clean and complete transactions therefore, collecting international payments often becomes a true "win-win" situation.

SHIPPING INTERNATIONALLY

With the money in the bank, the next hurdle to clear is packing and shipping your items for a safe journey to their new international home. Here again, service providers (eBay and elsewhere) have stepped up to assist sellers to smooth the rough spots formerly associated with shipping across the border and around the globe. Now we'll take a look at the similarities and the few differences to consider when shipping outside of your homeland.

Packing Concerns

The best news about shipping overseas is that packing requirements really aren't much different from shipping domestically, for which you also have to pack items securely inside and out to withstand the sometimes bumpy, jarring ride of transit. The key to successful international packing is not to overdo it. Some sellers will overpack an item, maybe wedging it *too* tightly into a package, which means that it will stand a greater chance of being damaged on its journey. Therefore, continue to use good interior cushioning (bubble wrap, foam peanuts, and so on) to protect your items. Then be sure to use new, sturdy outer boxes or cartons, dispensing with used, potentially banged up or weakened boxes that might not stand up as well to around-the-world handling. Of special note: be sure to use two address labels on international packages. Apply one to the outside of the shipping carton as normal but then include a second label *inside* the package just in case the outer carton ever becomes damaged or the package requires interior inspection.

Choosing a Carrier

You'll be glad to know that all the major carriers I mentioned in Chapter 12 also offer global shipping services, many as speedy and effective as domestic delivery.

- *United States Post Office (USPS).* The USPS offers incredibly reliable and cost-effective shipping services to international destinations. As a seller, you can easily offer a variety of international shipment services, offering your customers choices regarding the speed of delivery. Without much special effort on your part, you can easily offer Global Priority delivery, Global Express delivery, and standard Air Mail delivery, giving your customers pricing and delivery options to suit their needs. Personally, I've found Global Priority

delivery to be the best for my needs, costing about $8 for a one-pound package, with items arriving within about seven days after departure (sometimes sooner).

eBay TIP: While slower international shipping methods are certainly less expensive, understand that the sooner a package arrives, the less time it has to become potentially damaged in transit. Explain this to your customers as well so they can see the benefit of choosing a relatively quick delivery method.

- *United Parcel Service (UPS).* UPS also maintains an excellent track record of delivering items abroad quickly and safely. If you prefer UPS, you'll see they have you covered with several international shipping services. One thing to be clear about, though, is the additional customs and brokerage fees that UPS levies to package recipients. Be sure to fully review the UPS international fee chart on their Web site (*www.ups.com*) and communicate those fees, *in advance*, to your bidders and buyers so they won't be caught off guard.

eBay TIP: Whenever offering goods for international shipment, be sure to try to incorporate the use of the different shipping calculators, as explained in Chapter 12, to enable your shoppers to determine the shipping fees for themselves. This is one of the best ways to eliminate any confusion over the shipping charges you'll ultimately be collecting.

- *Federal Express (FedEx).* Federal Express also manages deliveries to other countries, though their service is somewhat more costly than other carriers. If you need an item to be delivered quickly, this is FedEx's specialty (hence, their name). Just make sure you understand their services and fees before you include FedEx into your overall selection of shipping services.

Offering Insurance

Just as with domestic sales, when you offer shipping insurance you're offering protection to international buyers in case something goes awry in the delivery process, such as the package and its contents becoming damaged or lost along the way. Really, there's not much need to alter your normal (domestic) shipping policy in this regard: offer insurance and require buyers either to pay the additional amount or bear all risk and loss for uninsured shipments. Be sure you clearly understand the insurance options of the carrier with

whom you'll ship and ensure your buyers are likewise aware as they determine whether or not they'll purchase the extra protection.

eBay TIP: Sometimes, as a seller, you may elect to make insurance mandatory, especially if you're shipping fragile goods. As a seller, that's entirely your prerogative, but be sure you clearly state this up front in your sales policy.

CAN YOU TALK THE TALK?

Finally, as you've mastered the ways and means to make yours a global business, ready and eager to serve customers from all around the world, give some consideration to the whole issue of communication, often referred to as the language barrier. While Americans are quite lucky (even spoiled) in rarely having to consider communicating in another language, many of your foreign customers *will* be faced with the challenge of communicating with you when

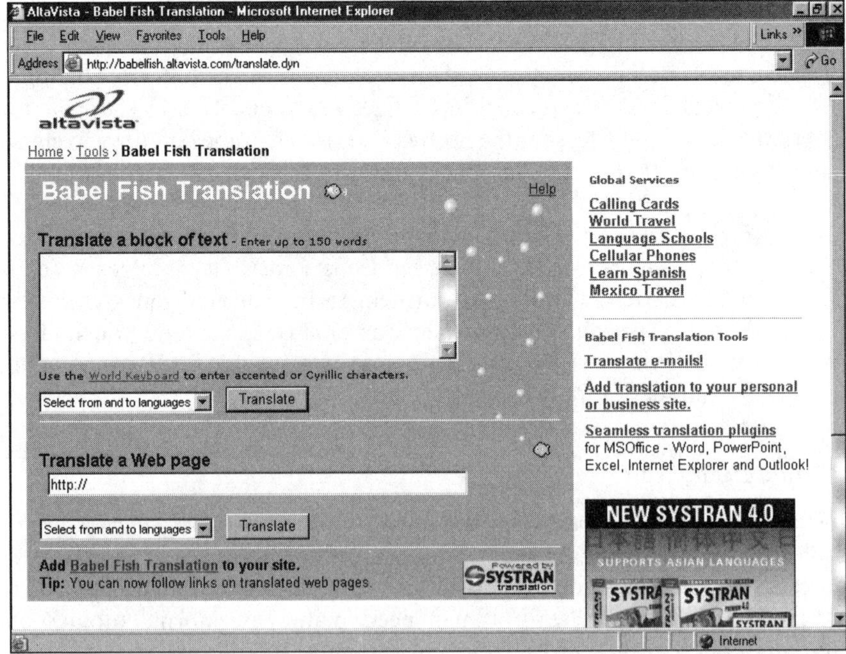

Figure 14-2 Make use of Alta Vista's Babel Fish translator to erase miscommunication when talking different languages.

they wish to purchase your goods. While you don't have to run out and grab all manner of learn-at-home language courses to serve the international community, there is something you can do today to help bridge the communication gap. Simply put, "put it simply." When you write the descriptions for your item listings, try to use very straightforward language that avoids too much slang or flowery phrases that may be difficult for non-English-speaking customers to interpret. If you find you're developing a significant international customer base, you may entertain the idea of creating localized versions of your listings by including translations into other languages within the listing body.

Even if you don't speak the language of your customers, there's a terrific tool for you and your customers to use that makes translations a breeze. Just visit Alta Vista's Babel Fish translation site (see Figure 14-2), plug in the text you want to translate, and select the language to translate to (or from). Babel Fish will make the translation for you, and instantly you're ready to communicate in a different language.

15

Using Third-Party Auction Tools and Services

Up to this point, I've shown you how you can easily and impressively set up, manage, and maintain an online venture using just the tools within eBay. From bulk listing tools like eBay's Turbo Lister to easy payment collection through PayPal and online postage purchase and shipping label creation, eBay has truly covered 90 percent of the bases that will help your business flourish. Still, there are some other tools out there that can also be a boost to your business and, as I'm not here to strictly rally for eBay alone (remember, it's *your* success I'm ultimately cheering for), this chapter will introduce a few non-eBay tools that you may find useful in managing and growing your business. While I don't believe you absolutely need these tools to gain success, I feel you'll want to know about them anyway, just so you're aware that other methods and mechanisms exist to help you along the way.

eBay TIP: Before rolling out a list of what I've found to be some of the better tools available for online businesses (and there are quite a few, believe me), I find I can best run my own operations when I can consolidate my efforts within a single platform. For that reason and because eBay has made some key acquisitions and developed some key partnerships, I'm finding more and more that I can manage most all my activities easily within eBay's walls. Yes, I know that's somewhat contradictory to my previous statement of not being an eBay-only cheerleader, but it's the truth. In my years of experience selling on eBay, I'm finding that eBay is responding to the needs of its user base and, though they do not always seem to have the small business in the forefront of some of their site policies and

politics, they've come a long, long way since the dot-com bust days of 2000, when every online business was just scrambling to maintain a profitable bottom line.

LISTING TOOLS

If you've been working online auctions for very long, you're probably somewhat familiar with the different auction management services available, suites of tools that have been designed to help small, medium, and larger businesses manage and maintain their flow of item listings and close transactions, all within a collection of integrated functions that smooths out the process and streamlines a business's ability to do fast and efficient business.

How Do You Know If You Need an Auction Management Service?

Once eBay had taken hold in Net shoppers' minds and became the de facto destination for online bargain hunters and entrepreneurial-minded sellers, it gave way to a service industry that sought to fill in some of the gaps in the still-developing site. With about 100 new auction management service sites (perhaps more) having crept onto the scene to tap this lucrative new market, interested sellers have understandably been puzzled over the different sites' services and the fees they charge for their tool sets. While all of these service providers promise the potential to make greater profits with less effort, sellers still are unsure if the services being sold are truly needed to succeed. With so many similar and some different tool sets being offered, you, the seller, need to assess if your business would benefit from the expense of an auction management service. Here are a few things to ponder as you try to determine if a third-party service is right for you:

- How many items will you list per week? If your business is so small (and not that there's anything wrong with that), you may not need to invest in a high-powered and higher-cost service (if you even need one at all).
- Where will you list items? Naturally, all the services are aimed at servicing the eBay seller, but will you list items elsewhere online, too? If you want to list items at Amazon Auctions, Amazon Marketplace (fixed-price items), Yahoo! Auctions, or at a Yahoo Store, be sure the service you're considering will manage the multiple venues you want to utilize. And what about a Web site of your own? If you're planning on doing significant business on your own site and already have a solution to manage your sales there, then introducing an auction management service might just complicate your overall business plan. Even if you'll be starting on eBay to grow your business, try to

think one to three years down the road as you decide if an auction management service is right for you.

- If you already have a Web site or storefront of your own, will you be paying for store-building features that you don't really need? Be sure to see if the auction management service you're considering allows à la carte pricing so you can purchase only the individual features you need.
- How computer and graphics savvy are you these days? If you can create nice HTML templates or Web pages already, why bother paying an auction service site for their canned templates? Of course, if such computer design isn't your bailiwick, perhaps an auction management service that provides such design tools is a good choice to help dress up your business.

Essentially, the key to effectively utilizing auction management services is to understand just how much *service* they'll actually provide to you. I'm of the mind to develop my own tool set or fully capitalize on services already provided on eBay and its partners' sites. If, however, I find tools that offer features I see as truly beneficial to my sales and business growth and are of a nature that is either beyond my current skill set or would be otherwise unfeasible for me to attempt, I'd look to the provider of that service as a good place to invest some of my business capital to help grow my profits.

Sifting through the Auction Management Services

Many of the numerous auction management service sites have dissolved in recent years, but a strong few have remained and developed some tools that truly are effective and efficient. In short order, here are the top three that currently have the best suite of services to perhaps help you in your business.

Andale (www.andale.com) First on the list is Andale (see Figure 15-1), an auction management service company founded in 1999 and one that's been around to ride and survive the dot-com boom and bust. Created with small businesses in mind, Andale offers a compelling à la carte list of services, including but not limited to listing tools, image hosting, checkout functionality, and e-mail services. The service most intriguing to me (and to any small business) is the variety of research and analysis tools the site offers. Although eBay now retains data on closed items for only 14 days rather than its previous 30 days, Andale has the rest of the historical data that can help you in your market-research efforts. In well-organized fashion, Andale research provides telling statistics, such as average selling prices of specified items, category statistics, one-year trending graphs, and even comparison data that will tell you how your items' pricing will stand up to

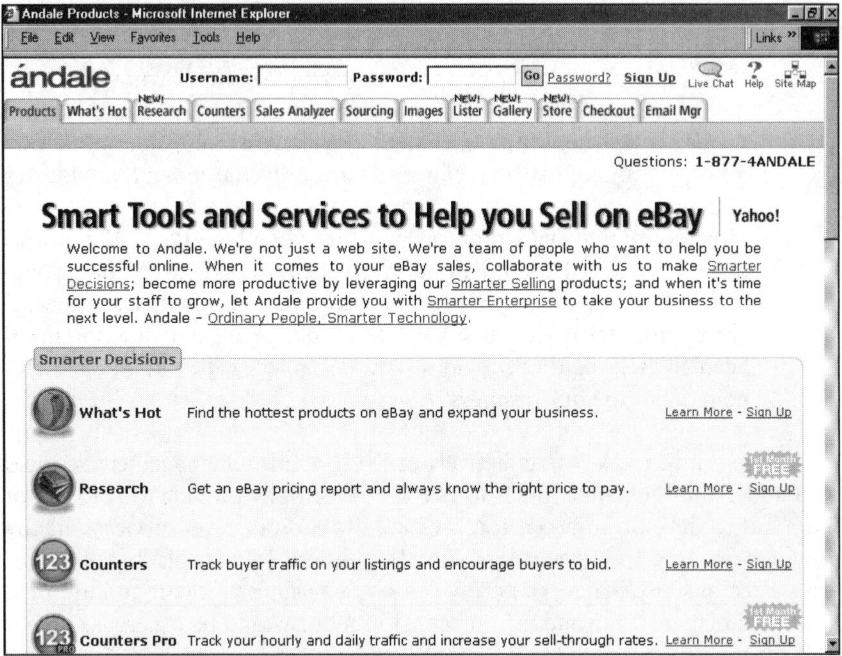

Figure 15-1 À la carte pricing and tight integration into eBay makes Andale my first choice in auction management services.

retail prices. To me, this is the best feature Andale has to offer, since eBay has adapted to provide all the other tools your business needs. And because you can "use only the products you need—and as much as you need," it's easy to pick and choose among Andale's tool set, keeping the services that you like and actually use and avoiding others that don't provide the results your business needs.

Vendio (www.vendio.com) Formerly known as AuctionWatch.com and originally launched in 1998, this is the most venerable of the auction management sites still around today. At its inception, AuctionWatch.com quickly became the premiere auction service site, not immediately for the tool set it offered but for the incredible amount of useful auction information, articles, and analyses of the online auction industry. The strong editorial content coupled with the most active online auction forum (even rivaling that of eBay's own community forums) made AW the first and last destination for auctiongoers seeking real-world insight and information. Of course, AuctionWatch grew to provide listing services, image hosting, and even payment services to help buyers and sellers get the most from their online

Figure 15-2 Longtime auction management service Vendio has your business's branding and market proliferation in mind to help grow your results.

auction efforts. In 2003, the company was renamed Vendio, Inc., and announced a further focusing of its services to help businesses "through the entire online sales process, including inventory management, online store creation, merchandise placement on both fixed price and auction marketplaces, customer communication, and order fulfillment." Vendio's services support the major online portals of eBay, Yahoo, Amazon, Froogle, and its own suite of Vendio Stores. For pricing, Vendio uses a variety of tiered payment plans and varied service offerings that, in my opinion, are a bit cumbersome to navigate. Still, with their experience in this realm of auction management services, Vendio definitely deserves a look (see Figure 15-2). Also, their online community forum is just as active as ever and brimming with great interactive auction information.

Marketworks (www.auctionworks.com) Last of the big three (again, in my personal estimation) is Marketworks, formerly AuctionWorks (see Figure 15-3). Something of a hybrid between Andale and Vendio, this site offers plenty of listing, hosting, and communication services that can be well-employed

Figure 15-3 Take a look at Marketworks for a simplified approach to auction management services.

by online businesses of all sizes, yet it projects the image of being very corporate minded. Marketworks was actually teamed with Disney to host a large offering of memorabilia from the Magic Kingdom, proving its mettle to serve even the biggest companies in their quests to enter the online auction fray.

Services include listing tools, image hosting, inventory management, and post-sale management and communication. The fee structure is much simpler at Marketworks, and for that reason it becomes one of my Top 3. Fees are 2 percent of an item's selling price, with a minimum of 10 cents and a maximum of $3. Image hosting can be purchased separately under one of four tiered plans. There are no listing fees to launch items from Marketworks, and that's a big plus.

Of course, there are numerous other auction management services out there to review and perhaps use. Study all sites' prices carefully, and calculate those costs as you work to project your operating costs accurately. Whenever possible, cut costs where they don't produce a noticeable (and calculable) positive impact on your business. Depending upon how well organized you already are and how well you're utilizing the built-in features of other computer-based tools you use every day (including e-mail tools, file-folder

tools, and even spreadsheets), you may find you're able to manage your business quite well without having to insert a third-party management service into your process. If so, that's terrific news for your business and a testament to your business prowess. Bravo!

eBay TIP: Something else you'll need to consider when determining which, if any, auction management service you'll use is the impact to your business if the service becomes unavailable. During the busy holiday season of 2002, Andale services were suddenly interrupted for 16 hours, affecting sellers' listings and confusing bidders and buyers who were receiving blank e-mail notifications and invoices stemming from the affected listings. Clearly, this sort of situation is the exception and not the rule, but it drives home the point that you also want to strive to make your business as interruption-proof as possible by eliminating reliance on too many other systems and servers and other such third-party tools that may go "clunk" when your business least expects it.

A NEW IMAGING TOOL

One of the most interesting new tools I've seen that is a definite candidate to add to your listing lexicon is the new VideoSnap imaging tool from Logitech. You may recognize Logitech as the designer and provider of what are called personal-interface products—for example, the ever-popular WebCams—which individuals use to communicate via video links for work or for play.

Logitech has now applied to the e-commerce industry the movement it gave to Web-hosted meetings and chats: streaming video for use in auction listings. VideoSnap allows you to include up to 60 seconds of full-movement video to provide on-screen demonstration and moving images so that you can better describe and detail an item listed for bid or sale (see Figure 15-4).

To add video to your next listing, just navigate over to *videosnap.logitech.com*, where you'll see how easy it is to bring moving pictures to your auctions and fixed-price listings. You can create video clips using any current USB (Universal Service Bus connection) WebCam in conjunction with the exclusive VideoSnap Composer, or you can choose to upload your own .avi video files. VideoSnap offers a simple video-editing tool for adjusting clips to fit within the 60-second time frame (allowing you to tighten up the presentation and weed out any unnecessary frames). Once launched, the video clip will remain available for as long as your eBay listing is active. How much does VideoSnap cost? Logitech charges just $2.49 per 60-second clip. A bit pricey when compared to other listing costs, but if your item stands to gain a good selling price because the detailed video will enhance it, it might be a well-

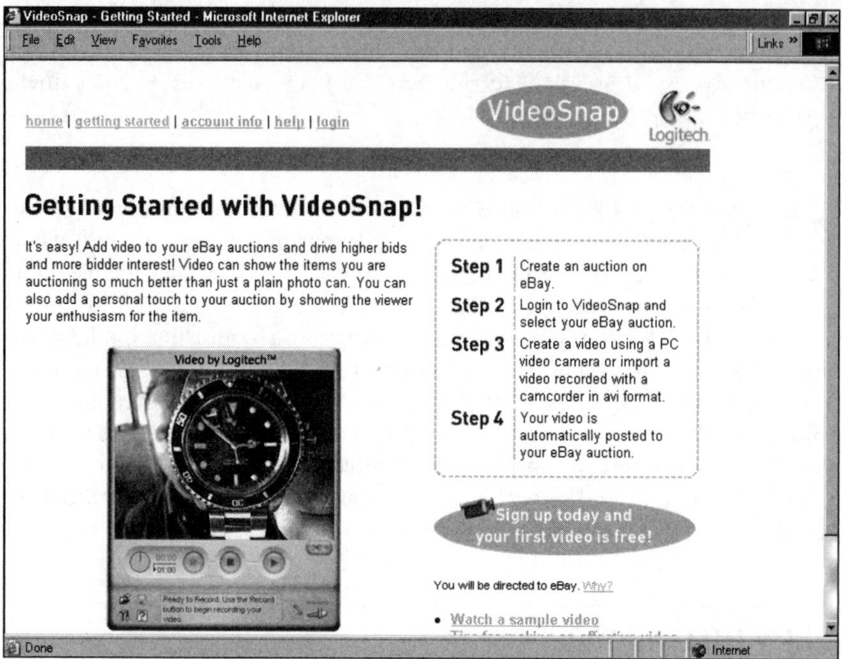

Figure 15-4 Logitech's new VideoSnap imaging adds multimedia to create compelling new online listings.

placed investment. As a bonus, Logitech has enabled easy PayPal payment from sellers who choose to use VideoSnap in their listings.

eBay TIP: Just as with still images, I expect to see moving images become increasingly more popular for online sales. Recall the days when it was a treat to find an eBay listing that actually contained a picture (circa 1996) and now see how prevalent—actually predominant—that feature has become. I see video proliferating in the same way and, as it does so, expect to see the price of creating and hosting such videos get much cheaper as more service providers step forward to offer their own branded solutions.

If you want to stay on the cutting edge with your listings and are looking for that certain something that will help your item listings stand out in front of the competition, VideoSnap may be that special ingredient that helps you woo more customers.

A FAVORITE BIDDING TOOL

Just because you're focusing your efforts on selling and growing your business doesn't mean you'll stop bidding. Whether it's for investment in business needs or inventory or for personal reasons, there's one bidding tool I have used for years and will continue to use since it helps me effectively launch snipe bids, those last-second stealth bids that can often establish you as the winner of an auction without allowing others time to bid against you. In the old days, the only way to launch a snipe bid at the end of an auction was to be "present to win," sitting by the computer at whatever hour (sometimes dreadfully late at night) to place that final bid. Thanks to eSnipe, there's an online tool that can do the sniping for you while you work, sleep, or play. eSnipe is a simple tool that allows you to specify the item number of an active eBay listing, specify the maximum price you'd be willing to pay (bid) for the item, and the number of seconds you want left on the auction clock before the snipe bid is placed. With that information, eSnipe's servers will monitor the auction for you and place the bid on your behalf. If your maximum bid holds up, you win! (See Figure 15-5.)

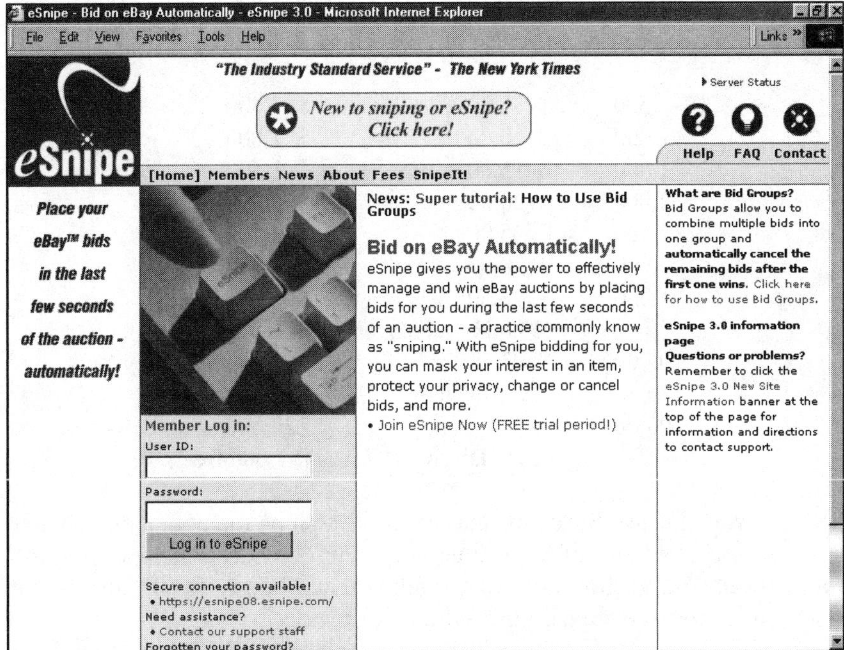

Figure 15-5 I use eSnipe to launch last-second bids, which helps me win items I want or need without having to be present at the time. That's convenient!

Aside from simply launching last-second snipe bids, eSnipe also features a unique tool called Bid Groups. If you're looking to snipe a particular item, say an Olympus digital camera or a Hewlett-Packard printer, eSnipe allows you to specify several auctions for the same item that may be running concurrently in a bid group. Now all you do is specify the most you're willing to offer in your snipe bid and eSnipe will systematically launch last-second bids for the items in the bid group until one of them is won. Once you've achieved a win, the snipe bids for subsequent items within your bid group will be cancelled.

As far as pricing goes, eSnipe's cost to use is practically negligible. At eSnipe, you purchase BidPoints that are consumed as you place winning snipe bids (if you don't win, you don't pay eSnipe—cool). Each BidPoint is valued at $0.01 each, and points are consumed in the following way:

- Auction wins under $25 cost $0.25 in BidPoint value (or 25 BidPoints).
- Auction wins between $25 and $1,000 cost 1 percent of the auction price in BidPoint value.
- Auction wins over $1,000 cost $10 in BidPoint value.

You can purchase BidPoints easily at eSnipe using any major credit card or by money order or check. BidPoints cost as follows:

500	$ 5.00	$ 500
1,000	$ 10.00	$ 1,000
1,500	$ 15.00	$ 1,500
2,000	$ 20.00	$ 2,000
2,500	$ 25.00	$ 2,500
3,000	$ 30.00	$ 3,000
5,000	$ 47.50 **(5% Discount!)**	$ 5,000 **($250 free!)**
10,000	$ 93 **(7% Discount!)**	$10,000 **($700 free!)**
20,000	$180 **(10% Discount!)**	$20,000 **($1,000 free!)**

As you can see, BidPoints can be used to snipe many auctions of low value or fewer auctions of high value or anything in between. Next time you want to snipe an auction but don't think you can be present to launch that last-second bid, let eSnipe do the bidding for you.

E-MAIL MARKETING TOOLS

One final third-party tool I want to bring to your attention is that of e-mail marketing. Yes, again we walk the fine line between what constitutes spam and what is a valid and useful marketing campaign tool. Sometimes it's difficult to sort out the two on your own, and that's when you should take a visit to GotMarketing at *www.gotmarketing.com*. As a leader in e-marketing, GotMarketing's Campaigner tool is an excellent solution to creating compelling and results-oriented commercial e-mail communications that are also well within the bounds of recent new antispam laws (see Figure 15-6). Utilizing only permission-based customer lists (those who have agreed to continue receiving communications), GotMarketing has likewise adopted and governs itself by the recent CAN-SPAM Act enacted by the U.S. Congress. In fact, GotMarketing was a founding member of the Email Service Provider Coalition, an organization of responsible e-mail-provider services dedicated to fighting spam through a concerted effort. Therefore, the CAN-SPAM Act has been important in defining what is and what isn't spam, and GotMarketing has been working to provide technological functionality that ensures that all GotMarketing campaigns (and, hence, its users) will automatically comply

Figure 15-6 If you want superior looks and results from e-mail marketing, look no further than GotMarketing.

with the legal stipulations to provide legitimate e-marketing communications. So what are these stipulations? Briefly, the CAN-SPAM Act requires commercial eMarketing campaigns, and GotMarketing's Campaigner requires that its clients:

- Must not present misleading information in the From field or header information. Campaigner sets the header information automatically and enables sending messages using only validated e-mail addresses.
- Must include a link for (and, of course, honor) unsubscribe requests. Campaigner automatically adds an unsubscribe link to every e-mail sent and manages the unsubscribe requests automatically.
- Must conspicuously state that all commercial, promotional mail is an advertisement, unless all recipients have opted in. Campaigner is designed for permission-based lists only. Subscription tools and intelligent list filters help ensure that mailing lists are strictly opt-in.
- Must include a valid physical address in all communications. Campaigner has included space where users can enter their mailing addresses.

So, with the whole worry of spam put to rest, take a look at what GotMarketing's Campaigner e-marketing tool can do for your business:

- Create professional-looking communications, leveraging from a variety of customizable templates and designs
- Build and manage opt-in contact lists, including managing bounced responses and handling unsubscribe requests automatically
- Measure the actual results of e-marketing campaigns by providing feedback to you about how many recipients opened your e-mail, who clicked what, who forwarded your message, and whether you've gained any new subscribers

This all sounds great, but what's the cost? Actually, this is where I was most attracted to GotMarketing's Campaigner. Figure 15-6 shows how inexpensive it can be to create and manage your own eMarketing campaign.

GotMarketing's prices are incredibly low when you consider the time,

Monthly fee	$25	$40	$75
Number of emails per month	2,500	5,000	10,000
Cost per additional email	$0.0125	$0.0125	$0.0125

Figure 15-7 Getting inexpensive marketing help is easy with GotMarketing's fantastic tools.

effort, and cost associated with sending out direct-marketing mailers, handing out handbills, or buying radio or TV air time. Really, this is a marketing campaign that can be used to identify, target, and build a lasting relationship with your key customers. Again, communication of your business and its products is crucial for success and growth. I heartily recommend you consider e-marketing using GotMarketing as you seek to get the word out. It's easier and less expensive than ever before.

PART 3

eBAY INNOVATORS: BUILD YOUR PROFITS USING THE NEWEST TOOLS AND STRATEGIES AVAILABLE

16

Other Inventory Sources You May Not Have Considered (or Perhaps Forgotten)

As your business gets going and gains momentum, you may find you're looking for new sources of inventory either to complement the great items you're already selling or help you determine new avenues of merchandising that could be well worth consideration. Perhaps you're still looking to start up and are concerned about what you might do if ever you run out of inventory. Well, regardless of whether you're still testing the waters with your toe or you're looking for new sources of goods to offer alongside what you're already selling, here are a few more places you should be looking as a source of tempting items your customers just may clamor for.

IF YOU'VE GOT KIDS, YOU'VE GOT INVENTORY

eBay established itself in our online consciousness largely due to its never-ending inventory of collectible goods, the sort of nostalgic stuff that you and I fondly recall from our youth. Memories can be marketable, but selling current goods for today's youngsters is also prime turf for booming business on eBay. If you have kids (or know someone who has), you'll know those little ankle-biters outgrow just about everything they're given within a few short months (especially during the rapid-growth ages from infant to seven years). This is perhaps one of the greatest sources of inventory if you're looking to establish or subsidize your other offerings, since the market for kids' items is always teeming with buyers looking for great deals on great items. While most parents have made it fashionable to regularly visit local consignment shops to buy and consign kids' clothing, shoes, toys, and just about anything else,

more and more shoppers have turned to eBay and, therefore, more and more sellers are finding a better profit to be made by selling direct as opposed to relegating themselves to the 50/50 split and delayed payment most kiddie-trade establishments offer to consignees.

As the children's clothing category on eBay is growing about as quickly as your little darlings, sellers have found fast profits by regularly raiding the kids' closets of outgrown fashions (or jettisoning some of those truly weird outfits from Grandma and Grandpa). Demand for name brand ensembles and separates from Gymboree, Old Navy, GapKids, and others are practically sure sells to the buyer with youngsters who trail yours by just a few months and are looking to avoid high retail prices for garments that will only be useable for about as long.

The key to turning good profits in kids' clothes is to ensure they're very clean and complete. If an item has stains, tears, or other unsightly signs of use, don't bother listing it, but if it still looks like it came off the rack (and so many of these items do, due to the brief period Junior will fit into them), it's the sort of thing you should offer quickly. Another key consideration with children's clothing is offering items in advance of the upcoming season. If last year's summer shorts still look like new but will no longer fit your little ragamuffin, clean them, iron them, and offer them in late winter or early spring, a time when most parents are looking to snap up quick purchases in advance of a weather change. Same goes for winter and holiday-themed clothing. And remember how I explained in Chapter 2 that wedding goods are great to sell on eBay? The same holds true for one-time-wear outfits for youngsters, such as Baptism gowns, party dresses, ring-bearer's suits, and so on.

When selling general assortments of kids' clothing, try to offer lots rather than individual items. Buyers will usually snap up a grouping called spring wardrobe that includes shirts, shorts, shoes, hats, and even sunglasses and other accessories when the ensembles are prematched and all of the same size. Beyond clothing, don't overlook the toys kids have outgrown, with special attention paid to Fisher-Price, Playskool, and Little Tykes items. Outdoor gym sets, those colorful, heavy-duty, plastic play-yard pieces, are always being sought out on the secondary market. Most buyers will pay the shipping costs for yours, since it can still likely come in at a price well under exorbitant retail costs. Riding toys, play-figure sets, videos featuring outgrown purple dinosaurs and other "gently used" kids' items are always great offerings on eBay and, if you have a household full of growing youngsters, you'll know that at least four times a year you have a slew of great items that need to be moved out (that is, kids seem subject to growth spurts with the turning of each season—though your actual results may vary). Move 'em on eBay for years of profitability.

TRASH *IS* TREASURE

Remember my discussion in Chapter 6 regarding "JoesCrap"? I hope you considered it beyond the apparent humorous value it may have offered, because your "crap" can be just as valuable and there's usually a steady supply of it. As we are creatures prone to acquire, oftentimes to upgrade or replace items already in our possession, this trait typically leads to incredible amounts of goods that always seem to gather in the closets and attics of our living spaces.

Although I'm very eBay-minded, I recently cleaned out the video closet of all the VHS tapes and laser discs, because I'd since upgraded to the DVD format. I wound up with two grocery sacks full of entertainment, ready to be lugged to the driveway to sell for 50 cents each at my next garage sale. Quickly, I thought better of it and decided to list the movies on eBay. My result: a fast $500 that would have only yielded maybe $25 dollars to the yard-sale crowd. Every year I seem to come up with another sack full of films, and every year I dispose of my outdated media on eBay for some good profits.

You see, your trash truly is treasure to many others out there who are either looking for collections of items or just looking for an old VHS copy of *Saturday Night Fever*. Videos, magazines, books, unwanted CDs, and other media are excellent candidates for eBaying and are the sorts of items that each of us typically stockpiles year after year. If you're something of a pack rat (and if you don't think you are, take another look around the house), your items are usually worth a few dollars each to the millions of online bidders and buyers. Recall that I said I believe each of us is surrounded with at least $3,000 worth of goods at any time—my grocery bag of videos quickly contributed to that dollar amount. Therefore, when it's time to clean up the clutter around you, be sure to give the goods careful consideration of their eBay-worthiness before you sell for pennies or toss the stuff in the trash.

eBay TIP: Although this comes awfully close to dumpster diving, let your family and friends know that you'd like to rummage through their castoffs before they haul them off to the dump. Sure, some will ask, "Why? Do you think it's worth a lot of money?" Perhaps yes, perhaps no. If they press to know why you want to sift through their items yet they're not prone to list on eBay themselves, you can arrange to split the profits with them. This, after all, is the concept behind consignment selling on eBay, a topic we'll cover more fully in Chapter 18. In the meantime, let those around you know that you'd be interested in looking at the items that no longer interest them.

GARAGE SALES ARE BACK IN BUSINESS

During eBay's early days, garage sales were the target supply source for online auctioneers, their virtual auction skills still unknown to many. When eBay became better known and more folks were ready to try their hand at making fast cash, garage sellers opted to list online rather than take paltry coins for their items. Soon, all the really "good stuff" formerly found on the driveways of America was being held back. To some sellers, this meant the end of their eBay businesses, but times have changed yet again. Although eBay is clearly a household name, most one-time sellers realize they won't be pulling down an immediate fortune with just a weekend's worth of listings; there's money to be made but, with an increasing supply of all sorts of odds-and-ends items, it takes committed sellers to make those profits. For that reason, I've seen those fly-by-night sellers go back to the garage and begin offering up good stuff at garage sales once again, believing it's now too much work to sell on eBay. For us consistent sellers, that's great news because the goods are getting good once more. Therefore, if you had turned away from garage sales of late, look again; there are plenty of great bargains and good finds out there. Plus, now that eBay has been around for a decade (and still going strong), the castoffs that folks lug out to their driveways are the kinds of items that will appeal to the next generation of eager collectors.

Remember the key tenets of successful garage sale shopping (in case you've forgotten):

- Check your local newspaper or online classifieds for listings of upcoming garage sales and plot out a course that will allow you to hit as many as possible on a time- and fuel-efficient route.
- Remember that upscale neighborhoods often have nicer items, but you'll likely be paying a bit more than at sales in more modest neighborhoods.
- Neighborhoods with older houses (and older people) often are treasure troves for vintage goods that may have been stored away for 30, 40, or 50 years or more. If you're hunting for vintage items, homes in these long-established neighborhoods will often have the goods you seek.
- Be early! Some listings wave off "early birds," but be there at least 15 to 30 minutes ahead of time to swoop in for the best items.
- Being late can be advantageous, too. Visit sales at the end of their run and see if the homeowner is willing to allow you to take a boxful or clear a table for cut-rate prices, since the goods probably will wind up in the trash, otherwise.

If you've stayed away from the garage sales of late, believing their time of fruitfulness has come and gone, look again. There's some great stuff show-

Figure 16-1 Who says you can't find great items at garage sales? This highly desirable though sometimes overlooked "Auto Race" lunchbox from 1967 was a recently found buried gem at a local thrift outlet.

ing up these days, just the sort that can help fuel your eBay sales (see Figure 16-1).

OTHER SOURCES TO REMEMBER FOR GREAT SECONDHAND GOODS

With garage sales looking promising again, other secondhand outlets are showing signs of paying off for astute sellers. When eBay was all the rage back in 1999 and was host to some incredible prices being realized for thrift-type goods, most secondhand-store owners were actively scooping up everything that came their way in hopes of making some big bucks quick but many, dabblers that they were, found they simply couldn't pull down the fabled fortunes they'd heard of in the news and elsewhere. When they attempted to boost prices of their thrift goods, they saw a drop-off in the rate of in-store sales. The market has since corrected itself, and the secondhand outlets are once again prime for some great goods. While you were right to steer clear of secondhand stores during the "I'm gonna get rich on this stuff at eBay" era (and in relative Internet years, it *was* an era), here are the key spots to hit again, as they also seem to be paying off for the sharp seller.

Flea Markets, Thrift, and Consignment Shops

After many folks realized how much work is involved in actually *running* an eBay business, most peeled away when they failed to make buckets of money overnight. But, just as I previously mentioned, the acquisitive nature we each possess means more goods are finding their way into the secondhand venues. To that end, flea markets are booming again, as are thrift and consignment shops. The key to finding the best items at these venues is to find those venues

that are clearly off the beaten path. Big antique malls and such are usually heavily trafficked and may not yield the sorts of goods you're truly looking to invest in. Look for those lonely spots, dig through your area phone directories if need be, and go see what's sitting and waiting to be discovered. Again, the goods are flowing as the next generations are turning their attention to mementos of their past. Look sharp in out-of-the-way curio shops and you'll more than likely begin turning up great goods once again.

Estate Sales

While estate sales were long sought as the source of great and authentic "antiques" (items that are, by definition, at least 100 years old or more), the newest trend in collecting yesteryear's items are those from the Eames Era (that is, from the 1950s and 1960s). Again, it's a generational thing, and those folks who are looking for what they consider antiques aren't even familiar with items from 100 years ago. Rather, this is the crowd more familiar with *Leave It to Beaver*, *Father Knows Best*, and the flagship retro-sitcom, *Happy Days*. Most of today's collectors are from this more recent era and are eagerly snapping up items that they found in their parents' homes or that they saw on sets of the popular sitcom shows. At estate sales, these are the items you're more likely to find today at reasonable prices and generally in plentiful quantities, because they're now leading the antique (in its expanded definition) market.

When shopping estate sales, skip those that are open to dealers before the general public (unless you are a dealer, but expect you will pay higher prices in general). Success at unearthing the best items at estate sales is generally found when you scurry into the back corners of the home, the attic, or the basement while others crowd the living and family rooms. Scour the kitchens and bathrooms, too, as much of the kitchy stuff buyers want is often related to these service rooms in homes of yesterday.

GOVERNMENT AUCTIONS WANT YOU

With eBay and other online venues having commanded so much of the public consciousness of late, many sellers looking for great inventory, either to use in running their businesses or to use as inventory for their business, have forgotten about police and government auctions. Government agencies of all types, from the U.S. Treasury and U.S. Marshals Service to individual counties, continue to populate private government auction sites to dispose of all manner of equipment and property quickly. Although you can look in your local newspaper to track down the local auctions in your area (and you should), take a look online where seized, repossessed, or otherwise surplus goods are available every day of the year. Already, a growing population of individual buyers and small businesses have found online government auc-

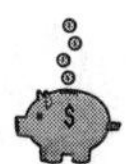

tions to be a great source of great items, new and used, that will keep the business running and the inventory flowing.

The best news today is that you no longer have to trek out to live auctions to collect up the excess or otherwise dispositioned goods available through government auction channels. Now, you can view the lots for sale from the comfort and convenience of your home computer screen. Begin with *www.GovLiquidation.com* and you'll find an incredible amount of goods for sale, some as previews of upcoming live auctions and others being offered for online bids.

GovLiquidation.com is a front-end clearing house (managed by Liquidity Services, LLC) that handles sales of goods for its stable of government clients (see Figure 16-2). From warehousing to sales to delivery logistics to customer service, Government Liquidation has made it easy for buyers (many of whom are online sellers seeking new inventory) to purchase surplus goods with the convenience of online shopping.

Bid4Assets Inc., another government-auction house, models its auction process after eBay's own, never taking actual ownership of the property it is disposing of. Every day there are thousands of items up for bid, from tax-

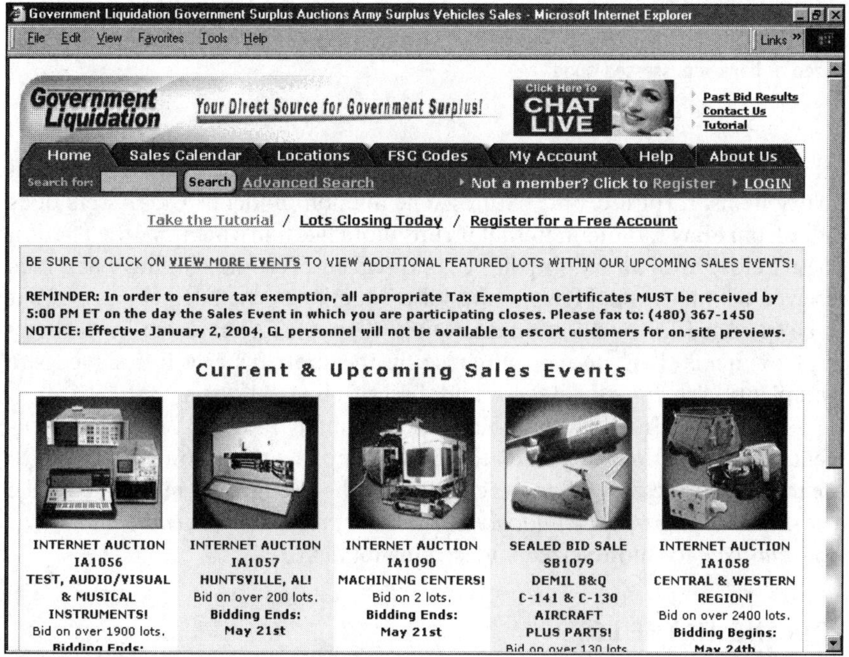

Figure 16-2 Visit *www.govliquidation.com* for a convenient way to shop government surplus auction goods.

Figure 16-3 Visit *www.bid4assets.com* to find even more government surplus or police-seized or bank-repossessed goods.

defaulted real estate to seized personal property like jewelry, collectibles, and luxury items, furniture, and fixtures. The auction model at Bid4Assets does differ from eBay's, though, in that it runs more like a live auction: the auction doesn't close until all bidding has ceased (called overtime bidding when bids received within the final few minutes of an auction's scheduled close causes it to be extended for an additional amount of time). The site also hosts many buy-now items that you can purchase on the spot. It's a well designed site with plenty of help, information, and, best of all, great items.

Search the Internet and you'll discover many more police and government surplus auction sites ready to serve you up great deals on good items to use in your business or sell to others. Besides the two already mentioned, take a visit to *www.governmentauctions.org*, *www.policeauctions.com*, and *www.ESurplus.com* for more seized and surplus-lot deals.

LOOKING TO THE LOTS

When you think of buying surplus goods as at the government auctions, you're thinking about buying items in quantity or lots. Many sellers keep

themselves happily stocked up in inventory by buying this way. And as I've shown you a few sites where you can readily find surplus lots, let me now lead you back to eBay itself and its ever-expanding Wholesale Lots area (see Figure 16-4).

Believe it or not, many long-time eBay sellers either overlook this area or simply don't know it exists on the very site where they're already doing business. When you visit the major category groups on eBay (such as *Books*, *Camera & Photo*, or *Consumer Electronics*, for example) look under the subcategories and most often you'll find a link to *Wholesale* or *Bulk* lots for the goods you're browsing. Savvy sellers have found that these wholesale or bulk lots harbor some excellent inventory in which to invest. Much of it is goods being offered from large companies eager to offload their surplus items (and that can make for good profit-bearing inventory if you remarket it properly) but, more compelling, there are many bulk listings being offered by individuals who have large collections or ensembles of items that they are eager to sell in one fell swoop instead of as individual listings. Look closely at the offerings, do a bit of piece-by-piece research and sales projection, and you'll find there's some great inventory just waiting to be scooped up.

Figure 16-4 Visit eBay's category pages to find the Wholesale Lots listings for excellent sources of inventory.

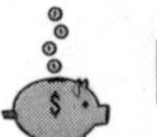

GETTING ON THE INSIDE TRACK AT OUTLET STORES

Finally, let's take a look at those now-pervasive "outlet stores," the stripped-down satellite versions of retail destinations for Nike, Gap, Sharper Image, and Bombay Home Furnishings. Outlet store malls became all the rage in the late 1990s and still seem to draw decent traffic on the premise that the goods for sale are at surplus or closeout prices. Sadly, this is not true. Many of the outlet store malls are merely hybrid stores that give you the feeling you've been allowed to root through the warehouse of goods at wholesale pricing, but actually you're paying much too close to retail price. There is, however, a way to find true outlet stores and great deals on potential inventory for your eBay business.

In my personal journeys, information I've gotten from several different folks and that I have found on my own has made it clear that real outlet buying entails shopping only where goods have been discounted below prices found in retail or catalog offerings. The goods being offered in these true outlet settings are of the following types: outlet stock, overstock, seconds, refurbished goods, and returns. With that, it all becomes suddenly clearer, doesn't it? Outlet stores should be in the business to sell goods that can't be sold in normal retail channels, thereby assuring discounted prices.

So what prices can you expect to find, and how will you know if you've found a true outlet? For starters, we all understand that it begins with the retail price that the manufacturer suggests and which retail stores will either sell at or discount slightly; this isn't the sort of price that allows you reasonable investment or profit.

When shopping outlet stores, you can usually expect to find outlet prices, which are discounted slightly more than retail prices, often 10 percent, and sometimes up to 50 percent, off retail. While you might find some good deals here and there, these prices usually aren't low enough to help keep your resell enterprise profitable.

The gold in the true outlet market is those items offered at "discount" or "closeout" prices. For goods that are severely overstocked or deemed surplus for whatever reason, you might find deep, deep discounts of up to 80 or 90 percent off retail. Now, before you buy up an entire stock of items because you found an honest-to-goodness discount price, be sure you can sell the items online. This means you'll need to be persistent with your research and, therefore, steer toward items that you've seen do well on eBay and elsewhere online. Of course, this works as a sort of catch-22, because when you stumble across such goods, you're often in the predicament of buying the items on the spot or else risk them not being available if you decide to return later. It's not uncommon, therefore, to see folks toting laptops with wireless Internet connections (either on their person or in their vehicles close by). On-the-spot

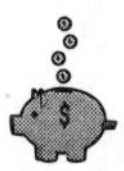

connectivity allows you to quickly research an item that you think may have potential, verifying if you think you can sell it at a reasonable profit.

And, having an on-the-spot mentality when considering new sources of inventory will keep you keen and nimble in recognizing potentially profitable goods and the out-of-the-way (sometimes *unusual*) new places from which you'll stock your inventory. Always keep your eyes and your mind open to new sources for goods to sell and you'll stand the best chance of growing and shifting your business to meet the demands of the marketplace.

17

Stockless Inventory: The Current State of Drop Shipping

Perhaps one of the most intriguing methods of selling items online is to sell those that you don't actually have. What? Although it sound like an utter scam, many online sellers are doing phenomenal business by offering items they don't actually inventory or ship—someone else manages that for them—and it's perfectly legitimate and satisfactory to buyers.

Drop shipping is enjoying a renewed boom thanks to the proliferation of e-commerce, marrying manufacturers or wholesalers with retailers ready to sell the products. Not relegated to just online sellers, drop shipping is also being embraced by brick-and-mortar business owners who are likewise eager to expand their product catalogs in serving the wants and needs of their customers. This chapter will explain how drop shipping works, how it can be managed successfully, and how you can reap the rewards of offering vast inventories of goods without spending a dime on product *until you've sold it*. This is no come-on; this is a real opportunity.

UNDERSTANDING VIRTUAL INVENTORIES

You'll hear it called by many different names: stockless inventory, drop-ship warehousing, or virtual order fulfillment. Whatever the name, the concept is simple: rather than investing in and storing inventory themselves, retailers (sellers) pass customer orders directly to a manufacturer or wholesaler who ships the products directly to the customer with the retailer's name or label on the package. When you establish this sort of supply chain, you present the item for bid or sale, you forward the buyer's address to the manufacturer or wholesaler, they drop ship directly to your buyer, and the whole time you pro-

vide the appearance of having fulfilled the order yourself. This is virtual order fulfillment.

The concept here is really nothing new, though. Drop shipping has been taking place for decades, formerly employed by catalogers, who traditionally publish listings of a large variety of goods for mail order. When customer orders are received, many are forwarded direct to the manufacturer, wholesaler, or other such order fulfillment point for processing and shipment. All along the way, the end customer was none the wiser and the cataloger (or "retailer") was never burdened with the cost of acquiring, warehousing, and shipping the goods.

PROS AND CONS OF DROP SHIPPING

Immediately, you'll be thinking, "what a terrific idea, and it's so easy!" Well, yes and no. Definitely, drop shipping is an excellent method of retailing and order fulfillment and seems tailor-made for online merchandising. While it has definite benefits that every online businessperson should harness and exploit, it does have a few "gotchas" that you'll need to understand before jumping headlong into the wide world of virtual sales.

First, let's consider the exciting benefits of virtual-supply-chain management:

- *Low to No Investment in Up-Front Inventory.* As you'll soon learn, legitimate drop shippers will not require you to purchase the items they ship until *after* you've sold them. This nullifies the risk of investing in inventory that might not sell.
- *Low to No Investment in Order-Fulfillment Processing or Capacity.* If you decide to sell medium- to large-size goods, you won't be bothered with the headaches of storing an inventory of gargantuan goods, nor will you need to worry about shipping such large items. The drop shipper will manage this for you (and your customers).
- *Ability to Offer Wider Product Selection.* If you're not hampered by inventory investment and management, you can easily increase the quantity and diversity of your product offerings without strain on your business's capital. You can easily shed items that don't sell while adding newer items that could become hot with your customers.
- *Elimination of "Shipping-in" Costs.* Immediately, you can reduce the overall shipping costs to your business, as you'll now be able to avoid paying to have goods shipped to you for warehousing; the drop shipper holds the goods until you have a buyer.
- *Potentially Lower Wholesale Costs Due to Economies of Scale.* Since most manufacturers and wholesalers serve multiple retailer relationships, they are typically dealing in sale and movement of larger

quantities of goods beyond just what you're selling. When the supplier can pool this aggregate demand, handling and warehousing costs typically decline.

- *The Often Unseen Benefit.* When you can free yourself from order-fulfillment duties, you can redirect that time and effort to more bottom-line matters, such as acquiring more customers and presenting more products in more compelling ways.

Already you must be itching to jump into the virtual fulfillment dream but, before you do, be sure you understand the flip side of this virtual treasure trove:

- *Loss of Profit.* This first one hits you right in the bottom line, and while not completely devastating, understand that you'll be paying between $2 and $4 per shipment as fee to cover the drop-shipping arrangement. The manufacturers and wholesalers are collecting a fee to make this all worth their while, and certainly this fee is often more desirable than an up-front inventory investment. Still, understand that the drop-shipping fee does come out of your profit.
- *Loss of Fulfillment Control.* This is perhaps the most frightening aspect of drop shipping: what if the customer receives a damaged item or doesn't receive the item at all? The customers won't be chasing down a drop shipper for an explanation (and perhaps a pound of flesh), they'll be chasing *you*, the seller. If something goes awry with the drop-ship fulfillment, it's *your* online reputation that will bear the brunt of a dissatisfied customer. (Don't worry, though, as I'll provide information on how to mitigate and minimize this risk a bit later in this chapter.)
- *Loss of Customer Information Control.* To some retailers, customer information is the most critical information to manage and control. As a seller, you'll learn about your customers, their buying habits, their likes and dislikes. As a savvy marketer, you keep this information closely guarded to prevent competitors from luring your loyal customers away. In a drop-ship situation, the drop shipper also has full access to this customer-purchase history, and some sellers fear they could be squeezed out of the relationship as an unnecessary "middleman" should the drop shipper ever decide to deal with the customer directly. Fortunately, most drop shippers are in the order-fulfillment business because they elected not to enter into marketing and merchandising.

While you can see that the pros outweigh the cons in this analysis, recognize that drop shipping will require hands-on management by you to ensure

that all goes well and that the fulfillment transaction remains transparent and satisfactory to your customers. The next logical question, then, becomes, Where do you find drop shippers?

eBay TIP: If you want to learn more about all aspects drop shipping's place in the order-fulfillment cycle, check out author Nicholas T. Scheel's book, *Drop Shipping as a Marketing Function* (1990, Quorum Books). Scheel is also founder and editor of the *Drop Shipping News* which has an online presence at *www.drop-shipping-news.com* (see Figure 17-1).

FINDING RELIABLE DROP SHIPPERS

As noted, the biggest risk you accept when you decide to include drop shipping in your business model is that of answering for the mistakes and mishaps

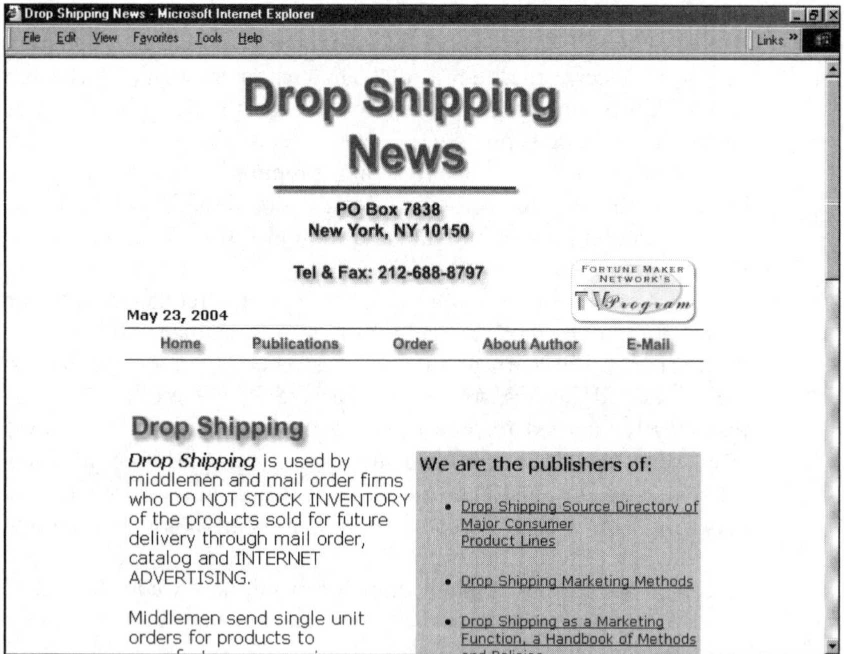

Figure 17-1 Visit *www.drop-shipping-news.com* to learn more about the methods and mechanics of drop shipping.

of a drop shipper. Although things will sometimes go amiss in even the best of retailer/drop shipper relationships, the key to avoiding most problems is to establish a partnership with a reliable source of supply at the outset. So where can you begin looking?

For starters, let me warn you that drop shipping has been afflicted with its own brand of scam: those who falsely present themselves as drop-ship sources or offer listings of drop shippers. Let's look at these two situations separately.

Drop-Shipping Charlatans

If you've done any surfing online regarding drop shippers, you likely found thousands of hits on your search, leading you in one of two directions: believing there are plenty of drop-ship sources available to help you or there are so many you don't know where to turn or whom to believe. If you thought the latter, good for you; there are thousands of posers pretending to be drop shippers and who promise to ship thousands of items for you, but it's not true. Any day on the Internet you can encounter plenty of cybercharlatans who are pretending to be drop shippers, promising tempting goods that you'll sell and they'll ship; all you pay is a setup fee. Look out! These are *not* legitimate drop shippers but, rather, middlemen who collect fees from you and merely forward your customer orders to the *actual* drop shipper. They're cutting into your profit by pretending to be the actual source of supply (which they're not).

The truth is, a legitimate drop shipper should *never* charge you an account activation or setup fee of any sort; they make their money when you *sell* the product, plus the drop-shipping fee. That's it. Anyone with a spiffy Web site or dazzling mailer is likely trying to step in between you and a real drop shipper, skimming your profits away in the process.

Lists of Drop Shippers: Let the Buyer Beware

Also be on the lookout for a person or fictitious business offering "the ultimate drop-shipping list in the world, ever!" Whatever the catchy come-on, many more folks out there are buying and copying and selling and reselling the same worn-out lists of drop shippers or wholesalers (have some of them gone out of business by now?), promising to have the critical contact information that will help you rocket your business to new heights. Recall those "work at home" scams where all you need do is stuff envelopes and send direct-marketing literature to a prepared list of ready customers. The customer list was usually horribly out of date or flat out phony, yet you paid a one-time set up fee of who knows what. You know what? The person who sold the list to you was the only one making money. The same is going on today under the guise of "ultimate drop-ship listing." Get it?

Finding the Real Deal in Drop Shippers

Well, that's all very enlightening but how, then, does a person find a *real* directory to *real* drop shippers? Have faith, because there is a legitimate path to follow: I've been there, walked it, and even interviewed the founders of these companies. My advice to you is to visit Worldwide Brands, Inc., online at *www.worldwidebrands.com*, and get ready to grow your business (see Figure 17-2).

I've had the good fortune to meet up with founder Chris Malta and his business partner, Robin Cowie, and have found them and their team to be committed to offering the most comprehensive and reliable directory to drop shippers available anywhere. They have made it their business to carefully select, screen, and recommend only the best drop-ship sources around while also going to great lengths to identify and disable scammers who attempt to repurpose the Worldwide Brands directory as a means to add some credibility to an otherwise illicit offering of information.

Most refreshing about the approach from Malta and Cowie is their generosity in providing real information about the entire drop-shipping process,

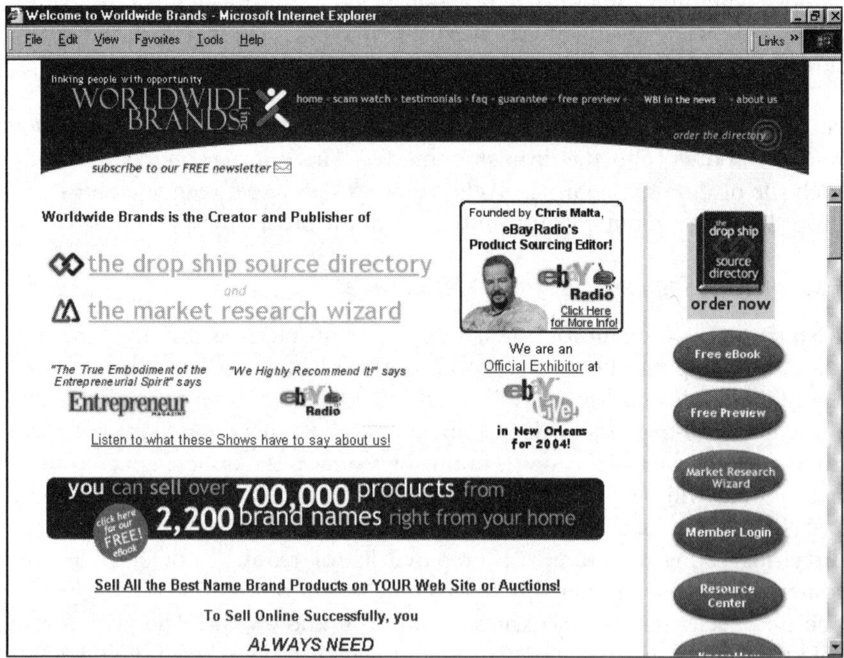

Figure 17-2 Visit *www.worldwidebrands.com* to access the best and most reliable listing of legitimate drop-ship suppliers available.

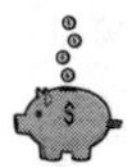

what to expect and what to look out for. They're very clear that drop shipping isn't any sort of panacea for real work; they're clear that you can't get rich sitting on your sofa clicking a TV remote while dollars magically roll in to your bank account. Drop shipping, like any other form of online selling I've been discussing in this book, requires real work but, if managed properly, it *will* pay real dividends.

So while investigating the scam-laden charges that some will try to levy on the unsuspecting newcomer, Malta and Cowie are very clear about the fees you should expect to pay when entering into a drop-ship relationship. Namely, that the drop-shipping fee I mentioned earlier is a real fee that you'll need to pay. Essentially, the fee (which I mentioned can run from $2 to $4 per customer shipment) covers the handling and fulfillment of the customer orders you forward. That, coupled with the carrier's cost of delivering the item, combines to form the shipping-and-handling fees you've heard about all these years. But, again, there should be no account-setup fees or other such surcharges.

eBay TIP: If you're concerned about that drop-shipping fee, you do have the option of passing that cost along to your customer. You can either offer an item for a retail price plus a shipping-and-handling fee that would cover the carrier's costs (buyers on eBay already expect to pay that) and the drop-ship fee. If you prefer, you can roll the drop-ship fee into the retail price of the item, therefore avoiding the whole What are you charging me for handling? debate.

KEYS TO MANAGING VIRTUAL ORDER FULFILLMENT

I previously mentioned the risks inherent in adopting a drop-ship source of supply for your online sales. Every opportunity has some sort of risk involved, but there are ways to control the potential troubles associated with drop shipping to make sure your customers are always satisfied and your business is always highly regarded.

Manage Your Inventory

But this makes no sense at all: manage inventory in a drop-ship relationship? Well, imagine the following scenario. The auction has just closed or a buy-it-now listing was just purchased, and your supplier utters the nightmarish words "out of stock." You don't physically possess the item, but it's your responsibility to ensure that the supplier has it ready to ship to your waiting customer.

Recall that the sources who will drop-ship goods to your customers are

also managing shipments to other retailers' customers. It's not uncommon that a supplier can become temporarily out of stock, especially if the item is extremely popular. Your customer, however, isn't interested in your order-fulfillment woes; that customer wants whatever was just paid for, and quick. What will you do? Here are a few suggestions to avoid those times when your supplier's shelves may have gone bare for the items you're actively selling online:

- Keep a few units on hand yourself. Though this flies in the face of the whole "stockless inventory" concept, if you have items that are particularly popular or upon which you base the core identity of your business, it's wise to have one, two, or three such items yourself to be used to fill a customer order if the supplier runs out.
- Identify backup sources who might be able to fulfill orders when your primary source is in a stockout situation. The principles of supply-chain management have long expounded the need to have multiple sources of supply, lest you become reliant on a single source (anyone remember the major shortages of computer chips in the 1990s, when the key source for chip epoxy experienced a factory mishap?). Though you'll likely lean to dealing primarily with one supplier over another—for reasons of pricing, reliability, or whatever—try to identify a backup source to avoid delivery disruption to your customers.
- Inquire whether you can reserve quantities of an item, to be warehoused at the drop-shipper's location. This will require that you pay for the goods in advance but, again, if the item's a good seller, you may want to maintain a store of goods that can only be used in fulfilling orders to *your* customers and that you could use and monitor as a safety stock.
- Consider suspending future sales of the item until you're assured inventory is once again plentiful enough to fulfill customer orders (otherwise, you truly are selling goods you can't deliver).

Manage Your Drop Shipper

Coming from a professional background that includes corporate procurement principles, I've learned that a well-managed supplier is one that believes and behaves as if you're in a type of business partnership. It's a symbiotic existence, really: the supplier needs retailers to help sell goods; the retailer needs suppliers to produce and provide goods to sell. Neither can exist without the other unless each wishes to assume the activities of the other (the manufacturer sells its own goods; the retailer manufactures its own goods). That, of

course, would be costly and inefficient. Therefore, establishing and nurturing a good working relationship with a drop shipper is essential if you're to succeed in selling and managing a virtual inventory. To that end, consider these key points in drop-ship partnering:

- Begin with a written contract, Memorandum of Understanding, or other such agreement that details what you can expect from the drop shipper and what is expected of you in return. Specify product specifications, that you require a stable source of supply, guaranteed pricing (at least for a fixed period of time), and expectation of order turnaround (fulfillment) time.
- Insist that no additional flyers, promotion slips, or other such literature be included in shipments to your customers other than what you might have requested or supplied yourself. Remember, you want to give the appearance the order came from you or your business, not a third party.
- Establish and update sales forecasts to your drop shippers so they can, in turn, adjust their stocking levels so product will be available to ship whenever needed. If you plan to introduce a new item that the drop shipper supplies, make that known to the drop shipper before you launch a number of listings. If your sales forecast then goes up or goes down, be sure to communicate that as quickly as possible to help the drop shipper adjust their internal operations appropriately. This is that all-important aspect of partnering by which you can garner from a drop shipper: equal consideration of your needs as they see how you're considering theirs.
- Define packing and shipping instructions to your drop shippers. Work closely with them to understand how they'll pack and ship an item (order it yourself first!) to be sure that what they ship—that which will bear your business's name—will be representative of the reputation you wish to promote.
- Communicate, communicate, communicate. When dealing with drop shippers, you'll likely work with a representative who will service your account, working with you to ensure your orders are shipped as expected. If there are any troubles or potential inventory shortfalls, you'll want to communicate regularly with your representative to try to identify and head off such situations before they have an impact on you or your customers. And, finally, let your representative know you're interested in learning about any other new products or pricing opportunities that would match the kind of business you're doing. Keep in close contact with your drop-ship representative and your business will likely come out much further ahead as a result.

Manage the Customer

Let's not forget the most important player in your business's supply chain: the customer. Not really a part of the chain itself but, rather, the recipient of its function, the customer needs to be managed well (without realizing he or she is being managed) in order for your business to flourish. Although drop shipping might be new to you, chances are your customers have been recipients of drop-ship supplied goods for decades (they just didn't know it). Your job, then, is to maintain that level of invisibility by offering reliable goods from reliable drop shippers and doing your work up front to manage the supply chain so the customer will remain none the wiser. One key aspect of drop-ship supply that you might need to communicate to your customers regards those who may purchase multiple goods that may be shipped in separate boxes from separate sources of fulfillment. If your customers will be receiving a separate shipment for a drop-shipped item, be sure to let them know, especially if the item will take longer to arrive than others they may have ordered (those that either you yourself shipped or were managed by other sources of supply, drop-ship or otherwise). Communication is generally the glue that binds all good retailing relationships together, supplier-to-retailer or retailer-to-customer, and it's something you'll want to do well if you wish to avoid fulfillment headaches while simultaneously instilling customer loyalty.

WHAT WILL YOU DROP SHIP?

Ultimately, it always comes back to the same question: What should I sell? Unfortunately, this is a question that can't be answered by means of supply process; you need to return to your business plan and marketing approach to help you decide which products you should offer as you seek to grow your business. However, drop shipping is an excellent solution to the problem of how to acquire costly or otherwise difficult-to-manage inventory items. If you've dreamed of going into the restaurant-supply business, assembling a stable of reliable drop shippers can allow you to do that very thing without having to beg for a mammoth start-up loan. More to the point, many brick-and-mortar business owners are learning that drop shipping can help them quickly increase their product offerings because they can selectively sell drop-shipped goods that would be too costly or too cumbersome to either inventory locally or expect a customer to transport themselves; the drop shipper can solve both the retailer's and the buyer's problem of how to get the thing to its final destination.

eBay TIP: Though it's very tempting to plunge into drop shipping head first, it's best to utilize just a few drop-ship sources initially as you venture into the realm of stockless inventory. Take

what many call the "hybrid inventory" approach by offering items you actively inventory along with those that you'll have drop shipped. In this manner, you can gradually experiment with virtual fulfillment while still maintaining a hands-on understanding of inventory and shipping practices as this virtual economy continues to grow and develop. As your business grows, you may find the need (read: opportunity) to establish employees who can focus solely on managing your drop-ship relationships and sourcing activities as you continue to develop new ways to market and promote your business.

18

Consign It

Now consider this situation: you're a seller who's looking for more goods to sell, determined to never run out of goods to auction or offer at fixed prices. You soon meet up with another person who has tons of great items to sell but just doesn't have the inclination, the time, or the motivation to list and sell the goods. The two of you should meet, and soon. The fact is, for every seller who's perpetually on the prowl for more inventory to offer, there are as many would-be (but, for whatever reason, won't-be) sellers who have gobs of stuff but just don't want to get involved in the whole online selling revolution. These folks would *love* to turn their trash into treasure, hearing how so many others have already done so, but they'd prefer it if maybe someone else would manage that for them, offering a cut of the earnings for the trouble. So comes the opportunity of eBay consignment.

WHY CONSIGN?

Well, for the situation just put forth, there are plenty of folks who have items to sell but either don't believe they can successfully manage the task (why, I don't know, but that's fine) or those who just don't have the time to do so. The trick is for sellers like you to find these people who may be sitting on a gold mine of goods and step forward to help them move their inventory while you earn a portion of the profits to put into your own bank account.

Computer technician and software specialist Mark Muñoz was doing well on eBay until he realized he was fast running out of his own castoffs to offer up. Rather than let his eBay account go idle and to supplement the supply of items he was picking up right and left at garage sales and flea markets, he decided to see if he could help others sell their items, have them do the shipping themselves (a drop ship of sorts) while earning a commission for his services along the way.

"I visited this great little thrift and antique shop, a real out of the way place," Munoz shared with me, "and the elderly woman running it said she knows about eBay but doesn't think she knows enough about computers to use it. I told her I could help her sell a bunch of her stuff if she wanted, and she couldn't start loading up boxes fast enough. Since meeting her, I've helped her make good money on the stuff that was just sitting around in her store. She's happy with the fact I'm selling more stuff for her, and I'm happy with the commissions I'm earning."

Muñoz is a grassroots example of the new industry that's springing up as a result of eBay, in the form of professionals who have found they can help others sell their goods on eBay—those items that are likely a bit too valuable to discard or sell for pennies on the dollar at a garage sale but that don't seem to be valuable enough to cart to a brick-and-mortar consignment shop. Muñoz and thousands of others just like him have stepped forward to fill the void while starting up a new venture for themselves. Much like the drop-shipping arrangement, Muñoz isn't required to invest in inventory, storing items, or shipping either. "With that first client, we agreed that she would store the goods and I would photograph and manage the eBay activity for her." These are among the services Muñoz offers to consignment clients:

- Reviewing and appraising of items to be offered (weeding out the items that either won't sell or perhaps won't earn enough to be worthwhile, also scouring clients' stores, garages, and other places for hidden treasures that could return big profits)
- Photographing and detailing items to be listed
- Launching auctions or Buy-It-Now listings, depending upon a client's wants and the market potential for the items
- Monitoring the listing and fielding all inquiries from potential buyers
- Collecting payment and delivering agreed-upon profit split to the client
- Providing ongoing consulting and assessment of future listings

Muñoz reports that his first client has already led him to others and he sees no end in sight to the potential to help more and more clients sell their goods. He invites others to contact him via e-mail at *BIDZ4ME@hotmail.com.* "For my clients, the headache to them was how to manage the eBay listing and payment collection. For me, the headache was storing and shipping the items. With this arrangement, everyone avoids the headaches and we each get what we want: sales and profit." Sounds like a match made in Heaven.

MORE TO CONSIDER ABOUT BECOMING A CONSIGNOR

While it sounds great to enlist the wares of those who are either time-crunched or eBay-phobic, and begin selling their goods for a well-earned commission, there are a few things you'll need to carefully consider and establish much the same as you established your sales policy when selling your own goods. Venturing into consignment selling requires you and your clients to be very clear about what services you'll offer, what will be expected of your clients, and at what rate of compensation you'll be working. Here are some consignment-policy terms to establish, communicate, and operate by.

Terms of Service

First and foremost, you'll need to determine exactly what services you intend to offer when acting as consignor of other people's goods. Really, this is up to you and how you wish to operate your consignment enterprise. So, if you're considering becoming a consignor, consider these aspects of service you may or may not provide:

- *Type of Items You'll List and Manage.* Will you offer to assess and sell all manner of items or will you narrow your focus to a certain type of goods? Consider your level of expertise for goods (that require either specified knowledge and/or in-depth research, the value of goods you're willing to manage (will you be responsible for high-value goods like diamond rings, vehicles, property, or artwork?), and the size and weight of items you'll manage. All of this needs to be clearly stated before you consider taking on other people's goods.

eBay TIP: Yes, operating as a consignor is a new business direction you can elect to take in unleashing the profit potential of eBay. As you read through this chapter, you'll see that consignment offers some interesting new twists to running an eBay business, and you may find that this approach could resolve some of your potential concerns regarding inventory acquisition and other aspects of selling and shipping goods via eBay.

- *Item Pick-Up and Storage.* Some consignors find they can attract more clients if they offer to pick up items from the client and store those goods during the run of an eBay listing. They also find it easier to write descriptions and answer bidder and buyer questions if the item is readily at hand. If you choose to offer this service, be clear in establishing the radius of area you'll travel to for pick-up, be sure

that you'll have appropriate storage facilities (don't forget about any special environment conditions you might need to maintain), and be certain you have an understanding of how you will be liable for items while they're in your possession.

- *Item Shipment.* If you take on the responsibility of shipping the goods, you'll likely attract that many more clients, ones who'd rather not bother. Of course, this can become a time-intensive effort and one you'll need to plan for, especially when servicing several clients simultaneously. If you determine that the item owner will be responsible for shipping the goods, make sure you stipulate proper packing and shipping procedures because, if an item arrives damaged or doesn't arrive at all, it will be *your* eBay ID that could receive a negative feedback comment.
- *Payment Schedule.* Although I'll talk about consignment fees in a moment, be sure to consider up front *how* and *when* you'll want to receive your payment for services rendered. Many consignors manage payment receipt from the eventual buyers and then pay the original owner of the goods the profit less consignment fees, so be clear about when *you'll* remit those payments.
- *Disposition of Unsold Goods.* As good as many consignors are at what they do, some items simply do not sell. Be sure you have an agreed-upon policy regarding what will be done with items that don't sell: relisting them, returning them to the owner (or having them pick them up from you) if you've been storing them, donating them to a charity, or discarding them. If there are any costs associated with the agreed-upon disposition method, be sure to get compensated for that.

Consignment Fees

So how much should you charge for consigning goods on eBay? That's an excellent question and there's no definitive answer; it's whatever you decide, based on your earnings goals and the level of service you'll provide. Generally speaking, consignors require item owners to pay the following:

- *All eBay Listing Fees.* Many consignors have designed listing types or styles that range from basic listings to those with more content, including listing upgrades and HTML design.
- *Final Value Fee.* Consignors likewise require item owners to bear the cost of eBay's commission assessed on the final price at the end of the listing.
- *Special Handling or Packing Fees.* If the item requires special pack-

ing, any costs above and beyond what can be covered in free carrier supplies will be covered by the item owner.

Now, in order to effectively attract clients, you'll probably want to provide a nice ensemble of services that will convince them you're the consignor who can get the best prices for the goods. To that end, before establishing your overall consignment fee beyond the eBay and possible special handling fees, consider offering the following services, and determine what these services will cost *you* in managing listings:

- *Item research and assessment.* If you're not an expert on an item a customer wants you to sell, and special research is required, you may want to factor that in.
- *Setting of Appropriate Listing Category and Opening Bid Price.* Some item owners need counseling here, and consignors can offer up their expertise to help the item succeed in gaining bids and a final price.
- *Item Photography.* How many photos will you take of the item? Your base fee could cover the cost of taking and hosting (where you'll store the item during the listing's run) a single photo, with additional photos incurring additional fees.
- *Competent and Compelling Item Descriptions.* Be sure you can offer great descriptions that will convince potential bidders and buyers that this is the item for them. Show your clients how you intend to market their item for maximum price potential.
- *Bidder and Buyer Correspondence.* You're managing the listing, so you'll also want to manage any inquiries.
- *International Buyer Support.* If you're going to offer to list items for worldwide purchase and delivery, be sure to consider the additional steps required and factor that into your commission fee.
- *Payment Collection.* If payment incurs fees (such as PayPal processing), you'll need to consider this in your base price.
- *Payment Disbursement to the Item Owner.* Establish the payment schedule so the item owner knows when their payment will be received.

eBay TIP: You can see that the business of consignment requires that many stipulations and terms be stated up front and agreed upon between yourself and your clients. For this reason, I strongly urge you to write all of this up in a contract or operating agreement before you engage in listing any goods for any clients. It can be a printed or electronic document that will be signed or otherwise accepted by both parties.

If you can have all the terms and understandings hammered out up front, you'll spare yourself any miscommunications or heartaches down the road.

As I said, establishing consignment fees is not an exact science and you'll need to decide for yourself how much you should charge for your services and eBay expertise. For this reason, research other consignors out there (visit eBay's Trading Assistant discussion board within the site Community area to see who's doing what) to help you decide on a fair and competitive fee and service schedule. Generally, consignors collect fees in the following manner:

- All eBay and other listing-related fees reimbursed
- A flat-rate fee charged for each item to cover the services provided (anywhere from $3.00 to $10.00 per item seems to be the norm), assessed even if the item does not sell
- A portion of the final selling price, usually between 20 and 40 percent, often dependent on the item's final selling price

Remember, you're now competing with other consignors, so you'll need to try to establish a competitive pricing structure that will attract clients but properly compensate you for the services and expertise you provide.

Will You Generalize or Specialize?

I hinted at this one in the previous chapter, and the same holds true for selling on consignment: you'll need to decide if you'll serve a "niche" category of goods (perhaps items you've developed expertise in yourself) or if you'll attempt to manage goods of all types. There are pros and cons to each approach, depending on the kinds of items you'll be managing. Consider the client base you hope to attract and the amount of fee you can expect to receive from the items you'll manage. If you look to sell high-end items (such as art, jewelry, antiques, and the like) and you have a proven expertise in these goods, you can likely earn good prices for your clients and good commissions for yourself. If your track record in selling such goods is impressive, you can market yourself as a specialized consignor and set your consignment service fees accordingly.

If you decide to generalize, you'll need to be prepared to manage all manner of goods (taking into consideration any specific items you decide *you* won't manage due to size, weight, or whatever) and be ready to learn quickly about the categories of items clients may bring to you. Most important here is that you'll need to be prepared to appropriately set clients' expectations about the potential prices they can expect to earn for their items. Sometimes it's difficult to let someone know their treasure is actually trash but, conversely, you stand a better chance of uncovering some real finds when you elect to represent a general assortment of goods.

Managing Your Consignment Account

Lastly, consider how you'll manage *your* activity and reputation as you embark on becoming a consignor of goods. Remember that, although the items you sell aren't yours, you *are* assuming all responsibility for their representation, accurate description, and successful transaction when you decide to manage them on consignment. To that end, some longtime eBay sellers have found it beneficial to create a unique consignment ID on eBay—in other words, registering under a new seller name with a new e-mail address and possibly credit card or bank account—to specifically manage consignment activity, while maintaining a previous account to use for personal business, buying or selling. This is allowed on eBay and fully within their rules, provided the new account is managed within eBay's normal user-agreement stipulations.

eBAY STEPS FORWARD TO HELP CONSIGNORS AND CONSIGNEES

If you're concerned about whether you can attract consignees on your own, look no further than eBay itself for a way to let it be known to millions of item owners that you're ready and able to sell their goods for them. In March 2002, eBay launched its Trading Assistants Program to help bring together experienced sellers and those item owners who either felt inexperienced or too time-constrained to manage selling activities on their own. The Trading Assistants Program allows item owners to search for experienced sellers by geographic location (utilizing ZIP codes) and allows registered users to connect and establish consignment relationships (see Figure 18-1).

That's the extent of eBay's involvement, though. Similar to its hands-off involvement in post-sale transacting, eBay likewise does not get involved in the consignment practices and agreements of its community members; individuals are free to negotiate and manage their business outside of eBay's monitoring. Of course, those who will be identified as trading assistants must qualify in the following manner:

- They must have sold at least four items in the past 30 days when requesting trading-assistant recognition.
- They must have a feedback rating of 50 or higher with at least 97 percent of overall feedback received being positive.
- They must have an account in good standing on eBay.

There are no special fees levied by eBay on trading assistants at this time so, in essence, it's a free service to give will-be consignors the ability to advertise their services and attract clients within eBay's vast community.

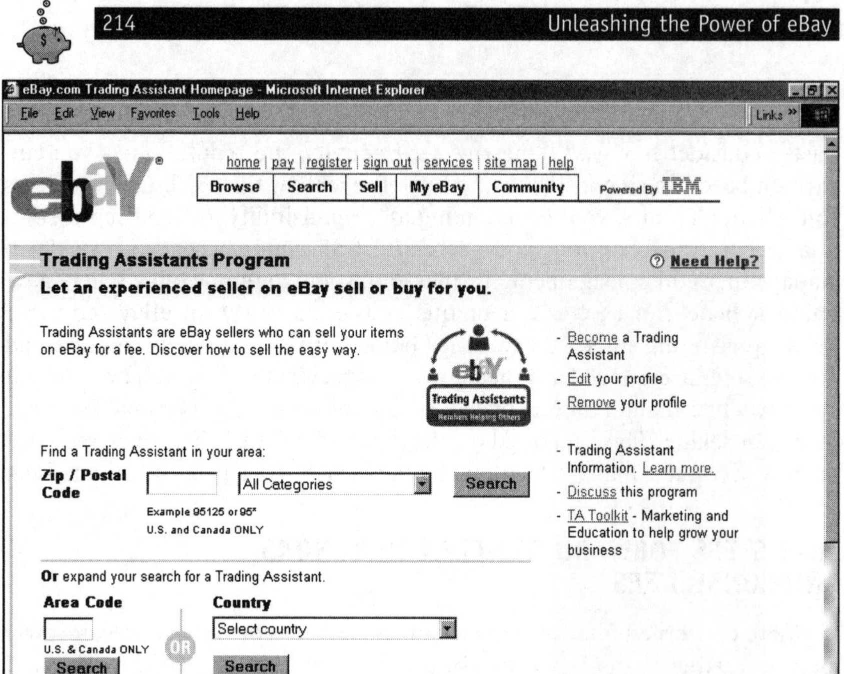

Figure 18-1 eBay's Trading Assistants Program helps item owners find experienced sellers to get top prices for goods.

INTRODUCING THE NEW INDUSTRY OF AUCTION DROP-OFF STORES

Just when you thought every market opportunity had been appropriately tapped within the online auction realm, a new industry is quickly emerging to take consignment to new heights. Auction "drop-off" stores are quickly popping up around the nation, offering a physical repository where item owners can literally drop off the goods they'd like auctioned, turning over the selling and transaction management tasks to a team of qualified auction handlers. In essence, it's the same concept as dropping off goods for donation, but there's a team of people on hand clients can talk to and who can help clients determine how auction-worthy their goods are. Clients then leave the matter to the drop-off site experts and await news of the profits earned.

Credit tireless entrepreneur Randy Adams for creating this new industry with the opening of the flagship auction drop-off store, appropriately named AuctionDrop (see Figure 18-2). Originally tasked with cleaning out his own garage of stuff, Adams got the idea that there must be others who would love to have their personal treasures or castoffs paraded in front of the

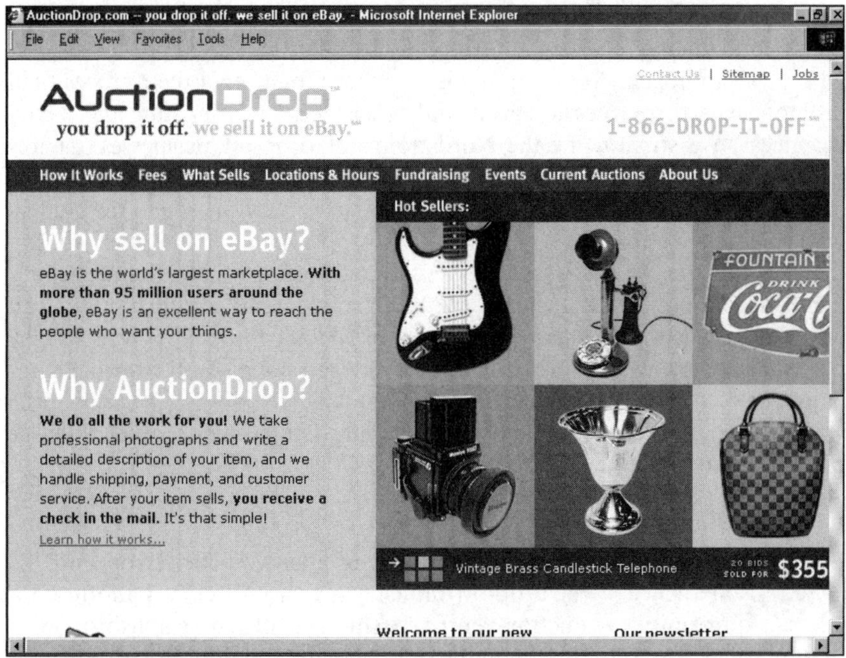

Figure 18-2 AuctionDrop (*www.auctiondrop.com*) provides clients drop-off locations where auctionable items can be left for the experts to sell.

hungry eyes of the eBay community without having to initiate and manage the entire process. The first AuctionDrop store appeared in March 2003 in the San Carlos, California, area and new locations are popping up throughout the San Francisco, California, Bay Area. Since opening its initial store, AuctionDrop has hosted over 20,000 successful consignment auctions and realized profits beyond $1 million already. Of its growing roster of clients, roughly 82 percent apparently have never sold on eBay, proving once again that there are still plenty of goods waiting to be traded and plenty of clients to be assisted in the eBay process.

The key to AuctionDrop's success and what I find most compelling about their operation amid the growing industry of drop-off sites is their unique centralization, or hub process. While customers can drop off goods at any one of roughly 20 (at the time of this writing) physical storefronts, all goods are transported to the company's 30,000-square-foot processing site where goods are transported via conveyor system to a number of item experts, who will assess the goods to be listed. AuctionDrop has wisely elected to establish specialists not only in terms of the goods themselves but also in terms of auctioning practices. Some employees specialize solely in professionally

photographing items, others in writing accurate and compelling descriptions, others in managing packing and shipping. Rather than attempt the "jack of all trades" approach, Abrams and his crew have found that their process will promote expertise, professionalism, and consistency in their listing and selling practices. "We strive to be the Nordstrom's of drop-off businesses," shares AuctionDrop's director of public relations, Andrea Roesch, "delivering superior services and person-to-person assistance to our customers and the bidders who show interest in the items we list." Most refreshing of the AuctionDrop model is that they've staffed themselves to handle actual bidder inquires about items the company represents and, with the actual items readily at hand, can quickly and accurately answer even the most detailed of questions posed by potential buyers, whether via e-mail or over the phone. And, with the company poised to open additional stores nationwide, the approach seems to be working well. As Roesch astutely notes, "AuctionDrop is here to offer a unique high-touch service in the virtual marketplace."

eBay TIP: What's interesting about AuctionDrop and the emergence of the drop-off industry is that it offers yet another opportunity for auction-centric businesspeople to establish or grow their presence and profitability in the online-auction realm. Most of the new drop off companies are readying to begin licensing franchised storefronts to ready-and-willing shop owners. Here again is another way the eBay economy is further shaping and driving the potential for business owners, online and off.

Of course, AuctionDrop isn't the only drop-off business in this emerging industry. While I find it has the best operating model of those I've surveyed, take a look also at AuctionWagon, Inc. (*www.auctionwagon.com*), QuikDrop, Inc. (*www.quikdrop.com*), and Snappy Auctions (*www.snappyauctions.com*). It's an exciting new venture on the rise and one to tap into early if you hope to make the greatest gains for yourself and your business.

19

A Never-Ending Supply: Selling Your Services

If you've been around eBay long enough, you've likely seen or heard of some of the more inventive or even curious goods being auctioned. I'm not talking about the human kidneys, bratty younger brothers, or professional baseball players' masticated bubblegum; there have been plenty of odd and outright "joke" auctions aplenty throughout the years on eBay. During the dot-com bust, though, a team of "techies" from South Carolina who lost their jobs decided to auction themselves off as a group for hire, ready to service the professional needs of any person or business that was willing to bid for their services. It seemed like a put-on initially, but others soon saw the opportunity to offer up a truly never-ending supply of goods: personal expertise and professional services (see Figure 19-1).

It makes perfect sense, really, when you consider the same had been going on during the dot-com boom as professionals were offering themselves up as high-priced consultants and analysts to businesses in need of guidance during the technological boom of the late 1990s. The South Carolina team simply decided to choose eBay rather than a placement service as the vehicle to announce their availability. Great idea. The group advertised themselves for an opening bid of $1 million and actually incited interest from several online banking outfits.

Although eBay was a little uncertain about how to respond to such auctions, debating whether to cancel them (many were canceled) or allow them to run their course, it soon realized this was a viable good (a service, actually) to offer on the site, a niche that attracted interested bidders. In response, eBay created a *Professional Services* category for more such listings. eBay took this a step further and created a sort of reverse auction (much like that used on

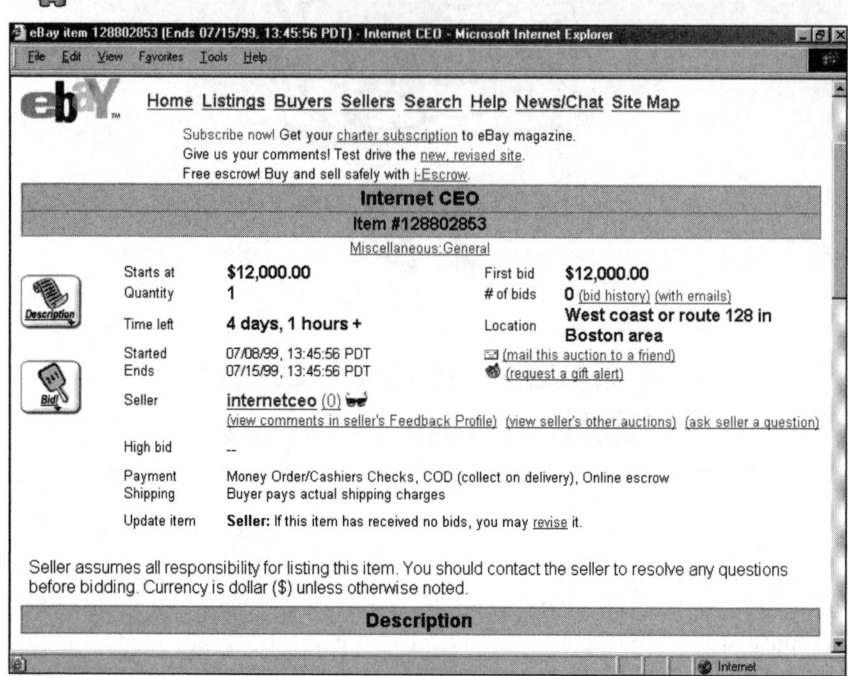

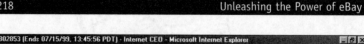

Figure 19-1 If you couldn't afford to bid on the entire tech team, how about this displaced CEO, who offered his services to the highest bidder.

Priceline), where clients in need of services post their requirements and professionals and other such service providers bid the job. In a deft move, eBay partnered with Elance, the online leader in freelance job bidding, and has presented both buyers and service providers with a new niche within the bustling auction space. If you have professional services you'd like to offer to the again-growing marketplace, from Accounting expertise to Legal training to Personal Development skills, take a look into eBay's Professional Services page at *pages.ebay.com/business_services/index.html* (see Figure 19-2) and see if what you might have to offer is already in demand.

eBay TIP: Everything's negotiable in the world of professional services, so be sure to consider whether travel and lodging will be required (if you intend to provide services outside your local area) and either charge separately to cover those expenses or roll them into your overall service price. Just be sure that if you only receive the minimum bid for your services that price will allow you to cover your costs and pull in a reasonable profit.

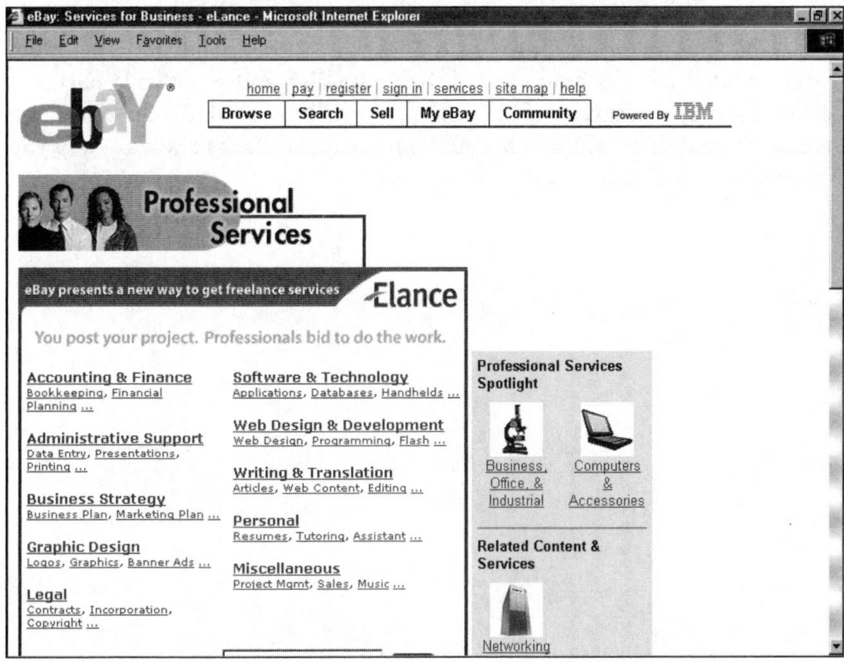

Figure 19-2 Partnering with Elance, eBay is actively hosting clients' jobs and giving skilled professionals the opportunity to bid for the work.

Of course, if you don't see a job posted that you'd care to bid on but still have services you would like to offer to the eBay community, visit the *Everything Else* category and drill into the subcategory of *Speciality Services*. A quick look today shows that professionals of all types are proactively offering assistance to those needing help with anything from graphic design, artistic services, resumé-writing assistance, and even custom clothing and jewelry design. With roughly 10,000 service listings available at any given time, professionals from all areas of expertise have found that eBay is yet another way to let the world know they're ready to help those in need.

eBay TIP: Are services truly in demand today? Forrester Research previously estimated that the U.S. market for selling services over the Internet will reach almost $250 billion by the end of 2004.

It all wraps up to illustrate once again how eBay has become the unbounded hub of business that has gone far, far beyond simply being a meeting ground to swap knickknacks and other such curiosities. eBay has

attracted and continues to sustain millions of people eager to do good business across the nation and around the world. At this point, it seems more than clear that eBay is ready to help you establish and grow your business, whatever it may be. Be creative, be inventive, and be excited. If you're ready to unleash the power of eBay to benefit your business, eBay's ready to help you succeed. Why not start today?

Glossary

A

Agreement An expression of mutual assent by two or more parties on a given proposition. Refer to *Terms of Service.*

Appraisal The act or process of estimating an item's value via expert *Authentication* and comparative pricing in the open market. Appraised values can change as the marketplace valuation of an item increases or decreases.

As Is Selling an item without warranties in regard to its condition and fitness for a particular use. The buyer is responsible for judging the item's durability and lifetime. Also known as "as is, where is," and "in its present condition." Typically, this is a sign that no return privileges will be granted.

Auction n (1) A method of selling a property in a public forum through open, competitive bidding. v (2) The act of putting an item up for sale in a competitive public auction.

Auction Block The podium or platform from which an auctioneer conducts a physical auction. Online, refers to a "live listing" to be found in a listing *Category.* To place an item on the auction block means to make it available for competitive bidding.

Auction Listing Agreement A contract executed by the auctioneer and seller, authorizing the auctioneer to conduct the sale. It also delineates the conditions of sale and the rights and responsibilities of each party. Also known as a *Listing Agreement.* Not to be confused with an online auction *Terms of Service.*

Auction Plan The itinerary for preauction, auction day, and postauction activities, set by the auctioneer and seller.

Auction Value The current price of a property during a competitive public auction. Also referred to as "Current Bid."

Auction with Reserve An auction in which the seller has set a minimum price for the item and reserves the right to accept or decline any and all bids that fail to meet that price condition. Also known as *Reserve Auction.*

Auction without Reserve An auction in which the property is sold to the highest qualified bidder with no limiting conditions or minimum price. Also known as a *Straight Auction.*

Authentication (1) The act or process of determining whether an auction item is genuine and accurately represented by the seller. (2) A mark on an article to indicate its origin and authenticity.

B

Bid An indication and offer on an item up for sale at a competitive public auction. Bids are typically made in predetermined *Bid Increments.*

Bid Cancellation The cancellation of a bid from a buyer by a seller. During online auctions, sellers can cancel any bid if they feel uncomfortable about completing a transaction with a particular bidder.

Bid History A historical list of bidding activity for a particular auction, viewable during or after the auction.

Bid Increment The amount by which a bid will be raised each time the current bid is outdone. It is predetermined by eBay based on the current high bid.

Bid Retraction The legitimate cancellation of a bid on an item by a buyer during an online auction. At eBay, bid retractions cannot be made within five minutes of an auction close.

Bid Rigging An unlawful practice in which two or more people agree not to bid against one another in order to deflate the potential value of an item. See *Collusion.*

Bid Shielding Posting extremely high bids (which are withdrawn at the last moment) to protect the lower bid of an earlier bidder, usually in cahoots with the bidder who placed the shielding bid.

Bid Siphoning The practice of contacting bidders during an active auction and offering to sell them the same item they are currently bidding on, thus drawing bidders away from the legitimate seller's auction.

Bidder Search An online search that will generate a list of items a user has bid on at an online auction service. Availability of this tool can vary from site to site.

Bidding Offering to pay a specified amount of money for an item that is up for public auction.

Big-Ticket Item An item with a bid of $5,000 or more.

Bulk Listing Listing a group of different items in separate *Lots* all at once using an eBay's bulk listing tool, Turbo Lister, or a specially designed third-party bulk listing tool.

Buying Up the Lot The practice of buying everything on offer in a Dutch auction, rather than bidding on some smaller number of the items. This is typically done for resale.

Buy-It-Now Auction Auctions with immediate-sell prices that, when agreed to, will halt an auction and prevent any additional bidding. Also referred to as *Fixed-Price Auction* or *Quick-Sell Auction.*

C

Category A logical item listing classification where similar or related items can be found. Many categories are further broken down into more granular subcategories.

Category Listings The categories in which an online auction site organizes its auctions.

Caveat Emptor The Latin phrase for "let the buyer beware." It is a legal maxim, meaning that liability is transferred from the seller to the buyer in regard to the quality or condition of the item or property up for sale.

Collusion An unlawful practice in which two or more people agree willfully and unfairly to manipulate the final price of an auction item.

Commission A fee paid by the seller to the auction site (i.e., eBay) at the completion of an auction, calculated as a percentage of the final sale price. Also known as the *Final Value Fee (FVF)*.

Contact Information The user information—generally name, street address, e-mail address, and phone number—provided when registering at eBay.

Contract A binding legal agreement between two or more persons or entities.

Cookie A piece of information sent from a Web server to a Web browser that the browser software saves and then sends back to the server whenever the browser makes additional requests from the server.

D

Deadbeat Bidding (Bidder) The failure to deliver payment on an item after securing the high bid in an online auction. Repeat deadbeat bidding will result in the indefinite suspension of a user from an online auction site.

Due Diligence The process of gathering information about the condition and legal status of items to be sold.

Dutch Auction An auction format in which a seller lists multiple identical items for sale. Varying price determination methods exist: "authentic" Dutch Auctions determine price by lowering the price of the item until all units have been claimed (bid on); contemporary and online auctions use a format where all winning bidders pay the same price, which is the lowest successful bid. Often confused with the *Yankee Auction* format.

E

Emoticons In-text icons created using common letters and punctuation marks to denote mood or attitude, for example:

:-) smiling face
:-(frowning face
:-P silly face with tongue sticking out

Escrow Money held in trust by a third party until the seller makes delivery of merchandise to the buyer.

Estate Sale The sale of personal property or real estate left by a person at the time of his or her death or incarceration.

F

Featured Auctions eBay's most prominent auctions of the day. Featured Auction status typically incurs a significant additional insertion fee.

Feedback One user's public comments about another user in regard to their auction dealings. Feedback comments cannot be removed or changed once submitted to an online auction site.

Final Value Fee (FVF) A fee owed by the seller to eBay at the completion of an auction, calculated as a percentage of the final sale price. Also known as a *Commission.*

Fixed-Price Auction See *Buy-It-Now Auction.*

FVF Refund Request A request to eBay for the crediting of a levied *Final Value Fee.* Usually granted in situations where an auction transaction is not completed (for example, because of a *Deadbeat Bidder*).

G

Grading Documenting the physical condition of an item with a specific set of labels, such as "Mint" condition or "Poor" quality. Different items have different grading terms. For instance, trading cards are graded from "A1" to "F1," while coins are graded from "poor" to "perfect uncirculated."

H

High Bidder The present or final bidder in an auction, who has bid a higher price than any other bidder.

I

Insertion Fee A fee paid by the seller to eBay in order to list an item for auction, calculated as a percentage of the opening bid or reserve price.

Item The thing being auctioned. May be a single unit or a set of similar or even mixed objects, as long as the whole group is being sold as a unit to one buyer. Also called a *Lot.*

J

Jump Bid A bid placed that significantly increases a current bid price over the established next *Bid Increment.* Used to scare off other bidders who might not be able to contend at higher price levels.

K

Keyword Spamming Deliberately placing a popular word in listing titles even though it is completely unrelated or irrelevant to the actual item being offered. Used to have items show up in the results of item searches.

Knock-Off Slang term for an unlicensed reproduction, or copy of an item that is made to appear as the real thing (such as brand-name watches, sunglasses, handbags, and so on).

L

Listing Agreement A contract executed by the auctioneer and seller, authorizing the auctioneer to conduct the sale. It also delineates the conditions of sale and the rights and responsibilities of each party.

Lot The single item or group of items offered in a given auction listing.

M

Market Value The highest price a property will bring in the competitive, open market.

Maximum Bid The highest price a buyer will pay for an item, submitted in confidence to eBay's automated bidding system to facilitate *Proxy Bidding.* The system's electronic "proxy" will automatically increase the buyer's bid to maintain the high bid. The proxy bidding system will stop when it has won the auction or reached the *Maximum Bid.*

Minimum Opening Bid The mandatory *Starting Price* for a given auction, set by the seller at the time of listing.

N

NARU'd An auction site term to describe eBay users whose memberships have been discontinued. NARU is the acronym for "not a registered user."

Neg Short for "negative user feedback."

Net Cops Auction users who actively seek out instances of fraud, such as shilling or bid shielding, to report to eBay.

Newsgroups Public discussion forums that number in the thousands and are dedicated to specific topics of interest and conversation. See *Usenet.*

NR Short for "no reserve." This indicates in the item description line that the auction has no reserve price specified.

O

Opening Bid The lowest bid amount accepted for a particular item. Also known as the *Starting Price.*

Outbid To submit a *Maximum Bid* that is higher than the one offered by another bidder. To "be outbid" indicates the reverse—someone who was the recognized high bidder has lost that status to someone else.

Outbid Notification Communication sent by eBay via e-mail or wireless modes notifying a bidder of being outbid.

P

Private Auction An auction in which the bidders' identities are hidden to preserve anonymity.

Proxy Bidding To submit a hidden *Maximum Bid* to eBay's automated bidding system. The system's electronic proxy will automatically increase the buyer's bid to maintain the high bid. The proxy bidding system will stop when it has secured the high-bidder status or reached the maximum bid.

Q

Quick-Sell Auction See *Buy-It Price Auction.*

R

Registered User A person who has registered as a member of eBay.

Relisting The relisting of an item occurs when it has not sold within its allotted auction time. An insertion fee is levied at the time of relisting but is refunded to the seller if the item sells.

Reserve Auction An auction in which the seller has set a minimum selling price for the item and reserves the right to accept or decline any and all bids that have not met the established reserve.

Reserve Price The minimum price a seller will accept for an item to be sold at a reserve auction.

Retaliatory The user term for retaliatory negative *Feedback,* posted by one user in response to another user's negative *Feedback.*

S

S&H Charges Shipping and handling charges.

Secure Server A server that uses Secure Sockets Layer (SSL) encryption technology to protect the users' credit card and other confidential information.

Seller List A list of items a seller has put up for sale at eBay.

Seller Search An automated search that retrieves a list of all the items a seller has put up for sale at eBay, active and completed.

Shilling Fraudulent bidding by the seller (using an alternate registration) or an associate of the seller in order to inflate the price of an item. Also known as *Bid Rigging* and *Collusion.*

Sniping Bidding in the closing minutes or seconds of an auction to outbid other buyers.

Starting Price The mandatory starting bid for a given auction, set by the seller at the time of listing.

Straight Auction An auction in which there is no reserve and where only one item is up for sale. This is the most common type of auction. The seller sets the opening bid and must respect the final price at the end of the auction.

T

Terms of Service (TOS) A legally binding agreement that outlines eBay's operations and policies. All registered users must agree to the site's terms before being allowed to participate.

Tie Bids Bids for exactly the same amount, submitted by two or more buyers at the same time. At eBay, the first bidder to have bid the amount will be declared the prevailing high bidder.

Troll A slang and somewhat derogatory term for someone who posts messages to public forums for the sake of stirring up tension, division, or confusion.

U

Usenet An online hub of *Newsgroups* where visitors are invited to read public postings as well as post comments and observations of their own.

User ID A moniker that identifies a user while on an online auction site.

User Information Personal data provided by a user when registering at eBay, including name, postal address, e-mail address, and phone number.

V

Verification Confirming the identity and evaluating the condition of an item.

W

Winner's Curse An oxymoron that indicates an overzealous bidder-*cum*-winner will be faced with paying his or her high bid—a bid perhaps placed during a moment of passion or excitement yet financially difficult for the bidder to honor.

Y

Yankee Auction An auction in which a seller lists multiples of an identical item. Unlike a *Dutch Auction* (in which all winning bidders pay only the lowest successful winning bid amount), in a Yankee auction each winning bidder pays the exact amount of their winning bid.

Index